Montgomery Throop

The future

A political essay

Montgomery Throop

The future
A political essay

ISBN/EAN: 9783337133870

Printed in Europe, USA, Canada, Australia, Japan

Cover: Foto ©Suzi / pixelio.de

More available books at **www.hansebooks.com**

THE FUTURE:

A Political Essay .

BY

MONTGOMERY H. THROOP.

Stay, my lord,
And let your choler with your reason question,
What 'tis you go about.
Be advised,
Heat not a furnace for your foe so hot,
That it do singe yourself.
K. HENRY VIII.

NEW YORK:
JAMES G. GREGORY.
1864.

W. H. TINSON, Stereotyper   C. A. ALVORD, Printer.

TO THE

HONORABLE ENOS T. THROOP,

WHILOM, AND IN THE HAPPIER DAYS OF THE REPUBLIC,

Governor of the State of New York,

THIS VOLUME IS DEDICATED AS A HUMBLE TESTIMONIAL OF GRATITUDE, REVERENCE,
AND AFFECTION,

BY THE AUTHOR.

PREFATORY NOTE.

THROUGHOUT the following pages, I have in general excluded from consideration such features of the existing situation, either with respect to our internal affairs, or our relations to the insurgents, as will exercise but an ephemeral influence upon the solution of the grand problem. But I have found it impossible always to avoid references to passing events, and conjectures respecting their results, the correctness or falsity of which a few months, perhaps weeks, will render manifest. It will therefore be necessary for the better understanding of some portions of this work, that the reader should bear in mind that it was prepared for publication during the months of November, December, and January last.

M. H. T

UTICA, N. Y., *March* 1, 1804

CONTENTS.

———•◦•———

INTRODUCTION.

CHAPTER I.

CHAPTER II.

CHAPTER III.

CHAPTER IV.

CHAPTER V.

CHAPTER VI.

CHAPTER VII.

CHAPTER VIII.

CHAPTER IX.

CHAPTER X.

CHAPTER XI.

CHAPTER XII.

1*

CHAPTER XIII.

THE FUTURE.

———•••———

INTRODUCTION.

The Object of the Work—The Propositions which it aims to establish—The Spirit in which the Author will endeavor to discuss them—The propriety and importance of such a Discussion at the present time—Practical Questions alone to be considered.

In one of the earliest of the diplomatic dispatches of the Secretary of State, the instructions to Mr. Dayton, dated April twenty-second, eighteen hundred and sixty-one, will be found this passage :

"The American people, notwithstanding any temporary disturbance of their equanimity, are yet a sagacious and practical people, and less experience of evils than any other nation would require, will bring them back to their customary and habitual exercise of reason and reflection, and through that process, to the settlement of the controversy without further devastation and demoralization, by needless continuance in civil war."

It is supposed, less from the context of the dispatch, than from the Secretary's well-known skepticism at that time, respecting the possibility of the

northern people feeling to any considerable extent
the pressure of the then impending civil war, that
the men of the South constituted that portion of the
American people to whom he particularly referred,
when he penned the sentence quoted. But his
remark is general, and the characteristics which he
ascribes to the nation are those to which the men
of the North lay peculiar, if not exclusive claim.

I propose to appeal to the "reason and reflection" of my "sagacious and practical" fellow-citizens, in a few earnest, but I hope calm and moderate observations. Assuming that we propose to
prosecute the war until the authority of the Union
is completely reëstablished in all the territory over
which it extended when the rebellion broke out,
and that the fortune of arms, and the course of
political events, have been such as to place such a
consummation within our reach, I will assign the
reasons for two conclusions to which I have arrived,
and to which it is the object of this work to lead
also the reader's mind. These are, first, that no
calamity could befall the nation, not even disunion,
which would compare in its disastrous consequences,
to a successful termination of the war, under such
circumstances as to leave behind it a permanent
feeling of hostility and hatred to the Government
of the Union, on the part of the people over whom
our victorious arms will have extended our sway;
and secondly, that such a feeling will naturally and

inevitably result from further persistence in many of the measures of civil and military policy which we have already adopted, and from adopting other measures, having the same general tendency which are now urged upon us by several leading states men.

Although I wish to expose my work to the charge of partisanship as little as the nature of the discussion will allow, I am fully sensible of the impossibility of gratifying that wish except to a very limited extent. I am not vain enough to suppose that I can succeed by any effort, however honestly and strenuously made, in divesting my own mind entirely of party bias, while treating of subjects which have provoked at such recent periods so much acrimony of debate in political conflicts, " quorum pars fui." And I know very well that at a time like this, when the passions of my countrymen are heated, as it were, to the boiling point, even if it was possible for me to bring to the discussion of my subject the calmness and impartiality with which posterity, aided by experience, will judge of the men and measures of to-day, I should appear to many honest, intelligent, and patriotic men, to have written purely as a partisan.

But I will approach as nearly to the accomplishment of my purpose as the adverse circumstances under which I write will permit. To that end, I will treat copiously of principles and sparingly of men, and when the nature of the discussion compels me to advert to the acts of individuals, I will avoid, as far as possible, captious and unfair criticism of their conduct and uncharitable construction of their motives. And I will advance no argument which I do not myself believe to be sound, and make no assertion, of the truth of which I am not myself fully persuaded. If, nevertheless, I shall justly expose myself to censure for the spirit in which I shall write, I can only plead the infirmity of human nature in extenuation of my fault.

The time has been when many men who would have agreed with me in some, perhaps all, of my general conclusions, would have deprecated this discussion, however moderate and candid might have been the spirit in which it might be conducted. They held that while the very existence of the Government was trembling in the balance, it did not become good citizens to criticise unfavorably well-intended, though possibly unwise measures, of those to whose hands was irrevocably confided the duty of preserving the nation from annihilation.

But the time has passed when such an argument had any weight. A presidential election is approaching, the result of which will determine the policy of the nation for four long years to come— years during which its destiny, as affected by the termination of the war, will be in all probability irrevocably fixed for weal or for woe. The powers

which the present national Administration have
wielded during the whole continuance of the war,
are now again to be committed to the hands of the
people, to be recommitted by the latter to such persons as they shall deem most worthy of the high
trust—that is to say, to the men whose principles,
as illustrated by their past conduct, and whose
pledges of future action shall be those which, in the
opinion of the people, will most conduce to the
national safety and prosperity. It is therefore no
longer possible, even were it desirable, to avoid the
discussion of the future policy of the nation, and
consequently of the measures which have already
been adopted. The wisdom of those measures, the
propriety of longer adhering to them, the adoption
of a permanent basis of the settlement of the controversy—these are the very issues which, divested
of extraneous considerations, are to be presented in
November next for direct adjudication at the bar
of public opinion. And all men, even those who
have heretofore believed that such discussion should
be discountenanced, must now form their own opinions respecting the future policy of the nation, and
act in accordance with their conclusions.

It will be my endeavor to avoid, as far as possible, all doubtful questions which are not of immediate and practical importance. And in general, I
shall also prefer to discuss such theories of constitutional law or of political science, as my subject will

from time to time force upon me, with reference rather to their practical operation, and to the results to which they will lead in the present state of the country, than to their abstract correctness or falsity as general propositions. The principal exceptions which I shall make to this rule, will occur when the proposition under consideration involves a question of right or wrong: that is to say, when it is or has been used to justify a particular measure or a general policy, and its decision is therefore necessary to determine whether the course which we have pursued, or which is recommended for our adoption, is a mere assertion of our unquestionable rights, or a lawless and unjustifiable usurpation. In such a case the question, however abstract apparently, will become practical in the course of the discussion: for although there are many among us who scorn to inquire what the Constitution requires at our hands in dealing with rebels, I shall endeavor to show in the progress of this work, that we cannot expect to secure the pacification of this distracted country, or to preserve our own liberties, if we allow our national Government to make the rebellion a pretext for disregarding its own constitutional duties, or assuming powers which the fundamental law has withheld from it.

There is one great question, the solution of which would be eminently practical in considering how we can restore peace and harmony to the country,

which I am compelled to ignore, except to a limited
extent, for another reason—it is, *what was the real
cause of the war?* By which I mean, not the
ostensible subject of the quarrel, for that was the institution of slavery ; nor the direct and immediate
causes which made that institution the subject of a
quarrel, for these may in general terms be stated to
have been dislike and suspicion of the people of
each section among the people of the other; but the
means by which those feelings were aroused and
the causes which led to them. If we could accurately ascertain the cause of the war, in that sense,
we should have made considerable progress in dis-
covering a remedy for our difficulties, and a basis
of lasting pacification. I shall make the attempt to
show how, when disunion was once determined
upon by the leading politicians of the ·South, the
masses of that section were induced to favor it.
But beyond that point the ground is too dangerous
to tread upon, with the hope of producing any satisfactory results in a work of this character, till the
excitement of the present shall have passed away.
Among those who sincerely deplore the commencement of the war, and long for its termination, in
such a manner as to secure future harmony and
mutual good-will among all sections of the country,
there is the widest difference of opinion as to the
degree of responsibility for its existence which at-
taches to particular men and particular factions.

The events are too recent, the actors in them are too closely connected with us in our every-day avocations, and the feelings which they have aroused are yet too keen, to permit of their being considered with the calmness with which I hope to be able to treat the subjects which I propose to discuss. All moderate men will concede that in both of the leading parties, at least in the North, there has been a sincere and unqualified attachment to the Union on the part of a vast majority; and that what has been done to destroy it, has been the result chiefly of passion, prejudice, ignorance, error, and timidity, and partly, but to a much less extent, of venality and unscrupulous ambition on the part of the leaders of public opinion, and the incumbents of public office. In what proportion these faults and errors are to be ascribed to particular factions or particular men, I shall not undertake to determine.

To that extent "forgetting those things which are behind and reaching forth to those things which are before," and asking my reader's forbearance and indulgence, if, as is probable in the present diversity of opinion respecting every measure of public policy, I shall fail to command his approbation in every particular, I invite moderate and thinking men to consider with me the all-absorbing FUTURE, and the mighty events which lie hidden beneath its veil.

CHAPTER I

THE doctrine of State sovereignty enters so largely
into the discussion of all questions connected with
the commencement or the termination of the war,
that it is essential in a work of this kind, to have a
clear understanding at the outset respecting its
soundness and the results to which it leads. Had
these pages been written a few months earlier, I
should have assumed that the sovereignty of the
States was so generally admitted by the public men
of the North, as well as of the South, that I could
proceed at once, without occupying the reader's
time with a demonstration of its existence, to con-

sider the consequences which legitimately flow from
it, and the perversions to which it has been subjected. But "the world moves," and it is not the
least significant indication of the manner in which
the passions generated and the new interests created
by nearly three years of civil war, have upset all
preconceived ideas of political science and of the
theory of our Constitution, that many of my fellow-
citizens are now questioning the soundness of a
proposition, which but a short time ago, they would
have treated as axiomatic. It is because this doubt
exists, that I am compelled, much against my
wishes, to defer the consideration of matters perhaps better calculated to interest the general reader,
till I have completed the discussion of this question
of constitutional law.

The most noticeable of the recent attacks upon
the doctrine of State sovereignty, as well from its
boldness and its elaborate character, as the reputa-
tion and position of its author, is to be found in an
article in a recent number of *The Atlantic Monthly
Magazine*, written by Senator Sumner of Massachusetts, and entitled "Our Domestic Relations."
I shall have occasion, in a subsequent portion of
this work, to consider some of the other propositions which the author of that article has attempted
to establish : at present I will confine my attention
to that portion of his argument which aims to prove
that State sovereignty has no existence under the

Constitution. As Mr. Sumner is beyond question the most distinguished of the champions of that doctrine, I presume that if I can successfully refute the reasoning contained in " Our Domestic Relations," I shall have overthrown the best argument which can be adduced in its support.

That part of " Our Domestic Relations" which is devoted to the consideration of what it styles " the miserable pretension of State sovereignty," refers also to the " pestilent pretension of State rights," in terms (not merely the different adjectives) which lead me to conjecture that the author draws in his own mind some line of distinction between the two supposed political heresies. But as he does not explain that distinction in such a manner that I have been able to discover of what it consists, I am compelled to consider the two doctrines as identical, State rights being, as ordinarily understood, the right of the States to enjoy unmolested that portion of sovereignty which the Constitution has not bestowed upon the Federal Government.

That no such right or no such sovereignty exists, is a conclusion which is announced in the article in question in the following words, succeeding a detailed statement of the origin of the Constitution and a recapitulation of its provisions respecting Congress and the States.

"Thus, whether we regard the larger powers vested in Congress, the powers denied to the States

without the consent of Congress, or those other provisions which accord supremacy to the United States,
we shall find the pretension of State sovereignty
without foundation, except in the imagination of its
partisans. Before the Constitution such sovereignty
may have existed ; it was declared in the Articles of
Confederation ; but since then it has ceased to exist.
It has disappeared and been lost in the supremacy
of the national Government, so that it can no longer
be recognized."

I shall consider separately the reasons which are
thus assigned for the disappearance of the sovereignty of the States ; but before doing so, it is necessary for me to have more satisfactory evidence that
such sovereignty existed under the Articles of Confederation, than is contained in the qualified and
hesitating admission of that fact, which the foregoing extract contains. For if it is distinctly understood that the States were sovereign when the Constitution was adopted, the argument will be narrowed down to the single question whether there is
such a radical difference between the relations which
now exist between the Federal Government, the
States, and the people, and those which existed between the Congress of the confederation, the States,
and the people, as to lead to the conclusion that the
Constitution has stripped the States of rights of
such incalculable importance, which they confessedly enjoyed under the Articles of Confederation.

By the Declaration of Independence, the colonies asserted that they were "free and independent States," and the Articles of Confederation, which were made in 1777 and ratified in 1778, purport to be the compact of the several States whose independence was thus asserted. It was expressly declared in them that "each State retains its sovereignty, freedom, independence," and every power, &c., not expressly delegated to the United States, and also that "the said States hereby enter into a firm league of friendship with each other." In the determination of questions each State had one vote in a congress consisting of one house only, and certain questions, enumerated in the Articles, could only be decided by "the assent of nine States," that is, by the vote of the delegations of nine States in the Congress. The President was merely the presiding officer of Congress, that body having executive as well as legislative authority, and the commander-in-chief was such military officer as Congress might appoint. The Union was to be indissoluble—that fact being asserted expressly and by implication no less than five times in the Articles of Confederation and their ratification. The title of the confederacy was, as the title of our present national Government is, "The United States," and the word "Union" was used as descriptive of the confederacy and of the bond by which the States were held together. Of course the constitutions of the several

States were appropriate for the exercise of that sovereignty which was expressly reserved to them.

After recapitulating some of these provisions, the author of "Our Domestic Relations" finds it impossible to withhold his unqualified admission that the States were then sovereign. He says, "The government thus constituted was a compact between *sovereign States*, or, according to its precise language, 'a firm league of friendship' between *these States*, administered in the recess of Congress by 'a committee of *the States*.'* Thus did State rights triumph."

The Union thus constituted is aptly compared in *The Federalist* (No. 18) to the Amphyctionic league, and the "weaknesses and disorders" which resulted from it were similar to those which afflicted the Amphyctionic states. They led to the calling

---

* I have copied the italics in the extract as they stand in the original text. The clear implication of this paragraph is, that the States themselves appointed a committee to manage the affairs of the Union during the recess of Congress. In truth, the "committee of the States" was merely one of the regular committees of Congress, consisting of one delegate selected by Congress from the delegation from each State, and empowered to act during the recess. The necessity of such a committee will be apparent, when it is remembered that Congress was the executive as well as the legislative authority of the Union.

There are other errors of a similar character in "Our Domestic Relations;" of course I assume that they result from carelessness in the author's mode of expression.

of the convention of 1787, which formed our present Constitution.

That instrument undertook to remedy the defects of the confederation, partly by enlarging the powers conferred upon the Federal Administration, but chiefly by enabling the latter to operate directly upon individual citizens and their property, instead of relying, as did the Congress of the confederation, upon the States to carry into effect most of its laws and mandates. In other words, the Constitution created *a government*, that is, *a sovereignty*, to which obedience, and therefore allegiance was due from each citizen within its territory, to the full extent of the powers conferred upon it. But those powers were expressly defined, and they were limited to the transaction of the external business of the nation, and to a few specified matters of internal administration, which it was necessary that the general Government should regulate, in order to enable it efficiently to fulfil its functions respecting external affairs, or which could not be committed to the separate action of each State, without producing confusion or internal discord. And it was expressly declared in an amendment which was in substance contemporaneous with the Constitution itself, that "all powers not delegated to the United States by the Constitution, nor prohibited by it to the States, are reserved to the States respectively or to the people." Bearing in mind, therefore, that

the States were sovereign *when the Constitution
was adopted*, it is manifest that all sovereignty not
granted to the United States remained in the States
themselves, and it is necessary to examine the instrument itself, to ascertain first, whether the sovereignty of the States was affirmatively ceded, and
secondly, if that was not the case, whether the
attributes and powers of sovereignty were so far
ceded that those which remained in the States constituted such a mere shadow of sovereignty, that
the name itself is no longer appropriate to describe
them.   The first question is speedily answered.
The Constitution itself nowhere uses the word " sovereign " or " sovereignty " when treating either of
the States or of the national Government.   It recognizes the former as then existing with certain rights
and privileges which it makes no attempts to define,
and it proceeds to *organize* and *create* the latter.
And an examination of the powers which it confers
upon the general Government will show very conclusively that its object was to effect what *The
Federalist* (No. 32) very correctly calls a " *division*
of the sovereign power."   They are far from being,
as the author of " Our Domestic Relations " calls
them, " all those powers which enter into sovereignty."   Let us divide them into two classes;
first, those which were precisely or substantially
the same under the two systems, and secondly,
those which are altogether new

The first class, those which were common to both systems, are the following : to borrow money on the credit of the United States; to pay debts; to appropriate money for the public expenses; to regulate commerce with the Indian tribes; to coin money and regulate its value; to fix the standard of weights and measures throughout the Union; to establish post-offices; to define and punish piracies; to enter into treaties and alliances; to declare war; to conclude peace; to grant letters of marque and reprisal; to make rules concerning captures by land or water; to raise and support armies; to appoint naval and military officers; to provide and maintain a navy; and to make rules for the government and regulation of the land and naval forces. Some of these powers were conferred upon the Congress of the confederation, in language varying somewhat from that employed in the Constitution, and the mode of execution of some of them was by means of the machinery of the State governments; but they were, nevertheless, POWERS granted to the Union under the former system, and the obligation of the States to carry into execution such of them as the latter were required to execute, rendered them theoretically as effective as they are at present. Upon this subject *The Federalist* may be consulted *passim*, particularly numbers thirty-eight and forty.

The second class, consisting of powers which Congress has under the Constitution, and which were not granted to the Congress of the confederation, are the following: to lay taxes, duties, imposts, and excises; to regulate commerce with foreign nations and among the States; to establish uniform rules of naturalization and of bankruptcy; to provide for the punishment of counterfeiting the United States coin and securities; to grant copyrights and patents to authors and inventors; to define and punish offences against the laws of nations; to provide for calling forth the militia to execute the laws, repel invasions, and suppress insurrections; and to provide for organizing, arming, and disciplining the militia—the power to train the militia and to appoint the officers being reserved to the States.

The restrictions upon the powers of the States which the present Constitution establishes may be classified in the same manner. Those which were common to both systems are the following: citizens of each State are to have the privileges of citizens of all the States; criminals fleeing from one State to another are to be surrendered; full faith and credit are to be given in each State to the records, acts, and judicial proceedings of the others; no State shall enter into any treaty, alliance, or confederation without the consent of Congress; nor without the consent of Congress keep troops or ships of war in time of peace, or enter into any agreement or compact with any other State, or a foreign power, or engage in war, unless actually invaded or in imminent danger. All these restrictions are established by the Articles of Confederation, substantially in the same manner, and in the same language, as by the Constitution. In two particulars there is a difference in the terms of the prohibition, without any substantial difference in its practical effect. The Constitution forbids any State to grant letters of marque or reprisal. The Articles of Confederation forbade such letters being granted, except by the consent of and under regulations to be established by Congress. The Constitution forbids the States to coin money; the Articles of Confederation vested in Congress " the exclusive right and power of regulating the alloy and value of coin struck by their own authority, or that of the respective States."

The restrictions upon the States, which were added by the new system to those which formerly existed, are the following : no State shall emit bills of credit; make anything but gold and silver a legal tender in payment of debts; pass any bill of attainder, ex-post facto law, or law impairing the obligation of contracts, or grant any title of nobility ; nor shall a State lay imposts or duties on imports or exports, or any duties of tonnage, without the consent of Congress; fugitive slaves escaping from one State to another are to be surrendered ; the United

States shall guaranty to each State a republican form of government. So far as the prohibition to pass acts of attainder, or ex-post facto laws, or grant titles of nobility, amount to an argument against the existence of sovereignty, the same prohibitions, in the same words, are made applicable to Congress; and generally it may be stated, that the law-making power of the Union is much more restricted by the Constitution, not only by the absence of grants of power, but by express prohibitions of particular acts of its exercise, than the corresponding power of the States.

Now, without entering into a detailed consideration of the nature and effect of the different transfers of power which have been effected by the Constitution, I think it will be very apparent, from even a superficial consideration of the classification which I have made, that with reference to the *extent of powers* granted to the Federal Government or denied to the States, the Constitution has made no *radical* change in the relation between the States and the central power. In truth, as I stated before, the great and essential difference between the Constitution and the Articles of Confederation is that the former creates a government to take the place of the "league of friendship" which formerly existed. It might, perhaps, open to an adept in the science of court etiquette a promising field for the exercise of his skill, to propound to him the

question whether, given a limited sovereign, it best
comports with "that divinity which doth hedge"
him, that he should be compelled to exercise certain functions of sovereignty at the will of another,
and without power to approve or disapprove, or
that his functions should be confined to those cases
in which he knows no master save his own will.
But as a question of political science, I apprehend
that it is of no importance whatever. Such is,
however, the principal change which has been made
in the former relations between the States and the
Government of the Union. For it is impossible to
lay the finger upon any *grant of power* to the new
Government which, as an attribute of sovereignty,
is not inferior in dignity and importance to many
of the powers conceded to the Congress of the confederation, or upon any *restriction* of the States in
the exercise of a power which, as an attribute of
sovereignty, is not at least equal in dignity and importance to some power which the States were restricted from exercising under the former system.
As examples illustrating simultaneously the truth
of each of these propositions I will refer to the
powers to declare war, to conclude peace, to maintain land and naval forces, and to enter into treaties
and alliances, all of which were granted to the
Congress of the confederation and denied to the
States as they are under the existing system. There
are no attributes of sovereign power which can out-

rank either of these; and we happen to have at hand (curiously enough), very conclusive evidence of the relative rank which the framers of the Articles of Confederation assigned to those very attributes of sovereignty; for in the Declaration of Independence, adopted by a Congress composed mostly of the same men who framed and recommended for the adoption of the States the Articles of Confederation, we find the united colonies first declaring in general terms that they are free and independent States, and then adding, " that as free and independent States they have full power to *levy war, conclude peace, contract alliances,* establish commerce, and to do all other things which independent States may of right do." There are thus four attributes of sovereignty which our forefathers deemed worthy of special mention in the great fundamental charter of their liberties, three of which they immediately granted to Congress, without any suspicion that such a grant affected the right of the States to complete sovereignty over the subjects of which they retained jurisdiction.

With reference to the *additional* grants of power made to Congress by the Constitution, I will copy from Number 46 of *The Federalist,* adding two short notes, intended to show how little reason there is to deduce a loss of sovereignty by the States, from the two most important of the additions.

" If the new Constitution be examined with accuracy and candor, it will be found that the change which it proposes consists much less in the addition of NEW POWERS to the Union than in the invigoration of its ORIGINAL POWERS. The regulation of commerce is, it is true, a new power, but that seems to be an addition which few oppose, and from which no apprehensions are entertained.*

"The powers relating to war and peace, armies and fleets, treaties and finance, with the other more considerable powers, are all vested in the existing Congress by the Articles of Confederation. The proposed change does not enlarge those powers : it only substitutes a more effectual mode of administering them. The change relating to taxation may be regarded as the most important,† and yet the pre-

* Among other arguments used elsewhere by *The Federalist* in favor of this clause of the proposed Constitution, it is mentioned that similar powers over internal commerce were then enjoyed by the federal authorities of Switzerland, Germany and the Netherlands. The author of " Our Domestic Relations " lays great stress upon the power of Congress " to put limits roundabout the business of the several States," but I opine that the king of Prussia would be astonished to learn from a grave senator of the United States, that his predecessors (Frederick the Great, for instance) were not sovereigns.

† Numbers 30 to 36 of *The Federalist* are devoted to the discussion of this power. Their object is to show the propriety of granting to the United States a " *concurrent* jurisdiction with the States in the article of taxation."

sent Congress have as complete authority to REQUIRE
from the States indefinite supplies of money for the
common defence and general welfare, as the future
Congress will have to require them of individual
citizens; and the latter will be no more bound than
the States themselves have been to pay the quotas
respectively taxed on them."

The new restrictions of the powers of the States
consist partly of such as were necessary to render
effective the new powers granted to Congress, and
partly of covenants or compacts that no State
shall exercise its powers so as to inflict certain
injuries upon the others. As I have already stated,
they exclude the States from but a very small portion of the privileges which were left to them by
the Articles of Confederation. In "Our Domestic
Relations" the powers of Congress are styled "that
commanding sovereignty which *embraces and holds
the whole country* within its perpetual and irreversi-
ble jurisdiction;" and those of the States are designated, by way of contradistinction, as "that special
local control which is essential to the business and
convenience of life." One would suppose that the

In Number 32 it is said, that such jurisdiction can never be
so construed as to interfere with the State right of taxation, because the possibility of inconvenience in the exercise
of its powers by the national Government could not "by
implication alienate and extinguish *a preëxisting right of
sovereignty.*"

latter sentence (even without dwarfing its subject
by juxtaposition with the "tumultuous grandeur"
of the phrase which precedes it) was employed to
describe a village corporation, instead of a State
vested with full legislative power over the lives,
liberty, and property of millions—power which is
absolute and supreme, except in the very few instances when it is specially limited by the Federal
Constitution. Let me again refer to *The Federalist*
for a proper description of the relative functions of
the National and State Governments; and as the
author of "Our Domestic Relations" cites Mr.
Madison in support of the theory that the States
are not sovereign, I will select my extracts from
some of the articles written by that distinguished
statesman.

From No. 45: "The powers delegated by the
proposed Constitution to the Federal Government
are few and defined. Those which are to remain
in the State Governments are numerous and indefinite. The former will be exercised principally in external objects, as war, peace, negotiation, and foreign
commerce, with which last the power of taxation
will, for the most part, be connected. The powers
reserved to the several States will extend to all objects which, in the ordinary course of affairs, concern the lives, liberties, and property of the people,
and the internal order, improvement, and prosperity
of the State."

2*

From No. 40 : " We have seen that in tne new government, as in the old, the general powers are limited ; and that the States, in all unenumerated cases, are left in the enjoyment of *their sovereign and independent jurisdiction.*"

From No. 39 : " But if the government be national with regard to the operation of its powers, *it changes its aspect when we contemplate it in relation to the extent of its powers.* The idea of a national government involves in it not only an authority over the individual citizens, but an indefinite supremacy over all persons and things, so far as they are objects of lawful government. . . . . *In this relation, then, the proposed government cannot be deemed a national one,* since its jurisdiction extends to certain enumerated objects only, and leaves to the several States *a residuary and inviolable sovereignty over all other objects.*"

I have thus considered all the grounds upon which the author of " Our Domestic Relations " bases his denial of State sovereignty, except the supremacy which the Constitution accords to the United States Constitution and to the laws "*which shall be made in pursuance thereof.*" But it is evident that this objection is already answered by what precedes. The real question is, have the States lost their sovereignty, or do they still retain it ? If, in fact, they retain " a residuary and inviolable sovereignty " it makes no difference that the

United States Government is supreme in the exercise of *that portion of sovereignty* which has been conceded to it.

The Federalist very correctly gives the reason why State officers are bound by oath to support the United States Constitution, while United States officers are not bound by oath to support the State constitutions, which is, that the State officers constitute an essential part of the machinery employed in the operation of the Federal Government, whereas Federal officers are not in any degree relied upon to keep in motion the wheels of the State governments. And as to the language of the clause of the Constitution which confers supremacy, it is but a mode of expressing the object to accomplish which both the Articles of Confederation and the Constitution were framed, that is, to cleave down *in certain particulars* the State constitutions. As *The Federalist* says (No. 33), the clause of supremacy " only declares a truth which flows immediately and necessarily from the formation of a Federal Government," and I may add, that it is a mere form of expression, scarcely available to settle a question of etiquette ; for while it provides that the national Government shall be supreme within its designated limits, the clause withholding from the Federal Government all powers which the Constitution does not affirmatively confer upon it, amounts to an assertion of supremacy in the States for all other purposes—a supremacy which the national Government must bow to as well as the humblest citizen, so long as the Constitution is not overthrown by force or by usurpation. Mr. Sumner has himself expressed the idea very appropriately in a speech delivered by him in the Senate on the 26th of August, 1853, in which he says, "While the nation within its wide orbit is supreme, the States move with equal supremacy in their own. From the necessity of the case, the supremacy of each in its proper place excludes the other." Here is the whole case in a nut-shell.

Let me now refer to a few of the express provisions of the Constitution itself. I have previously stated that while it organizes and creates the national Government, it simply recognizes the States as existing—and I may add, that it recognizes them as *governments exercising the attributes of sovereignty.* It speaks repeatedly of the States as political bodies possessing a "legislature," "executive," "executive authority," "executive and judicial officers," "judges," "constitution," "laws," "jurisdiction," "militia," "public acts, records and judicial proceedings," and, finally, a "form of government"—and in the latter connection it provides that these organizations, which we are now told are merely a species of corporations, shall not convert themselves into monarchies or aristocracies. It even goes farther, for it recognizes the possibility of the *crime of trea-*

son being committed by those whom the author of
" Our Domestic Relations" styles " the individuals
of whom the several corporations were composed,"
against the " several corporations" themselves. In
truth, the following extract from the second section
of the fourth article of the Constitution, contains in
itself a complete refutation of the theory that the
States lost their sovereignty when the Constitution
was adopted.

" A person charged in any State with *treason*,
felony or other crime, who shall flee from justice
and be found in another State, shall, on demand of
the executive authority of the State from which he
fled, be delivered up to be removed to the State
having jurisdiction of the crime."

This clause is not a transcript, but a remodelling
of a clause to the same effect in the Articles of Confederation, the language having undergone sufficient alteration to show that it had been carefully
revised. The significance of this clause as it stands
will become apparent, by considering what an argument it would have offered to those who deny the
existence of State sovereignty, if this word *treason*
had been omitted in the revision.

I have stated that the constitutions of the States
were appropriate to the exercise of that sovereignty
which they confessedly possessed under the Articles
of Confederation. It is another most significant
circumstance that those constitutions remained in

full force and unchanged for a long time after the
adoption of the Constitution. The constitution of
New York was not changed (save by certain amendments made in 1801 and relating exclusively to
matters of local administration) till the year 1823.
The constitution of Massachusetts remained entirely
unaltered till 1820, and with the exception of some
amendments, relating likewise to local matters, the
same constitution continues in force to the present
day. I copy two of its paragraphs, which yet remain a part of the fundamental law of that State,
whose senator has now discovered that it is merely
a political corporation.

"The people of this Commonwealth have the
sole and exclusive right of governing themselves, as
a *free, sovereign and independent State*, and do
and forever hereafter shall exercise and enjoy every
power, jurisdiction and right, which is not or may
not hereafter be BY THEM DELEGATED to the United
States of America in Congress assembled."—*Declaration of Rights, Article IV.*

"The people inhabiting the territory formerly
called the Province of Massachusetts Bay do hereby
solemnly and mutually agree with each other to
form themselves into a free, *sovereign and independent body politic or State*, by the name of the
Commonwealth of Massachusetts."—*Preamble to
Form of Government.*

In New York, we find in the constitution adopted

in 1846, the following : " The people of this State, in their right of *sovereignty*, are deemed to possess the original and ultimate property in and to all lands within the jurisdiction of the State."—*Article I., Section II.*

The legislation of the two States has been equally explicit.

" The General Statutes of the Commonwealth of Massachusetts," enacted in the year 1859, contain the following, which is a transcript from a law which has been reënacted in the same manner at every revision of the statutes of Massachusetts, since the foundation of the Government.

" The *sovereignty and jurisdiction* of the Commonwealth extend to all places within the boundaries thereof, subject to the rights of concurrent *jurisdiction* granted over places ceded to the United States."—*Part I., Chap. I., Title 1, Sec. 2.*

A statute of equal antiquity in the State of New York, reënacted for the last time in 1828, provides,

" The *sovereignty and jurisdiction* of this State extend to all places within the boundaries thereof as declared in the preceding title, but the extent of such *jurisdiction* over places that have been or may be ceded to the United States, shall be qualified by the terms of such cession."—*R. S., Part I., Chap. I., Title 2, Sec. 1.*

By subsequent sections it is made the duty of the Governor " to maintain and defend its sover-

eignty and jurisdiction," and "if any suit be commenced to recover lands held under a title derived
from the State under pretence of any claim inconsistent with its sovereignty and jurisdiction," it is
made the duty of the Governor to provide for the
defence of such suit.

But if these assertions of their own sovereignty,
made by the States, notwithstanding the number
of years during which they have passed unchal-
lenged, are unsatisfactory to the discoverers of the
new political theory that no such sovereignty exists, I will adduce in further evidence, an act of
the same character to which the national Government was a party. I refer to the proceedings by
which the district of Boston Corner was ceded by
the State of Massachusetts to the State of New
York, and the consent of Congress was given to
the cession.

The Massachusetts statute, passed May 14, 1853,
commences as follows : " Be it enacted, &c., Sec. 1,
Sovereignty and jurisdiction over that portion of
this commonwealth known as the district of Boston
Corner, situate, &c., is hereby ceded to the State
of New York, with all the powers, &c., now exercised over the same by this commonwealth."

The New York statute, passed July 21, 1853,
commences also :

"The people, &c., do enact as follows : *Sovereignty and jurisdiction* over that portion of the ter-

ritory of the commonwealth of Massachusetts known
as the district of Boston Corner, situate, &c., ceded
to the State of New York by an act of the legislature of said commonwealth passed, &c., and entitled, &c., is hereby accepted by the State of New
York."

Each of these acts was by its terms to take effect
only upon the consent of Congress being procured, it
being somewhat doubtful whether the third section
of the fourth article of the Constitution would not
apply to such a case. Such consent was accordingly given by an act passed January 3, 1855,
which recites that " whereas the commonwealth of
Massachusetts by an act, &c., ceded the *sovereignty
and jurisdiction* over that portion of territory
known, &c., to the State of New York . . . and,
whereas, the State of New York, by an act, &c.,
accepted the *sovereignty and jurisdiction* over that
portion of the territory of Massachusetts above described—Therefore, be it enacted by the Senate
and House of Representatives of the United States
of America in Congress assembled, that the consent
of the Congress of the United States be and the
same is hereby given to SAID CESSION and annexa-
tion."

If, therefore, the author of " Our Domestic Relations " is worthy of the honorable appellation of the
great man whose seat in the Senate he fills, we
have here the extraordinary spectacle of the legis-

latures of two of the principal States of the Union, the Congress and President of the United States, ignorantly or wickedly uniting to disgrace the statute books by an affirmation of the correctness of a doctrine which contravenes the whole theory of the Constitution, strikes at the very root of sound government, and if made the basis of practical action, would subject its advocates to the penalties of treason. For Mr. Sumner tells us distinctly that "the Constitution . . . can bear no sovereignty but itself;" that "there is but one sovereignty recognized, and that is the sovereignty of the United States ;" that "State sovereignty . . . has disappeared and been lost in the supremacy of the national Government, so that it can no longer be recognized ;" and that when "the Constitution was adopted . . . the miserable pretension of State sovereignty was discarded."

Who were the men through whose ignorance or corruption, if these sentences enunciate political truths, such a foul wrong was done to the majesty of the nation? I will not allude to the members of the two Houses of the Legislature or the governors of the two States, or to the Federal House of Representatives. I will content myself with referring to the United States Senate, a body which then comprised, to say nothing of men of lesser note, or men whose southern residence might lead to their rejection as expounders of constitutional law—Messrs. Hannibal Hamlin, of Maine; Charles Sumner, of Massachusetts; William II. Seward, of New York; Lewis Cass, of Michigan; Salmon P Chase, of Ohio; and Stephen A. Douglas, of Illinois. Mr. Rockwell, of Massachusetts, the colleague of Mr. Sumner, moved that the bill pass, and it was passed accordingly without debate, the ayes and noes not being called for. Why did none of these gentlemen rise and disclose the disorganizing political heresy, which we are now told is contained in the act referred to? Is it not clear that it was because the discovery of that heresy dates from the period when State rights became an inconvenient obstacle to the success of particular personal or political schemes? In truth, I have at hand evidence, in the published writings and speeches of each of the gentlemen whom I have designated by name, except Messrs. Hamlin and Chase, of his full concurrence in the doctrine of State sovereignty; and I doubt not that sufficient research would enable me to adduce evidence that those two gentlemen also hold, or at least held, the same doctrine.

Did space permit, I could furnish innumerable extracts to the same effect from the writings and speeches of the most illustrious jurists and statesmen from the earliest times to the present day. And it is a curious and significant fact that the researches of the author of "Our Domestic Relations" have enabled him to fortify his argument with no

citations to the point, except extracts from speeches
made in the Constitutional Convention by members
who, in their zeal for the new system of government,
were betrayed into saying that, even under the
then existing system, the States were not sovereign.

But a fear of wearying my readers at the very
commencement of my work, confines me to a few
extracts from a single speech, that delivered by
Senator Sumner, in the Senate of the United States,
on the twenty-third of February, eighteen hundred
and fifty-five. The subject of the speech was the
fugitive slave law, and the extracts will suffice to
show in what a different light he viewed "the pestilent pretension of State rights" as well as "the
miserable pretension of State sovereignty," when—
if the force of the expression will excuse its home-
liness—the United States bull was goring Mr.
Sumner's ox. The author of "Our Domestic Relations" then spoke as follows:

"Suffice it to say that it [the fugitive slave law]
is an intrusive and offensive encroachment on
State rights, calculated to subvert the power of the
States in the protection of their citizens.   .   .   .

"There is an argument against it which has espe-
cial importance at this moment, when the fugitive
act is made the occasion of a new assault on *State
rights*. This very act is an assumption by Congress
of power not delegated to it under the Constitution,

and an infraction of rights secured to the States.
You will mark, if you please, the double aspect of
this proposition, in asserting not only an assumption
of power by Congress, but an *infraction of
State rights.* And this proposition, I venture to
say, defies answer or cavil.

*   *   *   *   *   *

"And yet, sir, in zeal to support this enormity,
senators have not hesitated to avow a purpose to
break down the legislation of States, calculated to
shield the liberty of their citizens. 'It is difficult,'
says Burke, 'to frame an indictment against a
whole people.' But here in the Senate, where are
convened the jealous representatives of the States,
we have heard whole States arraigned, as if guilty
of crime. The senator from Louisiana has set forth,
in plaintive tones, the ground of proceeding, and
more than one *sovereign State* has been summoned
to judgment. . . . . .

"And now, almost while I speak, comes the
solemn judgment of the Supreme Court of Wisconsin, *a sovereign State of this Union,* declaring this
act to be a violation of the Constitution."

Verily the author of "Our Domestic Relations"
should have prefixed to his ingenious essay a quotation from a poetic *collaborateur*—

"Weep not that the world changes—did it keep
A stable, changeless course, 'twere cause to weep."

CHAPTER II.

The Constitutional Power of the General Government to suppress a Rebellion—That Power not affected by the unwarrantable sanction of a Rebellion by a State—The impossibility of a Constitutional Collision between the State and National Sovereignties—The course of the General Government in the Nullification Controversy—A similar course in this Controversy will not expose us to the charge of coercing Sovereign States—Consideration of the Doctrines of Forfeiture of State Rights by State Treason, of State Suicide, and of the Abdication by a State of its Place in the Union.

LET us now proceed to inquire what effect the doctrine of State sovereignty has upon the constitutional right of the general Government to use its military power for the purpose of reducing to obedience rebels against its authority, who plead the mandates of their own States in justification of their rebellion, and what objects the general Government can lawfully propose to accomplish by the use of force in such a case.

And first, has the general Government power to employ its military arm against rebels in any case whatever? I do not understand that there is any conflict of opinion among us upon this point. It is true that there is no express grant of any such power in the Constitution—the provision authorizing Congress to provide for calling out the militia " to execute the laws of the Union, suppress insurrections and repel invasions," being generally regarded as limiting the power of the Federal Government over the militia to those three cases, rather than as an affirmative grant of authority to do the several acts specified. Still those words lead irresistibly to the conclusion that the power " to suppress insurrections " is in fact lodged in the central Government ; and their connection with the rest of the sentence, and the ample powers which the States enjoy over their own militia, indicate very conclusively that the insurrections referred to, are those against the authority of the Union, and not of the several States. In truth, it is not necessary to resort to this clause, to justify the use of force to suppress a rebellion. Such a right results, by necessary implication, from the establishment of a government empowered to require the obedience of all its citizens, to the extent of the authority conferred upon it, and consequently entitled to their allegiance to that extent. Any such government, possessing a military arm, has the unquestionable right to use that arm to compel its subjects to obey its laws and respect its rightful authority, whenever the civil power proves to be insufficient for that purpose. We find accordingly in that part of the Constitution which treats of the powers of Congress,

a provision that the writ of habeas corpus shall be
suspended only when "in cases of rebellion or invasion the public safety may require it." And our
history shows that such a power was exercised in
the earliest days of the republic, and while the
Government was administered by the framers of the
Constitution, and their immediate contemporaries,
with Washington at their head.

Nor will the right to exercise such a power be
affected by the circumstance that the rebellion
purports to be justified by a State, when the insurgents are resisting the lawful and constitutional
authority of the Federal Government.

The doctrine of State sovereignty does not legitimately lead to any such conclusion, because it does
not require its advocates to deny the sovereignty
of the national Government. As stated in the
preceding chapter, the Constitution divides the
sovereign power, and allots distinct and different
portions of it to the Federal Government and to the
States respectively. It was evidently the design of
the framers of that instrument to render a conflict
of jurisdiction between the two impossible, by
drawing a clear line of demarkation, which should
restrain each within certain distinctly defined limits.
Every citizen of the nation was to owe a double
allegiance, that is, an allegiance to two separate
sovereigns—but this double allegiance was never to
require from him inconsistent duties and obliga-

tions. A clash of rightful jurisdiction between the States and the nation was rendered impossible by the enumeration of specific powers granted to the latter, and the provision that "the powers not delegated to the United States by the Constitution, nor prohibited by it to the States, are reserved to the States respectively or the people." And as it is entirely clear that no case of the exercise of authority can be suggested, which will not fall within one of the two classes, that is, powers delegated, or powers not delegated, it is apparent that the two governments can never rightfully require from the citizen obedience at the same time to two contradictory mandates. Whenever such a conflict apparently occurs, one of the two must necessarily be a usurper.

The fact that cases have continually arisen where each government claimed that the Constitution authorized it to exercise jurisdiction, does not militate against the soundness or the application of this principle. Such conflicts of authority have resulted, not from any actual omission in the Constitution to provide for every possible case, for, as we have seen, every possible case is provided for; but merely from the imperfection of human language, which has frequently rendered it impossible to ascertain immediately, by reference to the words used in the Constitution, whether in a particular case jurisdiction was granted to the Federal Government or re-

3

served to the States. A precisely similar state of things, and for the same reason, frequently occurs under the provisions of the constitutions and statutes of the different States, when the question arises between the State government and the citizen, or between different departments of the State government. In neither case was it intended that any doubt should exist; and in each case, when the question arises, the object of the tribunal which settles it is to ascertain, not how to provide for the contingency which has occurred, but how the constitution or statute in question provided for it; and when that is once ascertained, the effect is the same as if such a provision, for such a particular case, was incorporated into the body of the instrument itself. And the object of creating a national tribunal, with power to settle such questions as they might arise, was to avoid all danger of a resort to the sword, and to protect the citizen against the consequences of mistaking the sovereignty to which obedience was due.

It is one of the results of the impossibility that any conflict of rightful authority between the State and Nation should ever occur under the Constitution, that neither can, in any case, have the power to molest the other, or empower the common subjects of both to molest the other, in the full and unrestricted exercise of its allotted portion of the sovereign power. It is, therefore, clear that the doctrine of State sovereignty does not justify a rebellion against the rightful power of the general Government, notwithstanding that such rebellion may be sanctioned by the authority of the State.

The great point of difference between us and the South, respecting the constitutionality of the war on our part, arises not out of the doctrine that *the States are sovereign as to all matters not delegated to the United States by the terms of the Constitution*, but because the southern statesmen affirm the existence of *a State sovereignty which overrides the Constitution*. They contend that any State has the constitutional right to withdraw at pleasure from the Union; and that whenever it exercises that right, the allegiance which the individual citizen of that State owed, under the Constitution, to the national Government is at once dissolved, the *entire* allegiance of the citizen is *ipso facto* transferred to the State, thus rendered, by its own act, completely sovereign and independent; and an attempt on the part of the general Government to coerce obedience from the citizen becomes an act of usurpation. It follows from their premises that a war waged for such a purpose is a war of conquest merely, a striking coincidence with the conclusion to which those who deny the existence of any State sovereignty whatever have also arrived from *their* premises. It is by no means the first time that moderate men have had occasion to notice the remarkable similarity of the conclusions upon constitutional questions which the extremists of the northern and southern sections have reached, starting from premises as wide apart as the poles, and pursuing their converging course with mutual hatred and reviling.

I shall not encumber these pages with a dissertation upon the constitutional right of secession. So far as I am informed, no public man at the North maintains, at least openly, the existence of such a right, and its fallacy has been demonstrated repeatedly by arguments which appear to us to be entirely conclusive. It is impossible at present to procure the adjudication of the Supreme Court upon this question, and its consequent determination as a proposition of constitutional law. That tribunal is entirely competent to dispose of it (so perfect were the provisions which our forefathers made for the peaceful settlement of all our disputes), but the sword has been appealed to, and the sword alone can now decide the issue.

But it has been maintained, by statesmen of both sections of the country, that the Federal Government has no power to coerce the States, because the very idea of sovereignty is inconsistent with the right of coercion by any other power, and hence it is said that when a State attempts to exercise the pretended right of secession, the national Government is powerless to redress the wrongful act by force of arms. There would be considerable force in this argument, if it was necessary to assail the sovereignty of the States in order to reinstate the Federal Government in the exercise of its rightful jurisdiction over rebel territory. But no such necessity exists; we have only to follow out the principles which I have laid down to their legitimate conclusion. A State having, as we hold, no power to withdraw from the Union, its attempt to do so is simply an excess of jurisdiction, and therefore absolutely void, and to be treated in all respects as a nullity. The case is precisely the same as if it had undertaken to do any other act which the Constitution prevents it from doing. I need not resort to my imagination to suppose such a case, for it is well known that South Carolina undertook at one period of our history to nullify the laws of the United States providing for the collection of the duties upon imports. The United States authorities treated the act as entirely void, and proceeded to collect the revenue under the protection of the navy, at the same time menacing those who should resist such collection with criminal proceedings, and, if necessary, with the employment of the land forces. But these menaces were directed against *individuals* wrongfully resisting the Federal authority, the question whether they were or were not State officials being entirely ignored; and no suggestion was made that the State authorities should be deposed, or that the armed power of the nation

should be employed to coerce them, even to reverse the wrongful action of the State. This course
was perfectly consistent with the sovereignty of the
nation and the sovereignty of the State, and so long
as we pursue the same course in dealing with individuals who are now in rebellion, we are not justly
chargeable with coercing States; we are, on the contrary, "letting the seceded States alone," and merely
refusing to allow individuals to commit treason, and
justify themselves under an enactment which is
entirely void for want of jurisdiction.

It seems to me that these conclusions involve no
metaphysical subtlety or too finely drawn distinc-
tions: but if any portion of the argument is justly
chargeable with those faults, it is that which maintains the right of the Government to carry on the
war, notwithstanding the mandates of the States.
The proposition that the only legitimate object
of the war is to restore the " status quo ante bellum," by reëstablishing the Federal authority in
its original integrity over those individuals who
have rebelled against it, is but the natural conclusion to be drawn from the principles upon which
we defend the authority of the national Government to carry on the war at all. Whether we
deduce that authority from the implied right of
every government to cause its legitimate authority
to be respected by force, or whether we find it
in the clause authorizing the militia to be called

out " to suppress insurrections," it is manifest that the power is exhausted whenever the unlawful resistance is at an end, and the civil power of the Government has become adequate to the due administration of the Federal laws.

But some of our statesmen now contend that although such may be primarily the only legitimate object of the war, yet that as a necessary consequence of the attempt on the part of the States to secede, and their subsequently wrongfully making war upon the United States, they have forfeited their constitutional rights, and the restoration of their territory to the jurisdiction of the general Government will be unaccompanied with any constitutional restriction whatever upon the latter in the exercise of power within that territory. Several reasons are given for that conclusion. In the first place it is said that the States have committed treason by making war upon the nation. I have already shown that it is a constitutional impossibility that a State should make war upon the nation, and that if the forms of State authority are used by usurpers to carry on such a war, the national Government cannot recognize it as a war carried on by the State, and make even a defensive war upon the State in return, without committing an equally flagrant usurpation. But other principles, equally fundamental, forbid the conclusion that such a war can result in the loss of the constitutional rights of a

State. In the strict legal sense of the term it is
impossible for a sovereignty to commit treason;
still, it is not to be denied that in a federative form
of government, one of the members of the confederation may commit an offence against the federative
compact, which will have practically the same
consequences as the commission of the crime of
treason by an individual subject against his sovereign. Such were the offences which, under the
Germanic confederation, were punished by the
offending sovereign being placed under the "ban
of the empire," the consequences of which were the
loss of the sovereign rights and possessions of the
offender, to be enforced by the armed power of the
confederation, or of particular states to which the
execution of the decree might be committed.

But can an offence involving such consequences,
be committed against the federative compact by a
state possessing a REPUBLICAN form of government?
In a monarchy the crown is the individual inherit-
ance of the monarch, just as the dukedoms, mar-
quisates, &c., are the individual inheritances of the
nobles respectively, and the case may well occur
when it will be no offence against common right to
punish him for a crime by depriving him of the
dignity which he has abused. But those who administer the government in a *republic* have no personal interest in the government itself; they are
mere temporary occupants of public station; and

to deprive the State of its powers and jurisdiction for their misconduct is to punish the innocent commonalty, who have already been aggrieved by the unjustifiable acts of men who may have owed their positions to corruption, fraud, or perhaps violence, and who have certainly exceeded, in committing unconstitutional acts, the authority which was confided to them by the people. Nor would the case be altered by the submission of the ordinance of secession to the people themselves. The rights of majorities, as well as of public officials, are defined by the terms of the State and national constitutions, and for a majority to commit an unconstitutional act, in defiance of the wishes of a minority, is a usurpation of the same character as the commission of a similar act by a public official. But in point of fact, the ordinances of secession were adopted by the vote of the people in only two of the States.

I think, then, that the idea that a State can commit treason, in consequence of the unconstitutional acts of those who are administering its government, is utterly at war with the theory upon which our whole political system is constructed. But a consideration of the provisions of the Constitution, and of the principles to which I have already adverted, will make it manifest that no treason against the general Government can possibly be committed by a State. For the latter *owes no allegiance* to the general Government in any respect. As I have

3*

previously stated, the Constitution has provided for
such a perfect division of the functions of government between the two sovereignties, that neither
occupies a position of constitutional subordination
to the other. They are planets with entirely different orbits, which cannot by any possibility collide
with each other, until the whole system is wrecked.
The struggle on the part of the South is to wreck
the system, but we profess to be fighting to save it
from destruction. By recognizing the war, as made
by the States upon the general Government, we are
actually aiding the rebels in their unlawful purpose
to usurp in the name of the States a jurisdiction
which the Constitution has withheld from them.
To aid in that usurpation and to make it a pretext
to deprive the States of powers which they hold by
a tenure even stronger than that under which the
general Government holds all its powers, is first to
become parties to the conspiracy against the Constitution, and then to make the existence of the
conspiracy an excuse for a crime even more stu-
pendous than that which the original conspirators
contemplated. Such a course of conduct cannot be
justified by those who are equally unwilling to
allow the southern revolution to triumph, and to
become revolutionists themselves, unless it can be
shown that the States hold their reserved sovereignty under the Constitution during good beha-
vior—" quamdiu se bene gesserint "—or until it has

become an established maxim in political science and public morality that two wrongs make a right.

The same argument answers two other theories by which it has been attempted to establish the doctrine that the States have lost their rights in consequence of the rebellion carried on in their name, to wit, that they have committed political suicide, and that they have abdicated their places in the Union. These may, in fact, be regarded as two different methods of stating the proposition that they have forfeited their rights by their treason.

There are, however, other reasons assigned for the alleged disappearance of State rights, which call for a cursory examination. They will be considered in the next chapter

CHAPTER III.

Answer to Senator Sumner's Theory of a " Tabula rasa " in consequence of the vacancy of the State Offices—The unconstitutionality of the project to disfranchise Individuals or Classes by Act
of Congress—The recognition of the Insurgents as Belligerents
will not give us the rights of Conquerors over Territory wrested
from them—State Rights, not being derived from the Constitution, cannot be forfeited to the General Government—That Government has no power to disturb the balance of our Political
System by accepting such a Forfeiture.

THE author of " Our Domestic Relations " brushes
aside the theories of State forfeiture, State treason,
and State abdication, as " endless mazes in which
a whole Senate may be lost," and prefers to rest his
argument on the fact that the rebel States have
now no State officers who have taken the constitutional oaths of office; therefore, he says, their governments are vacated, and there are no officers who
are capable of superintending new elections, or of
administering oaths of office to such persons as might
be selected to fill the vacancies; and from these
premises he deduces the conclusion, that " the whole
broad rebel region is *tabula rasa*, or ' a clean slate,
whereon Congress, under the Constitution of the
United States, may write the laws."

I will not stop to consider the question whether, inasmuch as the requirement that an oath of office to support the Constitution shall be taken by State officers, is mandatory merely, and not made a condition precedent to the discharge of their official functions, an omission to comply with it authorizes the Federal authorities to treat the offices as vacant, while their functions are discharged by officers *de facto*, at least until the latter shall be ousted by legal proceedings; nor whether, if the Federal authorities would have such a right, the State officials may not at any future time qualify themselves by taking the oath required. No lawyer will hesitate to say that these are grave questions for the judicial department of the Government, and which it would be rash for executive or legislative authority to dispose of summarily; but it seems to me that there is an obvious answer to the conclusion, drawn from such questionable premises, which cannot fail at once to impress the general reader with its force. For the argument, resting as it does upon the mere fact of the State offices being vacant, and not depending (as indeed it could not depend without judicial convictions) upon the misconduct of the individuals who are *de facto* filling them, would be equally applicable to any other case where, by accident or from necessity, the terms of all the officers of a State had expired, and no constitutional elections had been held to fill the vacancies.

Therefore if it should happen, in the course of a war between our country and a foreign power, that one of the States should be invaded by an enemy, who should hold possession of the invaded territory for a period extending beyond the official terms of legislative and executive officers, superceding the local laws meanwhile by martial power, it would follow, if the argument which I am considering is sound, that upon the restoration of peace the State would present a *tabula rasa* upon which Congress might write the laws. And by a parity of reasoning, if the invasion should extend so far, and continue so long, that it should be impossible to obtain a quorum in the national Senate, House of Representatives, and the Electoral College, of members duly elected from the different States, the whole Government would be dissolved, the whole nation would become a *tabula rasa*, and the people of the United States, having ceased to possess any government whatever, further resistance to the invader would become the irregular act of an unorganized community, and therefore no lawful warfare. I am unable to see why the argument of a " tabula rasa," in consequence of vacancies in the public offices, does not lead to both of these conclusions, and many others of equal absurdity, with which I will not take up the time of the reader. The result is instructive, as showing into what quagmires of political doctrine men fall when they are no longer content "stare super antiquas vias," to cling to the old established doctrine of the limitation of the powers of the general Government and the inviolable sovereignty of the States.

It has also been said, that even if a State cannot theoretically forfeit any of its constitutional rights, yet that the general Government, after the rebellion is subdued, will be practically left free to accomplish such reforms in its Constitution as may be deemed advisable, because the whole community having committed treason, there will be no citizens, at least not enough to be worth regarding, who can insist upon a strict fulfilment of constitutional obligations; that the constitutional rights will therefore remain in abeyance for the want of the individuals to assert and exercise them; that Congress can provide by law for the exclusion of traitors from the exercise of the elective franchise; and that before the population which has committed no offence against the laws, will increase sufficiently to entitle it to resume the functions of self-government, the institutions of the State may be permanently modelled as may be desired. But a careful consideration of the subject will show that however plausible such a theory may appear, a palpable violation of the Constitution by Congress can alone reduce it to practical operation.

Among the various modes of exercise of legislative power none is more unequivocally condemned by the Constitution than that of passing acts of 'attainder, which was, till comparatively recently, the practice of the English Parliament, and the use of which disgraced even our own legislatures during the Revolution. Judge Rawle, in his treatise on the Constitution (p. 119) defines a bill of attainder as one " by which a person without judicial trial is declared by the legislature to be guilty of some particular crime ;" and he adds, that " the definition itself shows the atrocity of the act." Judge Story, in his treatise, says, that such an exercise of power in a free government would be intolerable ; and the most eminent modern jurists and publicists of all nations have condemned it. Accordingly, the Constitution, in its restraints upon the power of Congress, says explicitly—" *No bill of attainder shall be passed ;*" and it secures the citizen, by two separate and distinct provisions, against any punishment for crime, except upon conviction by a jury of the State where the crime shall be alleged to have been committed. So long as the Constitution is recognized as subsisting, it will therefore be impossible to declare any of the citizens of the southern States guilty of treason by act of the Federal legislature, or in any other way than in pursuance of the sentence of a regular judicial tribunal, and the verdict of a jury taken from the State in which the treason was committed. I doubt not that it will be practicable so to legislate as to procure a jury which will convict of treason in isolated cases, but I think that I need not spend any time in demonstrating the impracticability of indicting and convicting of treason the people of a whole State, or a sufficient number of them to make any appreciable difference in the number of those who will wield the political power of the State. Nor can the same result be accomplished indirectly by a test oath. The Constitution confers no power upon Congress, either expressly or by implication, to prescribe the qualifications of electors for members of the national House of Representatives, much less for members of the State legislature, or any of the State offices. On the contrary, those matters are expressly and exclusively left to State legislation. So palpable is the want of power in Congress to overthrow State power in the South by prescribing the qualifications of voters, that the author of " Our Domestic Relations " concedes the impossibility of effecting his cherished scheme by any such means.

It has also been argued that inasmuch as the southern people have been recognized as belligerents, not only by foreign powers but by the United States Supreme Court, and our legislative, executive and military authorities have dealt with them, in all respects, as if we were waging a foreign war, we shall enjoy at the conclusion of the war all the rights of conquerors, including the right of reorganizing the southern territory as we shall think proper. But the answer to this suggestion is that we have never treated our war as a foreign war, but as a civil war merely; and that the belligerent rights which we have assumed, and the belligerent liabilities to which we have held the insurgents, were imposed by us partly to mitigate the horrors of the war, by subjecting its operations to the rules of civilized warfare, and partly for our own convenience, and to increase the efficiency of our military operations. The necessity and convenience which led us to treat our adversaries as belligerents, did not at all depend upon the fact that the State governments profess to be actors in the war, but they arose solely from the magnitude of the scale upon which the war was waged. The result would have been the same if the State governments had been overpowered by the insurgents at the outset of the rebellion, and if the latter had attempted to obliterate the States entirely, and to set up an imperial government, embracing the whole insurgent territory, instead of a union of confederate republics similar to our own. And as we still profess that the restoration of the Union is the object for which we are fighting, the assumption of belligerent relations between us and the rebels is necessarily temporary only, and must be abandoned when the war results in the accomplishment of that object. This is, in fact, confessed by the confiscation and penal laws, and the avowed purpose of the administration party to punish the leaders of the rebellion for treason, if the fortune of the war shall place them in our power. I find the principles to which the decision in the prize cases leads, so ably defended in another recent decision, from the revolutionary imputation which it is attempted to put upon them, that I copy a portion of the latter. It is from the opinion of Judge Sprague, of the United States District Court, pronounced at Boston in April, 1862, in the case of the "Amy Warwick." He says :

"An objection to the prize decisions of the district courts has arisen from an apprehension of radical consequences. It has been supposed that if the Government has the rights of a belligerent, then, after the rebellion is suppressed, it will have the rights of conquest: that a State and its inhabitants may be permanently divested of all political privileges, and treated as a foreign territory acquired by arms. This is an error—a grave and dangerous error.

"Conquest of a foreign country gives absolute and unlimited sovereign rights. But no nation ever makes such a conquest of its own territory. If a hostile power, either from within or without a nation, takes possession and holds absolute dominion over any portion of its territory, and the nation by force of arms expels or overthows the enemy and suppresses hostilities, it acquires no new title, but

merely regains the possession of which it had been
temporarily deprived. The nation acquires no new
sovereignty, but merely maintains its previous
rights. . . . Under our Government, the right
of sovereignty over any portion of a State is given
and limited by the Constitution, and will be the
same after the war as it was before. When the
United States take possession of any rebel district,
they acquire no new title, but merely vindicate that
which previously existed, and are only to do what
is necessary for that purpose. Confiscations of
property . . . . are primitive, and punishments
should be inflicted only upon proof of personal
guilt. What offences should be created and what
penalties affixed, must be left to the justice and
wisdom of Congress within the limits prescribed by
the Constitution. Such penal enactments have no
connection whatever with the decisions of prize
courts enforcing belligerent rights upon property
captured at sea during the war."

I have thus adverted, I believe, to all the theories
by which it has been attempted to show that the
southern States have surrendered, abdicated, or
forfeited, their political rights, in consequence of
the war which has been carried on in their name.
That they are so numerous, so dependent upon
metaphysical subtleties, so conducive to political
disorganization, and in many instances so discord-
ant with each other, is, to say the least, strong

primá facie evidence that they have their origin in a lust of power, or in the real or fancied necessities of a faction, rather than in a calm and disinterested search after the truth.

The importance of the subject will, I hope, be a sufficient excuse for my adding to this discussion, already too much prolonged, a few observations which are applicable to each of the theories which I have thus separately considered. They relate to the origin and structure of the Federal Government itself, and their general design is to show that even if it was a constitutional possibility for a State to forfeit or abdicate its reserved rights, in consequence of the misconduct of the persons temporarily administering its government, the Federal Government is not the authority to which such forfeiture would enure.

In constitutional monarchies, even in liberally governed Great Britain, the constitutional rights of the subject are so many encroachments upon the prerogative of the crown, which is theoretically the source from which the liberties of the people are derived, and the ultimate depository of all power not delegated to the representatives of the nation. If, therefore, any portion of the people of such a country should rise in rebellion against the rightful powers of the sovereign, there might be some foundation for an argument that by their rebellion they had forfeited their own constitutional rights. After

it was subdued, the sovereign power might perhaps
legally declare the occurrence of such a forfeiture,
and in that case, as the forfeited rights would at
once revert to the source from which they were
derived, the sovereign would to that extent be
liberated from constitutional restraints in the exercise of power over the offenders and over their territory. But the same reason does not apply to a
similar case arising in this country, because the
process by which the existing relations between the
States and the people on the one hand, and the
Federal Government on the other, were created,
was exactly the reverse of that by which the relations between the sovereign and the people have
been created in constitutional monarchies. Instead
of the rights of the States and of the people origi-
nating in grants from the general Government, they
were derived from a successful rebellion against the
British crown, and the general Government was
created by them, for their own convenience, safety,
and prosperity, and all its powers depend upon
affirmative grants made by them. And instead of
the general Government being the ultimate depository of all power not delegated to the States and the
people, its powers are specifically enumerated, and
the States and the people are expressly made the ultimate depositories of all other powers. There is,
therefore, a complete failure of all analogy between
the relations which the general Government will

near to the southern States after the suppression of the rebellion and those which would exist between a victorious sovereign and discomfited rebels. There are, indeed, certain privileges and rights which are the creatures of the Constitution, and dependent exclusively upon it, and which a State or a people may therefore forfeit by its own misconduct. But these are merely the *benefits of the Union;* and the only method of enforcing their forfeiture, is to allow the State which seeks to secede to "depart in peace."

It is also evident that the constitutional limitations and expansions of Federal and State powers are graduated in accordance with the general interest, as well as the interest of the particular State. They therefore exist for the benefit of all as well as of each particular member of the Union. For instance, one State cannot constitutionally establish a monarchy, even if Congress, her authorities, and a majority of her inhabitants should agree to waive the constitutional requirement that her form of government should be republican, because the existence of the monarchical form of government within any part of the territory of the Union is prohibited, not for the benefit of a particular State, but as being prejudicial to the interests of all.* For the same reason, a State cannot

* " The more intimate the nature of such an Union may be, the greater interest have the members in the political

even with the consent of Congress and a majority
of her citizens, *voluntarily surrender to the Federal
Government any one of her constitutional rights.*
How, then, can she be deprived for any misconduct of her authorities, or even of her citizens, of
rights which she cannot voluntarily cede? It is
the right and interest of all the States that their
common Government shall not, anywhere in the
Union, exercise any other jurisdiction than such as
the Constitution has confided to it. Citizens of
New York, Ohio or Pennsylvania would be injured
by an expansion of Federal jurisdiction in South
Carolina, Georgia or Alabama, for many reasons,
which may be briefly comprehended in the general
expression that the whole balance of our political
system would be disturbed thereby. We have,
therefore, a right, for our own sakes, to insist that
the constitutional balance of power shall remain in
all respects intact throughout the whole territory
of the nation, and that it shall not be disturbed by
the central Government drawing to itself powers
and functions which our forefathers for wise reasons
denied to it. This is a right of which we cannot be

institutions of each other, and the greater right to insist
that the forms of government under which the compact
was entered into, should be substantially maintained. . .
' Greece was undone,' says Montesquieu, ' as soon as the
king of Macedon obtained a seat among the Amphyctions.' "
—*The Federalist, No.* 43.

deprived by any action of Congress, because that body has not been vested with power to give our consent to any such modification of the relations between the Federal Government and the people of any State. Such modifications can only be made by an amendment of the Constitution in the manner provided for that · purpose in the instrument itself.

THE FUTURE to which the nation stands committed by the instrument which alone legalizes the war, is therefore the restoration of the States and the people of the South to their former position in the Union, and that the former political rights and privileges of all the individuals within the seceded States shall remain intact, except so far as they may be affected through the regular operation of the ordinary courts of justice. I will now consider the manner in which we reaffirmed that pledge, and the circumstances which attended its reaffirmation.

CHAPTER IV.

The Theory upon which we entered into the War—The Assurances
respecting its Object and Termination which were given to Foreign Nations—The Adoption of the Crittenden Resolution—Its
Obligatory Character as a National Pledge.

When this war broke out, it is not probable that
one in fifty of the American people would have
hesitated to announce his perfect concurrence in all
the sentiments expressed in the two preceding chapters, and to ridicule the idea that the war would
result in the slightest interference with the constitutional sovereignty of the southern States and the
political independence of the southern people.

The Administration and its party, and a very
large number of the opposition, were firmly persuaded that outside of South Carolina, the condition of the South in 1861 was very similar to the
condition of England in 1688. It was well known
that a very considerable portion of the southern
people did not consider Mr. Lincoln's election a
sufficient cause for secession: that in every State
except South Carolina, the Union party was not
overpowered without a severe struggle: that in
several of the States a majority of the delegates to

the convention were elected as unionists: that in one of them the ordinance of secession was rejected by the people and then subsequently adopted by the convention : and that of the four border States which seceded after the outbreak of hostilities, in only two was the ordinance submitted to the people. In those two (Tennessee and Virginia) the State authorities had, in advance of the popular vote, assumed to form an alliance with the Southern Confederacy, introduced the armies of the latter into the territory of the State, and raised large forces of State troops for the confederate side of the war. Hence, although in Tennessee there was a majority of 57,675, and in Virginia a majority of 105,577 in favor of secession, it was argued that there had been no fair election, and that the expression of the popular will had been prevented in those States by the presence of the confederate soldiery, as it had been in other States by the treachery, timidity or venality of the members of the conventions.

The bulk of the northern people firmly believed that throughout the whole South a system of bribery and threats had been employed upon the members of the State conventions by desperate men, eager to convulse the country with civil war, in order to realize their own schemes of power and dominion ; and that by such means the conventions had been induced to adopt the ordinance of

secession contrary to the known wishes of the
people.

It was also believed that the executive and legislative departments of the southern States had fallen
into the hands of unprincipled men, who, having
obtained power, partly by misrepresentations of
their own intentions, and partly by artful appeals
to the prejudices, passions and interests of their
constituents, had first abused the confidence and out-
raged the loyalty of their people by assuming with
the assistance of the conventions, to precipitate the
States into rebellion, and had then suppressed the
indignant and active repudiation of their conduct
on the part of their betrayed constituents, which
would otherwise have followed, by crushing the
whole country under the iron heel of a military
despotism. Hence it was said that in every ham-
let of the South, aching hearts were looking eagerly
for that army of northern deliverers which was to
rescue the people from a hated bondage; and that
as soon as the national flag should be displayed,
supported by a sufficient force to form the nucleus
of an organization, hundreds and thousands of fighting men of the soil would array themselves under
the protection of its folds, break the military power
of their oppressors, inflict condign punishment upon
the leading traitors, and bring the great body of
their deluded followers back to their allegiance, by
exposing the frauds and deceptions by which the

latter had been seduced into the infamy and folly of rebellion.

My readers' recollection will bear me out, I think, in this statement of the opinions and expectations of the northern people, without incumbering these pages with extracts from speeches, newspapers and public documents. I shall content myself with a short quotation from one document, which, from the exalted position of its author, and the gravity of the occasion which called it forth, merits a peculiar distinction. It is from the message of President Lincoln to the extra session of the thirty-seventh Congress, held in July, 1861. Considering the caution with which a document of this kind would naturally be framed, the extract which follows may be regarded as an epitome of all the hopes, expectations, opinions and theories which I have stated more in detail:

"It may be well questioned whether there is to-day a majority of the legally qualified voters of any State, except perhaps South Carolina, in favor of disunion. There is much reason to believe that the Union men are the majority in many, if not in every other one of the so-called seceded States. The contrary has not been demonstrated in any one of them. It is ventured to affirm this even of Virginia and Tennessee; for the result of an election held in military camps, where the bayonets are all on one side of the question to be voted upon, can scarcely be considered as demonstrating popular sentiment. At such an election, all that large class who are at once for the Union and against coercion, would be coerced to vote against the Union."

Such a theory affords a full explanation of the conduct of the Administration which has been the subject of so much criticism in calling out seventy-five thousand men to serve three months, notwithstanding General Scott's opinion that the conquest of such a country as the South would require two years and two hundred thousand men. For it was not a war of conquest upon which the nation was bent, but a war of deliverance of oppressed millions, who wanted only a fulcrum to enable them to move themselves the mighty lever by which the usurpers would be overthrown.

Of course, under such circumstances, it would have been idle to suggest that the war could, in any contingency, result in a change of the relations between the general Government and the people of the South, or the injury of any of the citizens of the southern States, except those who might fall in battle, and the few leaders of whom even such a mild and lenient Government as ours, might find it necessary to make an example.

If the suggestion of such a result was made by any doubter in our own midst, it was considered as an indication of the weakness of his intellect or the depravity of his morals, and he was accordingly either ridiculed or denounced as a sympathizer with the enemy. But it was apprehended that foreign nations might not so readily discover the consistency between the absolute political freedom of the citizen and the reëstablishment of the Government by the bayonet, which this theory involved, and hence, at the very outset of the troubles, care was taken to set them right in that respect.

Before the actual collision of arms, and during the anxious days which elapsed between the sailing of the expedition for the relief of Fort Sumter and the attack upon that fortress, the Secretary of State gave the necessary instructions to Mr. Adams for the information of the English Government. I copy from his dispatch of April 10, 1861.

"He (the President) would not be disposed to reject a cardinal dogma of theirs (the southern States), namely, that the Federal Government could not reduce the seceding States to obedience by conquest, even although he was disposed to question that proposition. But, in fact, the President willingly accepts it as true. Only an imperial or despotic government could subjugate thoroughly disaffected and insurrectionary members of the State. This federal republican system of ours is of all forms of government the very one which is most unfitted for such a labor."

Equal care was taken to prevent the French court from misapprehending the character and extent of the rebellion, or the work which the seventy-five thousand men were expected to do. Immediately after the call for troops the Secretary wrote to Mr. Dayton a dispatch, dated April 22, 1861, from which I make the following extract:

"There is not even a pretext for the complaint that the disaffected States are to be conquered by the United States if the revolution fails; for the rights of the States, and the condition of every human being in them, will remain subject to exactly the same laws and forms of administration, whether the revolution shall succeed or whether it shall fail. In the one case, the States would be federally connected with the new Confederacy; in the other, they would, as now, be members of the United States; but their constitutions and laws, customs, habits, and institutions in either case will remain the same."

The battle of Bull Run gave a rude shock to the theory under which the war had been prosecuted up to that time; but it took not only weeks but months to shake the faith of the northern people in their favorite theory, that the mass of the people of the South were at heart pining for deliverance from the tyranny of the Confederate Government; and in fact there are many among us who have not yet abandoned that idea. It became very apparent however that the task before us was much more serious than had been at first supposed, and that it was indispensable to our success that the whole strength of the North should be united in moral and material support of the Government. Nor was any considerable number, either of the people or of their representatives, prepared at that time to sustain any policy looking to the overthrow of political institutions which they had been taught from childhood to regard as the very corner stone of the edifice of public liberty. Under such circumstances Mr. Crittenden had no difficulty in procuring a nearly unanimous vote upon the celebrated resolution which bears his name, which was introduced by him into the House of Representatives a few days before the battle of Bull Run, and passed on the day after that battle, the 22d July, 1861. It reads as follows:

" *Resolved by the House of Representatives of the Congress of the United States,* That the present civil war has been forced upon the country by the disunionists of the southern States, now in arms against the constitutional Government, and in arms around the capital: that in this national emergency Congress, banishing all feelings of mere passion or resentment, will recollect only its duty to the whole country: that this war is not waged on their part in any spirit of oppression, or for any purpose of conquest or subjugation, or purpose of overthrowing or interfering with the rights or established institutions of those States, but to defend and main-

4*

tain the supremacy of the Constitution and to preserve the Union, with all the dignity, equality and
rights of the several States unimpaired, and that
as soon those objects are accomplished the war ought
to cease."

This resolution was passed in the House by a
vote of one hundred and seventeen ayes and two
nays (Messrs. Riddle, of Ohio, and Potter, of Wisconsin, both republicans). A resolution in the
same language was introduced into the Senate on
the twenty-fourth of the same month by Mr.
Andrew Johnson, of Tennessee, and after a few
verbal alterations of no material consequence,
passed by a vote of thirty yeas to five nays (Messrs.
Breckinridge, secession democrat, of Kentucky;
Johnson, democrat, of Missouri; Polk, secession
democrat, of Missouri; Powell, democrat, of Kentucky; and Trumbull, republican, of Illinois).
Among the ayes in each House, are to be found men
of all shades of political opinion, and from all the
sections of the country which then adhered to the
Union. So anxious did all parties seem to be to
place the nation upon the platform of principle
which the resolution laid down, that notwithstanding the first part of the resolution was deemed offensive and objectionable by some of the democratic
members, because it failed to include abolitionists
and others of the North, in pointing out the origi-
nators of the war, and an unsuccessful attempt was

made to amend it accordingly, it commanded the votes of the extreme democrats of the slaveholding States, as well as the ultra-republicans, with the exceptions which I have named. And all of those who voted nay, in the Senate, except Mr. Johnson, explained their dissent as resting upon some objection to the phraseology of the resolution; so that there was no member of either House, except possibly Messrs. Potter and Riddle, who can be supposed to have dissented from the principles laid down in the resolution, as the only object for which the war could rightfully be prosecuted.

Thus did the people of the North, standing just within the threshold of this great convulsion, announce, through their chosen representatives, their unanimous adhesion to the political and constitutional principles which I have attempted to defend. The minds of the nation, differing upon almost every question of administrative policy, differing upon the meaning and effect of nearly every one of the principal clauses of the Constitution, by which the details of our scheme of government were provided for, nevertheless met upon one common ground in reaffirming distinctly the two grand principles which form the framework of the system. These are a *strict adherence by the general Government, under all contingencies, to the limitations of powers which the Constitution has prescribed,* and *the inviolability upon any pretext of the reserved rights of the*

States. I cannot regard this unanimous decision in any other light than as a final settlement of the questions which I have been discussing. The theories of State treason, State forfeiture, State abdication, State suicide, rights acquired by conquest, "tabula rasa," and congressional disfranchisement, all assume that the nation was in error when it adopted the Crittenden resolution as its declaration of principles, and that it has grown wiser by the lapse of time. But will it be pretended that the course of events since July, 1861, has been such as to justify men in deliberately discarding theories of political science and constitutional law, which more than eighty years of discussion and practical experience had impressed upon their minds, as the axiomatic rudiments of the science of republican government? Have the times been favorable to a calm review of our former political tenets, and to a discovery and correction of such of them as were erroneous? I assume that they have not, and of experience we have as yet had nothing, for while I write, the storm is yet raging in every quarter of the horizon, and the eye is strained in vain to discover the speck of blue sky which foretells the clearing. For these reasons I have not doubted that the new theories which I have been considering, however honestly entertained by many, were the products of the prejudice and passion excited by the civil war, cr, what is worse, the result of the selfish teachings of those who fear the loss of political power from the restoration of the Union of equal rights which formerly existed. To adopt those theories and to make them the basis of the future of the nation, will be to enter upon a career of never-ending agitation, by substituting a forcible usurpation in place of that lawful and constitutional Government, which alone can command the willing respect and obedience of the people of both sections, and insure the ultimate pacification of this distracted country.

But the Crittenden resolution is something more than a declaration of principles: it is a solemn pledge for the future. It went forth to the nations of Europe, together with the official dispatches of the Secretary of State, as a basis for the regulation of their conduct, in the course of a war so deeply affecting their own interests; and it undoubtedly had a powerful influence in contributing to avert an interference, which the prospect of the utter ruin of the South, by an attempt to reduce its citizens to political vassalage, might have rendered inevitable. It went forth to the men of wealth and high position in our own land, and produced among them a unanimity of all parties and of all interests to support the Government in the great crisis which was upon it—nay, a competition for the foremost place in tendering assistance. It went forth to the masses of the people, and an army of volunteers at once rose up in such mighty swarms, that the Government itself soon cried enough. It went forth to the border States, which were yet trembling in the balance, and enabled the noble band of Unionists in those States to decide the pending controversy in our favor. It stands now upon record as the solemn covenant of the nation with its citizens, with its enemy, with the world. Its violation, after we have acquired the object to attain which it was given, would be an act of perfidy which would break up all the foundations of future confidence in the nation's plighted word. And the retribution which would follow, would be swift and ample. But of that hereafter.

But adherence to the principles of our national pledge will not alone suffice to restore peace and quiet to the nation when the storm of war shall have passed away. In fact, its violation, the permanent usurpation of unconstitutional powers by the national Government, and the destruction of State institutions at the North and the South, are among the certain events of the future, unless the southern people can be inspired with affection for the Union, and a willingness to coöperate heartily with the national authorities in the work of administering the Government. The Crittenden resolution contemplates as the end of the war the restoration, to the very persons who are now engaged in carrying on the contest under the confederate flag, of the political rights and privileges which they formerly enjoyed. Their armies may be dispersed, their so-called government overthrown, their leading men executed or exiled, a Federal garrison stationed in every fortress and in every city, Federal gunboats in every river and in every bay, a Federal custom-house, defended by Federal guards, in every seaport, and yet the whole of that vast political power appertaining to the sovereignty of the State, will still be as completely in the hands of those who were so lately in arms against the conquerors, as the same power in the State of New York is now in the hands of our citizens.

I shall have occasion hereafter to examine the practical working of such a scheme in the midst of a hostile and exasperated people, and it is because a persistence in the policy which we have in fact pursued, can result in nothing but to produce and keep up a feeling of hostility and exasperation, and not by reason of objections to their legality, that I shall condemn the leading measures which make up that policy. There is one of those measures, however, which is open to graver objections than those arising out of considerations of mere expediency. I allude to the emancipation proclamation, as it is generally called, the lawfulness and effect of which I shall discuss in the next chapter.

CHAPTER V.

The Emancipation Proclamation as a War Measure—Consideration of the Rights of a Belligerent over the Slaves of Citizens of an Invaded Nation regarding them as Property—The same Rights regarding them as occupying a Peculiar Status under the Local Law—The Owner's Rights after the Restoration of Peace—Reasons why the Emancipation Proclamation exceeds the Rights of a Belligerent, and manifests a Revolutionary Intention on the part of our Government.

In treating of the emancipation proclamation, (including in that term the two proclamations of the President, dated respectively the 22d of September, 1862, and the 1st of January, 1863,) I shall not deny that martial law sanctions the suspension, within an invaded country, of the relation of master and slave, by the military edict of the commander-in-chief of the invader's armies, or in fact of any general having a separate command. And I shall also concede that a military commander can lawfully remove any number of slaves from the territory of an invaded nation whose laws sanction the institution of slavery, and thus enable them permanently to acquire their freedom. But I condemn the emancipation proclamation as going far beyond those limits, and manifesting a purpose on the part

of the general Government to overthrow the rights
and sovereignty of the States, and to inaugurate a
system of coercion of State action, revolutionary and
unlawful, and in its ultimate effects fatal to the
permanent pacification of the country.

This measure has become such a shibboleth of
party, and its discussion, even in grave state papers,
and official and semi-official documents and speeches
of the highest functionaries, has involved to such
an extent the consideration of the institution of
slavery in its religious, moral and politico-economi-
cal aspects, that it is exceedingly difficult to divest
the question of those features sufficiently to consider
exclusively its lawfulness as a military measure and
the line of policy which is indicated by it. Nevertheless I will make the attempt to treat it in that
aspect, asking from my readers no other admission
respecting the institution of slavery itself, than that
the Constitution grants to the Federal Government
no right whatever to interfere with it, in the States
where it exists, and that consequently its abolition
by Federal power, if lawful at all, is only lawful as
an exercise of the war power, the extent and nature
of which are not defined by the Constitution, but
are left to be gathered from the general rules of
international law, so far as the latter are applicable
to a contest of this nature. Upon this common
ground I can meet nine-tenths of my fellow-
citizens, the President included; the remainder

belong to that class upon whom argument is wasted.

Since the decision of the Supreme Court in the prize cases, it may be deemed settled law with us, that the Government may, notwithstanding its claim of sovereignty over the insurgents and their territory under the provisions of the Constitution, exercise in the course of the war, and while it lasts, all the belligerent rights to which it could lay claim in case of a war between it and a foreign power: or in other words that belligerent rights are temporarily substituted for the constitutional rights which the war is waged to reëstablish. Therefore whenever the Government lays claim to exercise during the war any particular power not conceded to it by the Constitution, it can justify itself in so doing, provided it can show a warrant for the exercise of that power in the rules of international law touching the rights of belligerents.

Those rights with respect to property real and personal, situated in a country invaded and occupied by a hostile army, are now well settled and defined. So far as they relate to private property and to the present subject, they are, in general, that private property must be respected, but the belligerent may take and use what may be needed by the invading army, and may destroy, retain or carry away whatever may be useful to his enemy for military purposes, with compensation to the owners in certain cases and without compensation in others.

What then are the rights of a belligerent over slaves, regarding the latter simply as the private property of the subjects of the enemy ? They are the same (subject to the laws of humanity) which he has over the horses and cattle found in the invaded country—that is, a right to take and use them himself in any way consistent with the objects of the invasion; and not forbidden by the rules of international law, or to adopt any means, within the same limits, to prevent their increasing the military efficiency of the enemy. Therefore, if the law of humanity did not forbid such barbarity, a belligerent might, if he saw fit, in order to weaken his enemy, destroy that species of property by the actual killing of the slaves, and he may, without violation of any recognized principle, carry it away with him, by transporting the slaves out of the country; or he may keep it from the use of the owners, either directly, by retaining the slaves in his own possession, or indirectly, by simply declaring them free for the time being and protecting them against their master's claims.

Such are unquestionably the rights of a belligerent over slaves, considered merely as personal property, but the owner's rights to the same kind of property after the return of peace are equally well defined by the law of nations. If provision is made respecting his title by the treaty of peace, of course no question will arise. And if the property has been actually and physically destroyed by the invader, there is no redress, and the owner must bear the loss, unless his own government remunerates him. The same result ensues if the invading army has carried the property to its own country. But on the other hand it is equally clear that if the property has been left behind by the invading army, it reverts at once to the possession and ownership of the person from whom it was originally taken. Martial law being ended, the civil law, temporarily interrupted, resumes its sway, and restores all rights of property to the "status quo ante bellum." No writer upon international or military law has ever advanced the proposition that a military edict can accomplish a *constructive* destruction of property, which remains physically intact, after martial law has ceased to operate. Regarding the slave therefore in the light of property, the United States, in the exercise of martial law can do nothing but suspend the master's power over him till the termination of hostilities, and when the sway of the civil law returns, the right and the ownership of the master will return with it.

But in treating a subject of this kind, we must also consider the slaves as *persons* occupying a peculiar status under the local law. This is the aspect in which the law of nations has usually considered them in modern times; and in fact, as we have already seen, it is impossible to lose sight altogether of their human character, even when treating them as property.

There seems to be no doubt that while the hostile occupation lasts, all the laws and institutions of an invaded nation stand or fall, in whole or in part, within the district occupied by the invader, at the will of the latter. This is the necessary result of that substitution of martial law for civil law which attends every invasion. The military leader of the conquering army becomes, for the time being, the autocrat of the country over which his occupation extends, and the only rule of action of all persons within that district is his will and command—"Sic volo, sic jubeo—stet pro ratione voluntas." But from the very nature of its origin, personal rights acquired during the existence of this anomalous state of things, are of a temporary character merely, and cease with the restoration of the suspended jurisdiction of the invaded nation. And therefore, although there can be no doubt that during the time while the hostile occupation lasts, every slave must be considered as a freeman if the military commander so orders, it seems equally evident that in order to entitle himself to a permanent enjoyment of his freedom, the newly made freedman must take care to keep himself under the protection of that law from which his freedom is derived, and out of the reach of that law under which he was a slave, and whose temporary suspension changed his status. This he can only accomplish by leaving the invaded territory, which he may do, either while the occupation lasts, or by accompanying the invading army, with the permission of its commander, when it shall return to its own country. At whatever time he may thus expatriate himself, he will still be under the protection of military law until he reaches the territory of the invader, and upon his arrival there, his title to freedom will become complete by the permanent cessation of the operation of that law under which he was a slave.

I am saved the labor of examining or citing numerous authorities to sustain these different propositions by the compilation made by Dr. Francis Lieber, and entitled "Instructions for the Government of the Armies of the United States in the Field," which were "approved by the President," and promulgated to the army by an order dated April 24, 1863. As this manual of martial and military law was specially designed for the present emergency, and "revised by a board of officers" after its preparation by its distinguished author, it unquestionably states the law as strongly in our favor, as the most liberal construction of doubtful precedents will warrant. I refer the reader, who wishes to examine the subject in detail, to paragraphs 1, 2, 3, 4, 6, 10, 14, 15, 20, 21, 22, 23, 31, 32, 37, 38, 42 and 43 of these instructions. It will be sufficient for me to copy paragraph 32, which reads as follows : " A victorious army, by the martial power inherent in the same, may suspend, change or abolish, *as far as martial power extends*, the relations which arise from the service due according to the existing laws of the invaded country, from any citizen, subject, or native of the same to another. *The commander of the army must leave it to the ultimate treaty of peace to settle the permanency of this change.*"

Our own history furnishes us two memorable instances of the temporary character of emancipation under martial law, not followed by transportation of the freedman to the country of the emancipator. In both of our wars with Great Britain, that of the revolution and that of 1812–15, our country was invaded, and numbers of negro slaves took refuge within the British lines, attracted by military proclamations offering them freedom. It was, in each case, made one of the terms of the treaty of peace which followed, that such of the refugees as had not left the country, should be delivered up to their masters, and this result was accomplished simply by an agreement on the part of the British that they should not be taken away

The provision to that effect in the treaty of Paris, dated Sept. 3, 1783, and bearing the signatures of

John Adams, Benjamin Franklin and John Jay, was as follows: "Article 7. His Britannic majesty shall, with all convenient speed, and without causing any destruction, *or carrying away any negroes or other property of the American inhabitants, withdraw all his armies,* garrisons and fleets from the said United States, &c." The treaty of Ghent, dated Dec. 24, 1814, and signed by John Quincy Adams, James A. Bayard, Henry Clay, Jonathan Russell and Albert Gallatin, provides in like manner: " Article 1. All territory, places, &c. . . . . shall be restored without delay, *and without carrying away . . . . any slaves or other private property.*" The negroes thus left behind were at once reclaimed by their masters, and no doubt has ever been suggested that, whether they were considered as property or as persons, the relation formerly existing between them and their masters was at once restored.

Thus it will be seen that the military power of the President, *as commander-in-chief of the army,* would extend no further than to proffer TEMPORARY freedom to such slaves as should be found within any territory occupied by our forces; and if deemed expedient, such safe transportation beyond the limits of the slaveholding States, as would ensure them against being reduced again to slavery, after the cessation of the war. Whether such protection could be secured on this side of the Canada line, need not now be considered. For no suggestion of the expatriation of the slaves, in any form or at any time, is made in the proclamations, and none of the preliminary measures have been taken by executive or legislative action, which such a gigantic task would require. On the contrary, the evident and openly acknowledged purpose of the proclamations is *permanently* to guaranty to the negroes their freedom and *continued residence* within the limits of the slaveholding States.

The proclamation of September, 1862, declares that on the first of January, 1863, " all persons held as slaves within any State or designated part of a State, the people whereof shall then be in rebellion against the United States, shall be *then, thenceforward and forever free*"—that such freedom will be maintained by the whole power of the United States, and that in due time the Executive will recommend that loyal citizens should be compensated by Congress for the loss of their slaves. The proclamation of the first of January, 1863, recites that of the preceding September, designates the States and parts of States within which all persons held as slaves " are and henceforward shall be free," renews the promise to guaranty such freedom by the whole military and naval force of the nation, exhorts the freed negroes " to labor faithfully for reasonable wages," and finally, " upon this act, sincerely believed to be an act of justice, warranted by the Constitution upon military necessity," the President invokes "the considerate judgment of mankind, and the gracious favor of Almighty God."

Reluctant as I am to attribute any intention to the President to overthrow the Constitution, or to violate the pledge contained in the Crittenden resolution and the dispatches written under his direction by the Secretary of State, I am unable to resist the conclusion, either that these proclamations were intended to delude the unfortunate beings for whose freedom he professed to make provision, by promises which he had no design or ability to fulfil, or else that they indicate his intention to continue the war till "the permanency of the change" has been settled by "the ultimate treaty of peace." A decent respect for the personal character of the President as well as the dignity of his office, forbids us to impute to him the base perfidy which the first of these alternatives implies. And as the "treaty of peace" to which the Crittenden resolution pledged the nation, would throw the negroes back into a state of slavery, from which he had power only temporarily to release them, it seems impossible to entertain the supposition that he intends or expects that the national pledge contained in that resolution will be redeemed.

I have said nothing respecting that extraordinary feature of the proclamation, extending the proposed emancipation beyond our military lines, and to States in which we have scarcely occupied an islet upon the coast or a narrow strip along the frontier. Its effect, as applied to those States, would be to prevent the restoration of the former constitutional relation between their people and the general Government, even if they should at once volunrarily abandon their rebellion and return to the Union. Grave, however, as this consideration would be under other circumstances, its importance nearly disappears in view of the fact that the so-called military measure is, even in districts in which our sway is undisputed, an act of permanent legislation, as revolutionary in its character as the act of secession itself.

But it will be said that the proclamations show on their face a design to maintain the constitutional rights of the States, for the September proclamation commences with this assurance, " that hereafter, as heretofore, the war will be prosecuted for the object of practically restoring the constitutional relation between the United States and each of the States and the people thereof, in which States that relation is or may be suspended or disturbed."

I know not by what process the President has satisfied his own mind that he can sustain his so-called military decree for the perpetual abolition of slavery, and yet restore the States, whose local laws he has thus permanently attempted to alter, to the full enjoyment of their rights and sovereignty as they existed before the war broke out. But I know of no rule of constitutional law or of martial law by which the two objects can be accomplished, so as to render the body of the September emancipation proclamation at all consistent with its preamble.*

---

* This chapter was written before the promulgation of the President's message and the accompanying proclamation, dated December 8, 1863. I will consider hereafter in detail the President's plan of reconstruction, and its practical effects. It suffices to say, in this place, that the documents referred to contain a substantial confession of the impossibility of fulfilling the guaranty of permanent freedom to the slaves, contained in the emancipation proclamation, without revolutionizing the States by military power. For the President's proposition amounts simply to this, that one-tenth of those who would be voters under the existing State constitutions, shall form a State government with a new constitution, " which shall recognize and declare their (the slaves) permanent freedom," and that the United States Government will sustain the government so formed as the lawful government of the State. What is this but revolution? Even if the coöperation of a majority of the voters was required, it would be revolution, though of course of a much less reprehensible character. But there is no substantial difference between the plan actually proposed, and one which should dispense altogether with the coöperation of any part of the citizens, except those who would fill the new offices. For there is no more consonance to the theory of republican government (the Constitution being entirely laid out of view) in allowing one-tenth to erect a government over the other nine-tenths, than there would be to confer the same privilege upon one-hundredth, one-thousandth, or even a smaller fraction.

I have intended to comment upon this inconsistency temperately and with the respect due to the President and his office, and thus to fulfil the pledge of moderation which I gave at the commencement of this work. But I will state a case, which is exactly parallel to the one before us, and which will give rise to no suspicion of bias, either for or against the person who represents the President, and let the reader decide it for himself. I will suppose that Great Britain had commenced a war with us to settle an international dispute—say respecting the construction of the extradition treaty—and, suspicions having been excited that she meditated to effect, by means of the war, a permanent conquest of a portion of the southern States or a forcible abolition of slavery, that she had solemnly pledged herself through her parliament, and by diplomatic communications to foreign courts, that the war was prosecuted for no other object than to obtain the delivery of the refugees, whose case had occasioned the dispute, and that it should cease when that object was effected. I will further suppose that she had invaded the southern States; that her armies held a portion of those States; and that the queen should issue a proclamation, declaring that the war would continue to be prosecuted, as it had been for the sole object of procuring the surrender of the refugees; and that as a military measure, *and as an act of justice*, upon which she

invoked the considerate judgment of mankind and
the favor of Almighty God, she declared all slaves
in the United States, whether within or without her
military lines, "*thenceforth and forever free*," and
would maintain their freedom with all the military
and naval force of the British crown.

I turn the English government, in this suppo-
sititious case, over to my reader for judgment. Let
him pronounce sentence, and then mete out the
same measure of justice to his own.

CHAPTER VI.

How the Southern People were induced to Favor the Rebellion—
Relations of the Slaveholders and of the Institution of Slavery to
the Masses of the People—Theories of the Constitution and of
Public Policy which were prevalent in the South—The Manner
in which the Southern Union Party was Extinguished—Action
of the Border Slave States.

I PROPOSE to examine in this chapter, how much
foundation there was for the opinion, which was so
generally entertained at the North, that the southern people were forced against their own will into
an attitude of rebellion, by the violence and usurpation of their leaders; to what extent a Union sentiment existed among them at the outbreak of the
war; and in what manner it was stifled or extinguished in the course of the events which succeeded
the commencement of hostilities. The object of
my work cannot be accomplished without making
this investigation, for it is impossible to form any
reliable opinion concerning the effect of the policy
which has been pursued, or to determine with any
accuracy the probable effects of any policy which
we may contemplate pursuing, without attaining,
approximately at least, a correct understanding of

these subjects. Many extravagant theories to account for the unanimity of the southern people in carrying on the war have been broached, and have found ready credence at the North. It is not difficult, I think, to ascertain the truth, if we will discard passion and prejudice from our minds, and conduct our investigations by the light of our reason, our common sense, and our experience of the operations of human nature, aided by our knowledge of the political and social institutions of the South, and the theories of government, political economy, and constitutional law, which were prevalent among the southern people when the war broke out.

I shall say nothing concerning the leading southern statesmen—those I mean with whose names we at the North have been made familiar, as conspirators of more or less recent standing, against the integrity of the Union, because it would be impossible for me to do full justice to the subject without entering upon a discussion, the reasons for declining which I have stated in the Introduction. And it is not necessary for the elucidation of the subject, within the limits to which I have confined it, to comment upon their actions or their motives : for my concern is with the great body of the southern people, who were honest and patriotic in intention, and actuated by feelings, passions, and interests, very similar to those which actuate corresponding classes of our own people. Nor are they upon the whole less intelligent or less capable of judging correctly of passing and future events, than the body of the people with us; for although education and information are less generally diffused in the South than in the North, they have not yet reached in either section that point which enables the masses to form their own opinions concerning great questions of international or internal policy. And although we are apt to plume ourselves upon the superior political sagacity of our people (which necessarily means the superior sagacity of those who give tone to public opinion), yet the South has always made the same boast on its part; and further information and calm reflection upon past events, may possibly lead each section to modify its extravagant claim of superior sagacity, as it has already modified an equally extravagant claim of superior personal courage and military efficiency.

In the State of South Carolina, a property qualification, or the payment of taxes within a year, is requisite to create an elector. In North Carolina, electors for the State senate must possess fifty acres of freehold land, and for all other offices must have paid a tax. With these exceptions, universal suffrage prevails in the South as with us, the elective franchise being extended to all adult white male citizens who have the necessary qualification of residence. Thus it will be seen that political power is practically lodged with the masses of the people

5*

at the South as well as at the North. With them as with us, a popular majority has always been essential to the success of measures of public policy, and to the gratification of the ambitious hopes of politicians. With them, as with us, there has been for years a great diversity of opinion upon political questions, and the people have been accustomed to be appealed to at short intervals through the press and upon the rostrum by candidates for their favor. With them as with us, there has been an enthusiastic and universal devotion to the principles of popular government and an exalted opinion of the rights of the people. And therefore it was quite as impossible with them, as it would be with us, that a few scores or even hundreds of scheming politicians could seize upon the reins of power, and without any standing army, or any accumulation of public treasure, could overthrow a republican government in all but the name, establish a practical despotism over a country far exceeding our section in territorial extent, raise an unprovoked rebellion against a Government enthroned in the hearts of the people, and carry on for years a war against overwhelming odds to sustain such a usurpation. The rebellion, unless it had commanded the support of a very large majority of the people, would have committed felo-de-se in the first month of its existence. Our seventy-five thousand volunteers would not have reached their destination in time to pull down the crumbling edifice: it

would have fallen from its own inherent weakness
upon the heads of its architects and builders, bury-
ing them forever beneath its ruins.

It is manifest, therefore, that for some reason, the
great body of the southern people either favored
the rebellion from its earliest stages, or were induced
to favor it by the events which immediately succeeded its inception. And inasmuch as it has
brought upon them hardships, which nothing but a
conviction of duty and patriotism, or a sense of
necessity would have enabled them to sustain, it is
also evident either that it still appeals successfully
to their convictions of right, or that they see no
way of abandoning it without dishonor, or exposing
themselves to greater calamities than perseverance
in the struggle will bring upon them. For although
the war has resulted, with them as with us, in the
discovery that the Government wields powers which
plain men would search the Constitution in vain to
discover; yet the basis of their system is also universal suffrage, and the legislative power of the States
and of the Confederacy, without the support of
which the war could not be carried on, is annually
or biennially renewed by the votes of the people.
Their government is also much more dependent than
ours upon the support of popular opinion for its
ability to carry on the war, not only because it is a
revolution struggling for existence against fearful
odds, and under almost hopeless financial embar-

rassments, but also because the principle upon which it was founded recognizes the right of every one of the members of the Confederacy to make a separate treaty for itself and return to the former Union, should it see fit to do so.

Let us therefore ascertain, in the first place, as well as the means of information accessible to us will allow, the process by which the people of the South were induced to believe originally that it was right and expedient to embark in the rebellion.

Although a philosophical observer may be able to trace the real origin of the dispute between the two sections back to differences of climate or race, or to radical defects in our system of government, it cannot be denied that the institution of slavery was the outward manifestation of the cause of the quarrel. Many of our people believe that the rebellion proceeded from a calculation, on the part of the slaveholders, of the comparative pecuniary profit and personal aggrandisement to accrue to them, as owners of slaves, from union or disunion; and that having reached the conclusion that the latter promised them more benefits than the former, they deliberately plunged the country into the miseries of civil war for the purpose of realizing them. This theory extends the number of selfish, unprincipled and calculating conspirators against the Union, so as to embrace not only the leading politicians, but also the great body of the slaveholders, or at least the principal slaveholders. But apart from the fact that the large slaveholders as a body include as many conscientious and patriotic men, as the social class which corresponds to them at the North, it will be apparent from a consideration of their relative numbers, as compared with the rest of the people, that it would be utterly impracticable for them to carry out any scheme to sacrifice the interests of their fellow-citizens in order to promote their own.

I have not been able to procure, notwithstanding considerable research, any reliable figures indicating the present number of slaveholders, and the amount of slaves owned by each, but returns of those statistics are contained in the census of the year eighteen hundred and fifty, which will sufficiently answer my purpose. From these it appears that the total white population of all the slaveholding States, including the District of Columbia, Delaware, Kentucky, Maryland and Missouri, was 6,222,418, of whom 347,525, or about one in seventeen, were slaveholders. But of the latter, 255,268 owned less than ten slaves, and only 92,257, or about one in sixty-seven of the white population owned ten slaves and upwards. Of course this proportion would be greatly diminished by rejecting those who are minors and women, and therefore incapable of exercising any political control over the rest of the people. But the aggregate number of slaveholders is in fact much less than the returns indicate. Mr. Helper, in "The Impending Crisis" (p. 147), states upon the authority of Professor De Bow, the superintendent of the census, "that the number includes slave-hirers," and further-more, "that where the party owns slaves in different counties or in different States, he will be entered more than once," and he adds (p. 148) certain data, from which he concludes that the number of slave-holders bears to the number of "non-slaveholding slave-hirers" the proportion of fifty-one to forty-three. It can hardly be supposed that the owner-ship of a less number of slaves than ten would create such an interest in the institution of slavery, as to induce a citizen to act against his own convic-tions of right and duty, in incurring the guilt of rebellion and the miseries and hazards of civil war, merely in the hope of realizing personal advantages by the increase either of his individual consequence, or of the value of his slaves, or of the security of that species of property. And the foregoing state-ment shows how powerless the larger slaveholders were to influence the course of public events, so as to promote their own interests at the expense of those of the rest of the community.*   And if we concede

---

* I might add that it has been repeatedly proved that the largest slaveholders were from the beginning opposed to the whole scheme of secession, either from patriotism or because it tended to the ruin, instead of the benefit of their

that their weaith and social position would give
them a greater influence over public opinion in their
own section, than the corresponding class could
command at the North, it is still impossible to suppose them capable of inducing such a large class of
their fellow-citizens, composed, measurably at least,
of intelligent and independent men, accustomed to
control the event of public affairs, to consent to

interests. I append two distinct admissions of this fact
from distinguished republican sources :

"Throughout all the agitations pending the outbreak of
the rebellion the more extensive and wealthy among them
(the slaveholders) steadily resisted disunion as involving
the overthrow of slavery. Governor Aiken, the largest
slaveholder in South Carolina, slipped away to Europe, if
we mistake not, very early in 1861, and there remains.
At all events, he has never had a word of cheer for the
rebellion. Governor Hammond, another South Carolina
patriarch, rich, shrewd, and a most intense devotee of 'the
institution,' has been ominously silent ever since Lincoln's
election. . . . . The men who had most at stake upon
slavery hesitated to play the desperate game to which they
were impelled, knowing well that by playing it they risked
their all."—*New York Tribune.*

" Every man acquainted with the facts knows that it is
fallacious to call this ' a slaveholders' rebellion.' . . . . . .
A closer scrutiny demonstrates the contrary to be true ;
such a scrutiny demonstrates that the rebellion originated
chiefly with the non-slaveholders resident in the strong-
holds of the institution, not springing, however, from any
love of slavery, but from an antagonism of race and
hostility to the idea of equality with the blacks involved in
simple emancipation."—*General Francis P. Blair*

commit treason and inaugurate civil war to the
direct ruin of their own interests.

The real explanation of the attachment of all
classes of society at the South to the institution of
slavery, is to be found, not in the tyranny over
public opinion exercised by a few selfish men, but
in the fact that the whole industrial system of that
section, comprising its manufacturing and trading,
as well as its agricultural interests, is based upon
the institution of slavery, precisely as our whole
industrial system is based upon free labor. Thus
the institution had intertwined itself with the interests of the whole people, whether slaveholders or
not, so that its violent overthrow would dry up,
temporarily at least, nearly every source of individual and public prosperity. It would besides, as
the southerner believed, transform a body of useful
and profitable laborers into a mass of shiftless,
thieving, idle paupers, a burden to the public and a
curse to the whole country in which they resided.
He was taught by his political leaders that the North
was endeavoring to accomplish this result, and that
Mr. Lincoln's election was the first step towards
its accomplishment.* Pride, self-respect, his very

* The theory upon which the South founded its fears
that the North would attempt the abolition of slavery, may
be found in the leading speeches made in the Senate by
Mr. Clingman, of North Carolina ; Mr. Mason, of Virginia ; Mr. Davis, of Mississippi ; and Mr. Douglas, of

attachments to the principles of self-government, combined with his own interest to attach him more firmly to the institution thus menaced from without, and to make him ready to resist by force of arms any attempt to ruin his section of the country, to deprive him of his constitutional rights, and to degrade him as a freeman, by compelling him to regulate his

Illinois, in the early part of the session of Congress, commencing in December, 1860. The argument was that Mr. Lincoln's election, and the manner in which the canvass in his behalf had been conducted, manifested a purpose on the part of the North to accomplish that object, and that the danger was only postponed, and not removed, by the fact that all parties agreed that Congress had no constitutional power to interfere with slavery in the States. The North had acquired by the admission of California, and the subsequent admission of Oregon and Minnesota, a clear majority in the Senate, as it had previously had in the House of Representatives and the electoral college. The South had failed in all its efforts to create any further slave States, and the recent election had settled the destiny of the vast territories of the United States. It was therefore evident that all the States which should hereafter be carved out of the vast tract of country yet remaining, would be non-slaveholding States, and that they would soon be sufficiently numerous to constitute, with the other non-slaveholding States, three-fourths of the whole number. By the provisions of the Constitution itself, it could be amended by a two-third vote of Congress and a three-fourth vote of the States, and hence it was only a question of time, and that not very distant, before the free States would have the power, as it was said that they had the disposition, to grant to Congress the constitutional right to abolish the institution of slavery in the States.

domestic institutions in accordance with the opinions
of others who had not the shadow of a right to
interfere.

Such were unquestionably the sentiments of a
very large majority of the southern people. That
there was not absolute unanimity among them we
know. Many southerners have long doubted the
abstract policy of perpetuating the institution of
slavery; a much larger number have doubted
whether it was worth preserving at the cost of disunion and civil war. The numbers of each of these
classes in any particular portion of the southern territory increased in magnitude in proportion to its
distance from the Gulf, and its consequent proximity
to the northern border; and in the States of Missouri and Kentucky, and in the mountainous portions of Virginia and Tennessee, they constituted a
preponderating majority of the people.*   But the

---

* The soil and climate of Western Virginia and Eastern
Tennessee are, it is well known, comparatively unfitted for
slave labor, and the institution of slavery has consequently
failed to procure in those regions a solid and permanent
footing.   The zeal of the people for the Union and their
determined opposition to secession, was, however, the indirect rather than the direct result of that fact.   For the
legislation of both of the States being controlled by the
more populous slaveholding sections, has been for many
years shaped by them so as to protect and foster their own
interests at the expense of those of the non-slaveholding
sections.   Strenuous efforts have been made by the latter
to correct this evil, but without success; and the result of

Union party included still another and much more numerous class of the people.

Throughout the whole of the southern section of the country there has always been a deep and earnest attachment to the Union, which, though greatly weakened by the slavery controversy, had undoubtedly in the winter of 1860–1861 a strong hold upon the great majority of the southern people, except in the State of South Carolina. In that State it would seem that the people had persuaded themselves that disunion was desirable *per se ;* but in all the other States it was regarded by a large majority of the people as a great calamity, an

the conflict has been to substitute a feeling of hostility to the institution of slavery, for that lukewarm interest which might otherwise have existed in its favor. The sympathies of Eastern Tennessee and Western Virginia have consequently been with the North, in the course of the slavery controversy which agitated the country before the rebellion broke out ; and when that event occurred, the people of those regions did not wait for the advent of our armies to rise in counter-revolution.

There are very few parts of the South where there was anything to prevent the same course of action on the part of the people, had the acts of secession been regarded as an attempt to sacrifice the rights and interests of the masses, for the benefit of a few politicians or large slaveholders. Even in Eastern Tennessee the Union feeling was far from being unanimous, for the sufferings of the Union men were due to a considerable extent to their own neighbors, and at the election held in February, 1861, for delegates to the State convention, there were 5,577 disunion votes polled in that section.

injury to all their material interests, and a violent
severing of ties endeared to them by the traditions
of their childhood and the associations of their
maturer years.   And among those who were prepared to resist by force of arms, if necessary, any
attempt to overthrow the institution of slavery by
the action of the northern majority, there were
many who doubted whether the election of Mr. Lincoln afforded sufficient evidence of the hostile intentions of the North, to justify them in seceding from
the Union and involving the country in civil war.
A large majority of the people of the border slave
States, who had an interest in the question of secession more direct and immediate than the people of
the Gulf States, were evidently unwilling to make
the result of the election the ground of dissolution,
and those States accordingly took action looking to
a reconciliation of the alienated sections, and to
obtaining such guaranties against interference with
the institutions of the southern section, as would
dissipate the alarm of the latter.   A large number
of the inhabitants of the Gulf States desired to await
the result of those negotiations before withdrawing
from the Union, and manifested that wish by their
votes when the elections for the conventions were
held.   But the fact that no considerable number of
the people of those States entertained any such
feeling of loyalty to the Union under all circumstances, as was supposed to prevail among them, is

sufficiently apparent by the designation which the opponents of immediate secession adopted. They styled themselves "Coöperationists," signifying generally by that name that they favored secession, only in case the border slave States would also secede, although a few of that party limited their requirements to the coöperation of all the cotton States.

In fact, no State except South Carolina seceded till after the failure of the committee of thirteen of the Senate to agree upon the Crittenden compromise. And whatever opinion may be entertained respecting the propriety of that measure; or the sincerity of the two principal southern senators (Messrs. Davis and Toombs) in the promise which they made in the committee to maintain the Union, if it should be adopted; or of the effect which its adoption would in fact have had upon the action of the seceding States, no candid man can doubt that the refusal of the incoming party to accept that measure as a basis of settlement, and the debates in the two Houses during the first six weeks of the second session of the thirty-sixth Congress, enabled the disunionist leaders to create the impression among their people that the door was finally closed against all hopes of reconciliation. That impression abundantly accounts for the trifling vote against the ordinance of secession which was cast in the different conventions of the Gulf States, notwith-

standing the results of the elections, without resorting to suspicions of bribery or threats on the part
of the secession party in or out of the conventions.
The members elected as "coöperationists," doubtless reflected the opinions of the mass of their party,
in believing that the events which had occurred
since their election, afforded a sufficient reason for
voting at once in favor of the ordinance of secession.
But whether that was or was not the case, the political training of the southern people was such, that
after the ordinance of secession was in fact passed,
and war ensued, all or nearly all of the former
opponents of the measure would become equally
unanimous and determined with its supporters in
defending their independence at all hazards. For
the *constitutional right* of a State to secede, and by
that act to absolve all its citizens from their allegiance to the general Government, was a cardinal
dogma of nearly all the southern people. And
those few who denied or doubted it, as an abstract
constitutional right, fully adhered to the doctrine
that the general Government had no constitutional
power of coercion in such a case, and that the successful exercise of coercion would result in the
destruction of State independence. These two doctrines, especially the latter, were as prevalent in the
border States as in the Gulf States, with the exception of the districts of Tennessee and Virginia, to
which allusion has been made. The zeal and unan-

imity with which they have been maintained by
southern statesmen, for many years past, are frequently considered as proofs that the leading politicians of the South have been for a long time
engaged in a conspiracy to break up the Union,
and that Mr. Lincoln's election was the pretext of
its explosion and not the cause of dissolution. It is
not impossible that such a theory may be well
founded; but whether it is correct or not, the fact
is well established that opinions such as I have
described, were universally held by honest and conscientious men as well as those who were neither.
And it would follow as a natural result of such
opinions, that as soon as secession became a *fait
accompli*, its original opponents would at once concede, as readily as their antagonists, that their
allegiance was rightfully due only to their own
State, and to the new confederacy of which she at
once became a part. Thus the act of secession
extinguished the Union party as soon as it was
adopted, except as a *reconstructionist* party, in
which form it continued, though much enfeebled,
to exist till after hostilities commenced. One of the
best known illustrations of the working of this doctrine is afforded by the conduct of Mr. Alexander
H. Stephens, who, while the question of secession
was yet open, was one of the most decided Unionists
and a bitter assailant of the secessionists. Nevertheless he gave in his adhesion at once to the new

order of things, and so little doubt was entertained of his sincerity, that he was elected the first Vice-President of the new confederacy.

General Lee, Stonewall Jackson, and many others of the most eminent military and civil leaders of the Confederates, were also decided Unionists, down to the time of the actual passage of the ordinance of secession by their respective States.

The border slave States, Virginia, Tennessee, North Carolina and Arkansas, remained in the Union till the President's call for troops in April, 1861. Without attempting to criticise the policy of that measure, I may say that with the opinions which they held, it was as certain to lead to a war with those four States as with the States which had already seceded.

They immediately seceded also, and joined their fortunes to those of their sister States; and similar causes produced results similar to those in the Gulf States in destroying the Union party, at least for the time being, excepting of course in the mountainous region. Maryland and Kentucky would have gone too, but the gripe of the armed hand of the nation was upon the throat of Maryland, before she could act; and Kentucky was saved by the statesmanship of a few of her noblest patriots, chief among whom was the honored and lamented John J. Crittenden. They succeeded in inducing that State to assume for a time an attitude of neutrality in the war, whereby the people of the State gained time for reflection and the subsidence of their angry passions, and the Union party gained time for organization; and the result was, that the prominent secessionists were driven out, and the State was saved to the Union—let us hope forever.

I may remark here that there is no evidence to show that the sentiments of the citizens of Tennessee and Virginia were not correctly expressed by the votes of those States, to which reference has been made. The natural result of an attempt to coerce the seceded States, would be to precipitate the border slave States into the arms of the Southern Confederacy. In truth, that is the only intelligible explanation of the remark of Mr. Lincoln, which I quoted on page 78, from his message in July, 1861. "At such an election, all that large class who are at once for the Union and against coercion, would be coerced to vote against the Union." The coercion upon the voter would however be that of circumstances merely; it would exist because he had no choice between secession, and submission to and participation in a policy which he regarded as unconstitutional and destructive of public liberty.

The vote of the two States does not indicate any other kind of coercion. The total vote of Tennessee for President in 1860, was 145,333; the vote upon the secession ordinance in 1861 was 152,151,

over a third of which was in the negative, and the
negative vote was not confined to Eastern Tennessee, but a fair proportion of it was cast in all parts
of the State.   These figures show that there was a
full vote upon the ordinance, and that the negative
vote, though doubtless affected by the circumstances
of the election, was not excluded.   If a strong current of public opinion or fear of personal consequences deterred any considerable number of people
from voting in the negative, they could not have
been prevented from staying away from the polls,
and consequently if there had been a very large
party opposed to secession, the result would have
appeared in a diminished aggregate vote.   In Virginia the vote for President in 1860 was 167,223,
and upon the ordinance 146,323, of which 20,373
votes were cast in the negative.   When it is remembered that all of Western Virginia was then occupied by our troops, and the votes of that region
were consequently not counted, it will be seen that
the figures lead substantially to the same result as
in Tennessee.

As has already been intimated, the collision of
arms could not fail at once substantially to extinguish the Union party in the South.   In truth it
accomplished more.   The original opponents of
secession would deem themselves at once called
upon, actively to participate in what they regarded
as a righteous war of self-defence, against an attempt

on the part of our Government to accomplish by the conquest of their country the overthrow of public liberty. No doubt there were some who remained unconvinced and dissatisfied. But they constituted throughout the South generally too insignificant a proportion of the population to produce any effect upon the course of public affairs, or even to raise their voice above the din of arms. The mass of their fellow-citizens, however great might have been originally their disapproval of the measures which led to the collision, and their want of confidence in the men by whom those measures were carried through to their consummation, found themselves compelled by their ideas of duty, patriotism, self-interest and self-protection, to join heartily and actively in supporting their new government in its struggle for independence. Our own Congress having disclaimed, by the passage of the Crittenden resolution, any design in prosecuting the war inconsistent with the supremacy of the Constitution, the people of the North found themselves impelled by the operation of precisely the same causes, to give their united support to the Government of the Union, irrespective of differences of opinion touching the conduct of the Administration, and the men of whom it was composed. And thus each section confronted the other in battle array, substantially with the united strength of its whole people.

CHAPTER VII.

Effects of the Policy thus far pursued by our Government towards the People of the South—The "Anti-Rosewater" Military Policy—The Penal, Confiscation and Exclusion Statutes—Result of those Measures in arousing the Resentment and Hatred of the Southern People—Falsity of the Theory that the Masses at the South will regard with complacency the Ruin and Outlawry of their principal Citizens—Exaggerated Effects attributed at the North to Dissensions between the Confederate Authorities and their People—Practical Results of the Policy of Severity in the Districts which we have already conquered.

WE know, not from conjecture but from positive evidence, that a very large proportion of those southerners who could discover no course of action consistent with their ideas of duty and of self-protection, but to unite with the rest of their fellow-citizens in prosecuting the war, did so with extreme reluctance, and in the hope, desperate as it might seem, that some avenue of reconciliation might yet be opened. But such a hope, and even such a desire, was speedily extinguished, partly by events which were the natural consequence of a civil war, and partly by an unwise legislative, executive and military policy pursued by us, which will be the subject of comment in this chapter.

At the commencement of the struggle, great pains were taken, by order of the President, to observe the usages of modern warfare in our invasion of the southern territory, and our commanders were instructed to assure the southern people, by acts and by words, that we meditated no infringement upon their constitutional rights, and were animated by no spirit towards them inconsistent with the restoration of those fraternal feelings, which were then deemed essential to the existence of our form of Government. But the whole South was soon filled with the mourning relatives of those slain in battle, and with tales of suffering from the waste and destruction, which are inevitable accompaniments of the passage of ill-disciplined armies through a hostile territory. The sympathy excited by the tears of mothers, widows, and children, and the distress of families plunged at once from comfort and opulence into destitution, could not fail to be joined with a deep feeling of indignation against those by whom these acts were perpetrated, in a lawless attempt, as the southerner regarded it, to prosecute a scheme of conquest of his country. Increased and constantly renewed by fresh appeals to his sympathy, and a constant widening of the circle of sufferers, this feeling would naturally become intensified into active hatred of the authors of these misfortunes, and a burning desire for vengeance upon them.

More fuel was added to the fire by the language of many of the newspapers, civil and military officials, and other representatives of public opinion among us. The war produced its natural effect in increasing their hatred towards the South, which found vent in the most intemperate invectives against the people of that region, and ferocious threats of servile insurrection, indiscriminate slaughter, and spoliation during the war, and judicial massacres and political degradation in case of its successful termination. The newspapers and public speakers of the South, actuated by a precisely similar spirit, carefully culled and spread before their readers the choicest of these flowers of rhetoric, and retorted upon their opponents by similar denunciations, taunts and insults, which formed the occasion of renewed outbursts of fury on the part of the latter. This process was repeated *ad infinitum*, till the people of each region were taught to consider the people of the other as ferocious, blood-thirsty, and implacable enemies, bent upon gratifying the most cruel instincts of savage hatred without restraint from the laws of man or the laws of God. And in truth the South was soon able to point to more than words as evidence that such were the feelings of the North. The policy of moderation and restraint at first imposed upon our troops, was attacked with the utmost vehemence by men and presses whose counsels ultimately became dominant, and so the "rose-water system of warfare," as it was called, was abandoned, and the doctrine introduced that "rebels have no rights which even a negro is bound to respect." A shameful series of outrages ensued, I hope not with the direct sanction of the Executive, but with the sanction of his most trusted advisers and commanders, and without rebuke, punishment, or check from himself.* Their horrors for a

* I regret my inability to exonerate the President in stronger terms than I have employed, from responsibility for the inauguration of the barbarous system of warfare, which for a time disgraced the nation ; but General Pope was his chosen commander and trusted friend, and in daily, almost hourly, communication with him, while the "anti-rosewater policy" was in operation in Virginia. That the excesses to which it led were contemplated either by the President or his general, I have no reason to believe ; but they might have been and should have been foreseen, and I know of none, even of the worst offenders, being punished.

I do not overlook the fact that the Confederate forces were guilty in the early stages of the war of excesses of the same character ; although their conduct in the Maryland and Pennsylvania invasions refutes the charge that they only wanted an equally extensive field of operations to pro-duce an equally disgraceful record. I am merely consider-ing the effect which such acts on our part would naturally produce upon the minds of the people of the South—an effect which would not be diminished by proof, were it pos-sible to make it, that their own forces had committed equally atrocious excesses. The indignation which has been aroused at the North by stories of outrages of the same kind committed by their troops, has not been at all dimin-

time made the title of American citizen a by-word
and reproach throughout the civilized world, and
ultimately caused a reaction in public opinion
among ourselves, which has led, it is hoped permanently, to their suppression. But it is their effect
upon that portion of the southern people who
regretted the continuance of the war, and looked
for reconciliation and reunion, that I have principally to consider. It may well be imagined with
what emotions they would hear the sad history—
how not only isolated dwellings and public build-
ings, but whole villages and cities were wantonly
burned to the ground; public and private libraries
scattered to the winds; scientific collections and
apparatus destroyed; churches sacked and profaned
with every conceivable insult to the majesty of God;
elegant mansions pillaged of their contents, the
family paintings and rich furniture hacked to
pieces or burned; the jewels, pianos, and even
dresses of the ladies carried away (frequently by
officers of high rank); the crops, orchards, and agricultural instruments of the farmers destroyed;
cattle and other farming stock killed in very wan-
tonness when it could not be consumed; robbery,
abuse, insults, not unfrequently murder, perpetrated

ished by the fact that we have retaliated these injuries,
either to a greater or less degree than we have received
them, and the same effect "mutatis mutandis" would be
produced upon the southern people.

upon unoffending non-combatants; in short, of every horror which attended the marches of Tilly and Wallenstein, except one crowning disgrace, from which the early education of all Americans saved us, that of outrages upon women. And while so much of our open warfare has been of this savage character, the conduct of many of the pro-consuls, to whose arbitrary rule the people of such regions as we have conquered have been delivered up, has been such as to intensify the feelings which the excesses of our marching armies aroused; to satisfy the southern people that our tender mercies to the vanquished were even more to be dreaded than our hostility to those who resisted; and to convince those who had entered with doubt and reluctance into the struggle, that their leaders had not misapprehended or misrepresented the malignancy of the northern people towards them.

But our national Executive and our national legislature removed all doubt, if any yet remained in the southern mind, that there was no hope of personal safety or of political liberty in the future, except in successful resistance. The former issued the emancipation proclamation, in which he announced the intention to guaranty to the negroes FOREVER, that liberty which he could only permanently secure to them by an overthrow of the State constitutions, and an abolition of the right of self-government. The latter, in a series of acts justly styled " incendiary

6*

and infernal " by one of the ablest men of the dominant majority, closed the door of return in the faces of the southern people. Abolition of slavery being the first subject of their attention, laws were passed to accomplish indirectly that object in every conceivable method, short of an act of direct emancipation, the unconstitutionality of which had been declared by Congress in the days when the true policy of the nation was supposed to be to restore a Union, resting " upon the consent of the governed." But destruction of the slave property of the citizens of the seceded States, irrespective of their actual complicity in the rebellion, was not sufficient. Provision was made to strip every man who had been engaged in the rebellion, no matter what might be his social or military rank, of everything which he possessed; to render the tenure of the lives and liberties of a whole people dependent upon executive clemency; and to complete their political and social degradation even beyond the reach of executive clemency. The severity of the punishment of treason, and the rules of evidence applicable to trials for that crime, rendered it certain that if the rebellion was suppressed, only the few leaders could be punished. Hence to reach all classes of the community, an act was passed in July, 1861, to punish a conspiracy to overthrow the Government, by a fine of from five hundred to five thousand dollars, and imprisonment from six months to six

years; and in the succeeding year, full provision
was made for the punishment of every case from
"assisting" any rebellion up to actual treason, by
fines and imprisonments graduated according to the
offence and in the discretion of the court. A
sweeping system of confiscation was also established. At first, provision was made whereby each
State's proportionate share of the direct tax, was to
be levied upon the real estate within any district
which might be occupied by our forces, and the
property was to be sold to the highest bidder, and
not to be redeemed without proof that the owner
had taken no part in the insurrection. This was of
itself a very ingenious scheme for rewarding the
loyal and punishing the rebellious at the same time.
But a more sweeping statute for that purpose was
soon passed, whereby all the property of those who
did not return to their allegiance within sixty days
after a proclamation (which has been issued), was
forfeited, and it was made the duty of the President
to seize and sell it, and apply the proceeds to the
support of the army.

Such acts would be considered bad policy in any
constitutional monarchical government, endeavoring
to suppress a rebellion; but one would suppose that
even a despotism would endeavor to make it for the
interest of rebels to abandon or betray their associates, and for that purpose would desire in some
cases to grant a full amnesty for all offences, and to

appoint the repentant rebel to office. But our
legislature has provided that even the President
and the people of the whole nation shall be unable
to bestow a public office upon any person, who has
been in any way, no matter how remote, impli-
cated in the rebellion; nor can such a man ever
serve as a juror in any of the Federal courts. By
the act of June 17, 1862, it is a ground of disquali-
fication to any juror, not only that he has himself
been engaged in the rebellion, but that he has "given,
directly or indirectly, any assistance in money, &c.,
or anything whatever, to or for the use or benefit"
*of any person whom he knew to be a rebel or to be
about to become a rebel;* and the act of July 2, 1862,
provides that no person can hold office without
taking an oath that he has never borne arms against
the United States, or "given aid, countenance,
counsel, or encouragement to persons engaged in
armed hostility thereto."

It is manifest that these acts cover the case of
nearly every individual within the limits of the
seceding States, south of the Tennessee line and
east of the Blue Ridge; and that the result has
necessarily been to join despair to supposed patriotism, love of liberty, pride, self-respect, self-interest,
and human sympathy, in inspiring the people of the
South with the resolution to endure every sacrifice
in the struggle for independence, rather than to
suffer the degradation, tyranny and ruin which sub-

mission to the Government of the Union would bring upon them.

Is it possible to remove this feeling and to arouse anew in the hearts of the southern people that affection for the Union and loyalty to its Government which prevailed among them before the outbreak of the rebellion? This is a grave problem, the solution of which will require the patient and cautious labor of the ablest, purest, wisest and most moderate statesmen. I shall throw out in the concluding chapter a few suggestions, which may assist the reader in forming some conclusion as to the practicability and the proper mode of attaining such a result. For the present I must confine myself to such observations, as will show that it never can be attained by the policy which we are now pursuing. And first, let me glance at the theory, which is held by many, that the miseries and calamities which the rebellion has brought upon the people, and its failure to attain success, will turn a current of public indignation against the leaders of the insurrection, and lead the masses to cling to the old Government as the source of the prosperity and happiness which they formerly enjoyed, and which they will expect to see equalled or even exceeded in the future.

I have repeatedly said that I should not discuss the conduct or the deserts of the leading southern politicians, and the same reasons which led me to refrain from so doing, will exclude from my consideration the question, whether it is possible by any line of policy which we may adopt, so to separate the feelings and interests of the people, from those of the few leaders who rendered themselves most prominent before the war broke out, that the former would look with complacency upon the ruin of the latter as the result of a rebellion instigated by them. For that question is wholly irrelevant to the present subject of inquiry. The policy which I am condemning does not contemplate the punishment of a few of the leading conspirators merely—for the former laws punishing the crime of treason were ample and more than ample for that purpose—but its object is to reach all classes of the community. Not that I suppose that its authors intend actually to fine, imprison, or execute all the white people of the southern States, but they evidently do intend to strip a great part of them of their property; to render them all incapable of holding office; to punish criminally such of them as they shall select as fit objects of their revenge; and to hold a sword forever suspended over the heads of every man who shall be spared, to fall whenever his conduct shall fail to meet the approbation of those in power. Else why were the laws passed; and why are the confiscation acts being daily put into operation in such regions of the country as we have conquered?*

* I have heard the policy of these laws defended by men

It is evident that the result of carrying out such a policy will be, as it has been heretofore, to identify the people in feeling with the leaders against whom

who freely concede the impossibility of putting them into practical operation after the rebellion shall have been quelled, on the ground that they were *temporarily* necessary to prevent disloyal men from filling public office while the war was progressing, and to increase the motives for the insurgents to return to their allegiance. If it was conceded that they were merely temporary measures, many of the objections to them would be removed, for the discussion respecting the policy of such laws would be confined simply to their effect upon the *duration* of the war, a subject which I have considered already. But they are in no sense temporary by their terms, and although the President has been authorized by one of them, "to extend to persons who may have participated in the existing rebellion pardon and amnesty," the power to dispense with the two test-oaths has not been confided even to him ; and many of those who enacted the penal and confiscation laws, and sustain the policy which they indicate, openly support them as permanent measures, indicating a permanent policy towards the people to be conquered. The reader will find a few pages further on an extract from a speech of General Butler, in which he announces as his plan of *pacification* that the property of all who have taken part in the rebellion shall be divided among the volunteer soldiers of our army. The proofs that the laws in question are regarded by many public men as the permanent policy of the Government, might be indefinitely multiplied, but my space confines me to two short extracts from " Our Domestic Relations," which will at least satisfy the reader that I am not fighting a shadow. Mr. Sumner says : " Holding every acre of soil, and every inhabitant of these States within its jurisdiction, Congress can easily do, by proper legislation, whatever may be needful within rebel limits in order to assure freedom and save

it is expected that their indignation will be directed.
A tolerable familiarity with the workings of human
nature and the lessons of history, will show that
the result will be precisely the reverse of that which
was anticipated from their enactment. Among a
people thus consolidated by common suffering and
a common political ostracism, the man who has
suffered most in the common cause, will be the man
who will arouse the deepest emotions of reverence,
admiration, and affection, and his martyrdom will
efface the memory of all his faults and all his
crimes. Men are never convinced that opinions
are erroneous by persecution and suffering. And
if we wish to make the name of Davis awaken in
the hearts of the present and future generations of
southerners, the emotions which that of Emmett
awakens in the hearts of Irishmen, the true method
to attain the object is to execute him and enforce
the savage penal and confiscation laws against the
citizens of the South.

society. *The soil may be divided among patriot soldiers, poor
whites, and freedmen.*" Further on, after reciting the substance of the disqualifying acts he adds : " This oath will
be a bar against the return to national office of ANY who
have TAKEN PART with the rebels. It shuts out in advance
the whole criminal gang. But these same persons rejected
by the national Government are left free to hold office in
the States ; and here is a motive to further action by Congress. The oath is well as far as it goes : *more must be
done in the same spirit* "

Nor will the case be altered if the poorer classes of the community are suffered to retain their lives, liberties, and humble property, and the penalties of the confiscation laws (either with or without those of the penal laws) are visited only upon the principal citizens of each neighborhood. For the South is preëminently *not* one of those communities in which the rich and the poor occupy a position of antagonism with respect to each other. That antagonism, which the institutions of all other countries develop to a greater or less degree, is replaced in the South by an antagonism of race. The prevalence of universal suffrage, in connection with the existence of slavery, has created a species of aristocracy of color, in the real or fancied glories of which all of the whites have participated, and which has served to bind them together in a species of clanship. Hence, whatever exceptions may exist in isolated cases to the general rule, the ruin of the principal men, so far from awakening a feeling of complacency in the hearts of their fellow-citizens, will excite only the sympathy of the latter, and compassion for their sufferings will be mingled with hatred of the Government which inflicted them, and of those who will profit by the misfortunes of martyrs to a common cause. Nothing but radical antagonism of class could produce any other result.

Indeed, the idea of having been blindly led into the commission of a political folly by the sophistry

and misrepresentations of a superior, is one of the
most offensive which can possibly be presented to
the mind of a free citizen of Anglo-Saxon blood, at
the North or at the South. His pride—perhaps it
might be rather styled his conceit—revolts at the
suggestion that he has been made a tool in the
hands of another, and impels him to defend the wisdom and propriety of the course which he has pursued, and to regard every circumstance which is
urged as a demonstration of its folly, as patent
proof to the contrary. I suppose that no man will
contend that even if the rebellion had resulted in
the South conquering us, the mass of the Republican party would have rejoiced at the execution
or the ruin of the leading politicians who urged
them, in 1860, to bid defiance to the threats of the
South ; laughed at the suggestion that civil war
would ensue as the result of Mr. Lincoln's election ;
and assured them that the only fight which we
should have would be a contest among the southerners for the offices at his disposal. Much less would
they have sympathized with the spoliation of the
property-owners among their own neighbors. The
case supposed would not have been at all beyond
the limits of possibility, had the war been followed
by foreign intervention, and it will present precisely
the same case which will occur in the South after
its conquest, when the penal and confiscation laws
shall be enforced against the men who have at-

tained social, political, or financial preëminence in their respective neighborhoods.

The vindictive policy, which we have thus adopted as the foundation of the future relations between us and the southern people, after the war shall be closed, must necessarily stifle any attempts, pending the war, to organize a peace party in the southern States, if any disposition to do so exists in consequence of the subsidence of the angry passions which were at first aroused, and the apparently impending failure of the insurrection. It has already, in all probability, produced that result in North Carolina, in portions of which State the nucleus of an organization was formed, having as its object, not the unconditional submission of the South, but the inception of negotiations for the purpose of agreeing upon terms of submission. We have no means of determining with exact accuracy why the project was abandoned, but there are adequate reasons for its abandonment, which, in the absence of certain information, we must conjecturally assign as those which prevailed. It is hardly possible that the men by whom this project was inaugurated, comprising the governor and several of the members of the North Carolina legislature, should ever have contemplated a voluntary submission to a government which had already excluded them forever from public office and from the juries in its courts, and offered them no other

terms than enforcement of the penal and confiscation laws, and the overthrow of the right of self-
government implied in the emancipation proclamation.*

The fact that the door to the restoration of such
a union as formerly existed has been effectually
closed, is continually overlooked by our people
when speculating upon the present as well as the
future disposition of the people of the South, to end
the war by submission to the Government. Hence
they overestimate the significance of those jars in
the working of the machinery of the revolutionary
government, which are continually occurring in
every country in times of great public excitement,
and from which our own section of the country is
only comparatively more exempt than the other.
Riots in the leading southern cities, evasions of and
acts of violent resistance to the Confederate conscription law; collisions of opinion between the central Government and the governments of the States;
dissatisfaction with particular measures or the general policy of the Confederate administration, expressed in emphatic terms through the public press
or upon the rostrum; the unpopularity of certain
officers, civil or military; the longing for peace

* The exceptions in the President's proclamation of
amnesty, dated December eighth, eighteen hundred and
sixty-three, will exclude from pardon most of the men who
were said to be the leaders in this movement.

which evidently pervades all classes of the people; occasional acts of mutiny and insubordination in the Confederate army; flattering stories of deserters, refugees and "intelligent contrabands" anxious to propitiate favor in their new homes; individual acts of Christian charity and human sympathy towards prisoners of war captured from us; kindly intercourse between the soldiers of both armies; and the occasional discovery of an unquestionable unionist in the South; all these things have been so exaggerated by our credulous people, that the belief that the southern people are suffering from a military despotism which they are eagerly longing to shake off, still retains, absurdly enough, a hold upon the minds of many men, who, in cases in which their feelings and hopes are not so strongly enlisted, are cool and sagacious observers.*

These men overlook the fact that when the fortunes of the war were apparently against us, a very similar state of things was continually occurring upon our side of the lines, and that to a considerable extent we can yet match the same indications of popular discontent in the South with similar incidents of our own history. In truth the South has had nearly if not quite as much reason to believe from external indications that we are crushed by a military despotism, which the majority of our peo-

* See Note at the end of this chapter, page 152.

ple are longing to throw off, as we have to entertain the same belief concerning them. In the South
as well as in the North the proof that the hearts of
the people are yet in the war, is to be found in the
fact that the war is sustained by the representatives
of the people elected at frequently recurring intervals.

As an ounce of experience is said to be worth a
pound of theory, let me now consider whether our
occupation of certain portions of the southern territory, furnishes us with any indications concerning
the probability of regaining the affections of the
people, by the policy which we have been pursuing.
We have a few data from which to form an opinion
upon that subject, but they will enable us only to
approximate to correctness, for we have not yet
occupied any portion of the southern country, under
the same conditions which will present themselves
when we shall have subdued and occupied the
whole, and this for the reason that the *intellectual
and physical flower of the people* fled before us
when the Confederate army retired, except in the
State of Tennessee, where a peculiarity of circumstances has existed which will mislead us, if we take
that State as a standard of comparison. For the people of Tennessee, as late as the ninth of February,
1861, declared in favor of remaining in the Union
by a vote of nearly four to one, notwithstanding

that the Gulf States had then seceded.* And the comparatively early occupation of a large portion of the State by our forces; the exemption of the inhabitants from many of the mortifications of conquest by the embodiment of Tennessee troops in the army of occupation; the comparative discipline, good order, and respect for private property which have characterized the military administration; and above all, the assurance, implied by the exemption of their State from the emancipation proclamation, that they will ultimately be permitted to govern themselves, have subjected the Tennesseans only in a minor degree to the operation of those causes which have elsewhere influenced the southern people. So that although thousands of her most valued citizens have fled the State and cast their fortunes with the Confederates, and it has not been deemed safe after a year and a half of occupation to commit the civil government to the hands of the people, it seems probable that the State of Tennessee has been permanently saved to the Union with the approbation of a majority of its inhabitants. But this result is not due to the general policy which I have

* The vote in detail was as follows :

	Union.	Secession.
East Tennessee	30,903	5,577
Middle Tennessee	36,809	9,828
West Tennessee	24,091	9,344
	91,803	24,749

Majority for the Union, 67,054.

been condemning. It has occurred because a different policy has been pursued in that State. The people of Kentucky are almost unanimous in their condemnation of the measures which I have criticised ; can we doubt what is the public opinion of Tennessee respecting them?

Our principal acquisitions in Arkansas are too recent, and we still hold too little of North Carolina, South Carolina or Georgia, to render popular indications of any value in either of those States; but we shall find a tolerably fair indication of the probability that a vindictive policy will restore the affections of the southern people to the Union, in the results which ensued from pursuing the same policy after our occupation of Louisiana. New Orleans was captured in April, 1862, and the policy of severity was at once put into full operation by the military commander of that department, his theory of private rights under martial law having been stated by him in a speech delivered at New York in April, 1863, in the following words :

" They " (the conquered people, whom he styles alien enemies) "have the right, so long as they behave themselves and are non-combatants, to be free from personal violence ; *they have no other rights ;* and therefore it was my duty to see to it, and I believe the record will show that I did see to it (great applause and cheers). I did see to it that order was preserved, and that every man who behaved well and did not aid the Confederate States should not be molested *in his person.* I held *everything else they had was at the mercy of the conqueror* (cheers). . . . Has it not been held from the beginning of the world till this day, from the time the Israelites took possession of the land of Canaan, which they got from alien enemies, has it not been held that *the whole property of those alien enemies belonged to the conqueror*, and that it has been *at his mercy and clemency what should be done with it?* For one, I would take it and give the loyal man, who was loyal in the heart of the South, enough to make him as well as he was before, and I would take the balance of it and distribute it among the volunteer soldiers who have gone (the remainder of the sentence was drowned in a tremendous burst of applause)."

Let us see how far the policy thus announced has tended to produce such a state of public feeling in New Orleans, as to authorize us to expect that the loyalty of the people of Louisiana will soon be sufficiently aroused, to enable a civil government to assume the reins of power and to support itself, without relying upon the military forces of the Federal Government, by the voluntary action of the citizens. In none of the seceding States except Tennessee was there a district in which we should have expected to find as large a proportion of

7

Unionists as in that which comprises the city of New Orleans. A considerable proportion of the population of that city has always consisted of men of northern birth or northern education, and its commercial and financial relations with the North and the Northwest have been of such an intimate character, as to render it the first and greatest sufferer by the war, among the principal cities of the South. Very soon after its occupation, its citizens were required to choose between taking an oath of allegiance to the Union, and registering themselves as "enemies of the United States." Large numbers took the oath, many no doubt from sincere conviction and with a purpose to keep it honestly, many others simply because they had to choose between doing so and submitting to military plunder with a prospect of exile. In truth, the "registered enemies" were afterwards exiled. To the immense force which the United States sent to the city and the military department, were added several regiments raised in Louisiana, white and black, the latter consisting chiefly of New Orleans negroes and colored people, the most intelligent of the black population of the whole South. And yet, after more than a year of occupation, the purification of the city from all the friends of the rebellion who could be discovered, an immense influx of northern men, and the transfer of the chief command from General Butler to a gentleman whose humanity and modera-

tion none will question, it is found necessary for the
public safety and the preservation of public order,
notwithstanding the overwhelming military force
within the city, to adopt measures even more stringent than the Austrian military regulations in
Venice. Witness the following order:

"HEADQUARTERS DEFENCES OF NEW ORLEANS,
NEW ORLEANS, *July* 3d, 1863.

"GENERAL ORDERS No. 18.

"Hereafter no public assemblages, except for
public worship, under a regular commissioned priest,
will be allowed in this city, for any purpose or
under any pretence whatever, by white or black,
without the written consent of the commander of
the defences of New Orleans: and no more than
three persons will be allowed to assemble or congre-
gate together upon the streets of the city. Whenever more than that number are found together by
the patrol, they shall be ordered to disperse, and
failing to do so, the offenders shall be placed in
arrest. All bar-rooms, coffee-houses, stores and
shops of every description will be closed at 9 o'clock
P.M. All club-rooms and gambling-houses are hereby closed until further orders. No citizen or other
person except the police and officers in the United
States service, or soldiers on duty or with passes are
to be allowed in the streets after 9 o'clock P.M.

"By command of Brigadier-General EMORY.
"W. D. SMITH, Lieut.-Col., A. A. A. G.'

So much for the progress which has been made in re-kindling the extinguished flame of loyalty in the hearts of the people of Louisiana. In other regions which we have occupied for a sufficient length of time to develop public sentiment, the result has been simply the depopulation of the country, or an obstinate refusal to acknowledge the authority of the Government by any participation in the administration of public affairs. In the city of Norfolk, two hundred and forty votes were cast for mayor at the spring election of 1863. The city contained in 1860 a population of eleven thousand three hundred and twenty-five, exclusive of slaves, or a little less than two thousand voters. In Alexandria, our first capture, nestling under the very wing of the Federal Government, the successful candidate for the mayoralty received at the same election thirty-seven votes and his opponent thirty-one. The city contained in 1860, eight thousand seven hundred and fifty-two inhabitants; deducting people of color, the voting population would be between twelve and fifteen hundred.

In cities, the means of enforcing strict military law and the habits of the people are such, that it is only by such indications as I have mentioned that it is possible to ascertain the real feelings of the inhabitants. In the rural districts there have been greater facilities for determining the sentiments of the people by their conduct, and those

have been expressed in a manner which renders
it impossible to mistake them. It is true that when
resistance has become hopeless, we have been able
to enforce peaceable submission; that fear has
induced many to take the oath of allegiance, and
that occasionally our troops have fallen in with men
who profess themselves, some of them doubtless
with sincerity, to be our friends, and render us
services which secure them protection, and generally lead to their pecuniary profit. But the great
body of the people have been too sincere to feign
what they do not feel; and what they do feel, they
have expressed so as to render it evident that the
Federal rule over them was sustained by force and
fear only; that they were subdued, not regained to
the Union; that their country was subjugated, not
their hearts. Our armies have been received upon
their arrival with the sullenness of fear and hatred,
and with the most unequivocal assurances in words
and by deeds that their presence was accepted as a
forced necessity. Even the love of gain has generally proved insufficient to induce the inhabitants
voluntarily to supply the wants of our men, and
the stringent laws of war have been futile to restrain
them from acting as spies and informers for the
Confederate army. When reverses have overtaken
us and necessity has compelled our retreat, the
fierce and vindictive exultation of the people has
been too great to wear a mask; and while the men

who remained in the country have drawn forth
their rifles and fowling-pieces from hidden recesses,
and sallied forth to cut off stragglers, not even the
natural timidity of the sex has restrained the women
along the line of march from heaping curses and
taunts upon the heads of their hated enemies as our
forces passed by. Neither the events of the past,
nor the light which they cast upon the dark and
momentous future, authorize us to reject as exag-
gerations the statements and predictions contained
in the following extracts from a recently published
address of the southern clergymen of all denomina-
tions, to Christians throughout the world :

"Though hundreds of thousands of lives have
been lost, and many millions of treasure spent;
though a vast amount of valuable property has
been destroyed, and numbers of once happy homes
made desolate; though cities and towns have been
temporarily captured, and aged men and helpless
women and children have suffered such things as it
were even a shame to speak of plainly; though
sanctuaries have been desecrated and ministers of
God dragged from sacred altars to loathsome
prisons; though slaves have been instigated to
insurrection, and every measure has been adopted
that the ingenuity of the enemy could devise, or
his ample resources afford by sea and by land ; yet
we aver without fear of contradiction, that the only
possession which the United States hold in the Con-

federate States, is the ground on which United States troops pitch their tents; and whenever these troops withdraw from a given locality in our territory, the people resident therein testify a warmer devotion to the Confederate cause than even before their soil was invaded. Nothing is therefore conquered—no part of the country is subdued; the civil jurisdiction of the United States, the real test of their success, has not been established by any force of arms. Where such civil jurisdiction exists at all along the border, it has existed all the while, was not obtained by force, and is not the fruit of conquest. . . . .

"Notwithstanding the gigantic exertions of the United States, they have not been able to secure the return of a single county, or section of a county, much less a single State that has seceded. No civil order and peace spring up in the track of their armies. All in front of them is resolute resistance, and behind them, when they have entered our territory, is a deep, uncompromising opposition, over which only military force alone can for a moment be trusted.

"The only change of opinion among our people since the beginning of the war, that is of material importance to the final issue, has been the change from all lingering attachment to the former Union, to a more sacred and reliable devotion to the Confederate Government. The sentiments of the people

are not alterable in any other respects by force of
arms.

"If the whole country were occupied by United
States troops, it would merely exhibit a military
despotism, against which the people would struggle
in perpetual revolutionary effort, while any south-
rons remained alive. Extermination of the inhabitants could alone realize civil possession of "their
soil."

Note.—If our people would but carefully consult the
history of our revolutionary war, they would find it studded
with warnings against many of the errors, civil and military,
into which we have fallen during the present contest. The
obstinate attachment of the ministry of George III. to a
policy which appealed only to the fears of the Americans,
was caused to a considerable extent by a total misconcep-
tion of the feelings which prevailed among the people ; and
it rendered irreparable a breach, which the seasonable
adoption of wiser and more moderate counsels would have
closed. The embarrassments of the Confederate Government, referred to in the text, are strikingly similar to
those which Congress encountered in all except the earliest
and latest stages of the revolution, and the significance of
the latter was misinterpreted by the British ministerial
party, precisely as the administration party now misinter-
pret the significance of the former. The reader will find,
in the ninth chapter, a passage from Botta's History,
which describes some of the dangers to which the American cause was exposed, immediately after the battle of
Long Island, in consequence of the fears and despond-
ency of many of the people, and the remnants of the
spirit of loyalty to the crown which the war had not yet
extinguished. I will here add a brief outline of some of
the subsequent events, with extracts from the same work.

On the 30th of May, 1777, Lord Chatham was carried from his sick-bed to the House of Lords, where "in a strain of admirable eloquence" he delivered an address in favor of repealing the laws which had occasioned the dissatisfaction in America. In the course of his remarks, he said: "It is difficult for government, after all that has passed, to shake hands with the defiers of the king, defiers of Parliament, defiers of the people. I am a defier of nobody; but if an end is not put to this war, there is an end to this country. . . . . But you would conquer, you say! *Why what would you conquer, the map of America?* . . . . If you conquer them, what then? You cannot make them respect you; you cannot make them wear your cloth. *You will plant an invincible hatred in their breasts against you.* . . . . We have tried for unconditional submission; try what can be gained by unconditional redress. We shall thus evince a conciliatory spirit, and open the way to concord. . . . . Mercy cannot do harm; it will seat the king where he ought to be, throned in the hearts of his people; and millions at home and abroad, now employed in obloquy and revolt, would pray for him. The revocation I propose, and amnesty, may produce a respectable division in America, and unanimity at home. It will give America an option; she has as yet had no option. You have said, 'Lay down your arms,' and she has given you the Spartan answer, 'Come—take.'"

But all was in vain. The ministry would hear of nothing but unconditional submission. Botta continues: "Neither the authority of such a man, nor the force of his speech, nor present evils, nor yet fear of the future, were sufficient to procure the adoption of his proposition. Those who opposed it contended that it would by no means satisfy the Americans, since from the outset they had aimed at independency. They talked of the dignity of the nation, ... of the number of loyalists ready to declare themselves, the moment an occasion should offer itself; they harangued upon the tyranny of Congress, already

become insupportable to the Americans, upon the empti-
ness of its treasury, and the rapid depreciation of bills of
credit ; finally they enlarged upon that impatience, which
was universally manifested for the return of order, and the
blessings enjoyed by the rest of the subjects of the British
government."—*Otis's Translation*, vol. ii., pp. 73–75.

So another grand effort was made to "break the back-
bone of the rebellion" by the force of arms alone, the
ministry having perfect confidence that it could be accomplished in *one more* campaign. That campaign ended in the
surrender of Burgoyne at Saratoga, and the fruitless
British victory of the Brandywine, which, as Botta says,
only resulted in procuring good winter quarters for Howe's
army. The dreadful winter of 1777–1778 followed, made
memorable by the encampment at Valley Forge, in which
Washington's army endured hardships which the Confederate soldiers have not yet even dreamed of. The success
at Saratoga fixed the wavering resolution of the French
court to declare in favor of the colonists, and in February,
1778, the treaty between France and the United States
was signed. *Then* the British ministry began to perceive
the consequences of their infatuation, and made an effort
to be reconciled with the colonists. Having procured
unofficial knowledge of the execution of the treaty, they
introduced into Parliament a bill to appoint commissioners
to settle the differences between the colonists and the
mother country, on the very basis proposed by Lord
Chatham in the preceding year, to wit, the repeal of the
obnoxious laws, the surrender of the right of taxation, and
a universal amnesty. The bill passed, but on the thirteenth
of March, before anything was done under it, official news
of the treaty was communicated to the British court. A
resolution to test the sense of the House of Commons on
the subject of declaring war against France was introduced by the ministry on the seventeenth of March. It
was at once alleged by the opposition that the propositions
for reconciliation with the colonies were now too late, and

it was proposed that before fighting France, England
should rid herself of her American enemy by acknowledg-
ing the independence of the United States. The answer
of the ministry showed that their erroneous opinions
respecting American affairs had become too inveterate to
be overcome even by the experience which they had undergone. The speech of Mr. Jenkinson, the minister of war,
bears a striking resemblance in many features to those
which we now hear every day in Congress. He calls the
exposé which had been made by the opposition of the
blunders of the government, and the disasters to which
they had led, "indulging their favorite whim of *reviling
their country*, expatiating with apparent delight upon its
weakness, and magnifying the power of its ambitious
enemy :" he assures the House in the most confident manner that if the colonists decline the proposals of accommo-
dation, *one more* campaign MUST crush the rebellion, an
opinion which he supports in the following language :

"I shall begin with asking these bosom friends of rebels,
if they are certain that it is all America, or only a seditious
handful, whose craft and audacity have raised them to
the head of affairs, who claim independency? For my
own part, I confess that this independence appears to me
rather a vision that floats in certain brains, inflamed by the
rage of innovation, on that side of the Atlantic as well as
on this, than any general wish of the people. This is what
all men of sense declare, who have resided in the midst of
that misguided multitude ; this is attested by the thousands
of royalists who have flocked to the royal standard in New
York, and who have fought for the king in the plains of
Saratoga, and on the banks of the Brandywine. This,
finally, is proclaimed by the very prisons, crowded with
inhabitants, who have chosen rather to part with their
liberty, than to renounce their allegiance. . . . . There is
every reason to think that to such subjects as remained
faithful until England set up the pretension of taxation,
many others will join themselves, now that she has

renounced it ; for already all are convinced how much better it is to live under the mild sway of an equitable prince, than under the tyranny of new and ambitious men. . . . . Nor should I omit to mention a well known fact ; the finances of Congress are exhausted ; their soldiers are naked and famishing ; they can satisfy none of the wants of the State ; creditors are without remedy against their debtors ; hence arise scandals without end, private hatreds, and unanimous maledictions against the Government.

"There is not an individual among the Americans, but sees that, in accepting the terms offered by Great Britain, the public credit will be reëstablished, private property secured, and abundance in all parts of the social body restored. . . . . Yes, methinks I already see, or I am strangely mistaken, the people of America flocking to the royal standard ; everything invites them to it ; fidelity towards the sovereign, the love of the English name, the hope of a happier future, their aversion to their new and unaccustomed allies, and, finally, the hatred they bear to the tyranny of Congress."—*Id.*, pp. 90–99.

It is well known how conclusively the result proved that Mr. Jenkinson and his associate ministers *were* "strangely mistaken." May God grant that the people of my unhappy country may not need a similar catastrophe to open their eyes to the consequences of a similar folly !

CHAPTER VIII.

The impossibility of Governing the People of the South by means of State Governments, depending upon the Popular Vote, without allaying their Discontent—Results which attended the Attempt in Utah to maintain the Federal Government over a Dissatisfied People—Collisions which a similar Attempt in the South would provoke—The impracticability of introducing a new Element of Political Power, by means of the Blacks, or of Foreign Immigrants, or of Immigrants from the North—The practical Result of the Power of Government, popular in Form, to coerce its Subjects to obedience, compared with the Theory—Action of President Jackson in the Nullification Controversy—His Opinion respecting the possibility of maintaining the Union by Force alone—Madison, Benton, Everett, Douglas and Webster's Opinions upon the same subject.

LET us now examine what prospect a persistence in the policy which I have discussed in the preceding chapters, holds out of securing the ultimate pacification of the southern country, after the people shall have been subdued by the complete victory of our arms, and State governments controlled by the free and unbiassed votes of the whole people, shall have been established over them. Such, as has been fully stated in chapters iii. and iv., is the conclusion of the war which the Constitution requires, to which the Government has pledged itself to foreign powers, and which the Crittenden resolution contemplates.

In the language of that resolution, "the war is not waged for the purpose of conquest or subjugation, or of overthrowing or interfering with the rights or established institutions of those States, but . . . to preserve the Union, with all the dignity, equality, and rights of the several States, unimpaired, and that as soon as those objects are accomplished, the war ought to cease." In the language of Mr. Seward, if the revolution fails, "the condition of every human being" in the seceded States "will remain subject to exactly the same laws and forms of administration" as before, and their "constitutions and laws, customs, habits and institutions will remain the same."

If these words mean anything, they mean that as soon as the Federal armies have driven the Confederate armies out of the field, the people of the southern States are to resume the right of being governed by a governor and legislature, freely elected by themselves, and possessing, so far as any interference by the United States is concerned, unlimited power to raise money by taxation, and to appropriate it to any purpose whatever; to embody the people into a military force, and organize and arm them; to regulate the police system, the tenure of property, internal trade, and all the details of internal government. They will also possess a judiciary, elected or appointed by themselves, and empowered to decide (in most cases ulti-

mately and without appeal) all controversies which
may arise between inhabitants of the State; and
finally, they will have their proportionate vote in
the election of the President and their proportionate part of the members of each House of
Congress, to whom is confided the national Government of themselves and their conquerors. As
I have shown in the third and fourth chapters,
there is no method known to the Constitution
and laws of the country, whereby such of the
southern people as may escape the sword, the
gibbet and the prison, can be deprived of the full
exercise in their States of all the rights which freemen in the loyal States enjoy; and however great
may be the thirst of the conquerors for vengeance
upon their conquered enemies, the instinct of
humanity and the public opinion of the civilized
world will revolt against its gratification to an
extent which will appreciably diminish the population. The men who have composed the armies
which have hitherto retired before us, and those
other men, more or less prominent by their social
position, their wealth, their talents, their acquire-
ments, and their virtues, who have accompanied
them, will return to their homes and resume their
former occupations. The vast powers to which I
have already referred, are therefore to be exercised
by a proud and high-spirited people, who will be
animated with the spirit towards the North and the

Federal Government, which has been already described, and which will naturally be greatly intensified by that crowning mortification to any free
and sensitive people, a foreign conquest. The circumstances necessarily attending such a conquest—
the grief and mourning for those who have fallen
in battle, the impoverishment of the country by the
annihilation of its currency and the miseries of invasion—and the national humiliation which the fact
of conquest involves, would render the attempt to
reconcile such a people to their condition a trying
task for the ablest statesmen. But the idea of *reconciliation* is to be completely ignored; on the contrary, the policy marked out for us, is one calculated
to render that condition absolutely intolerable,
which under the most favorable circumstances
would be extremely galling. The leaders of this
people, whom they regard with a reverence and
affection which living statesmen and warriors cannot hope to inspire, except in revolutionary times,
are to be brought to the block or exiled; the system
of labor upon which all the industrial interests of
the country are founded is to be destroyed; an
immense portion of the property of the country is
to be swept away beyond the reach of even Executive clemency; the remainder and the lives and
liberty of each individual are to be held at the
mercy of the conqueror; and all are to be inexora-
bly excluded from filling any office whatever under

the Government of the conqueror, or from sitting as jurors in his courts. If some of them shall by a pardon earned by early submission be relieved from the weight of such of these hardships as are capable of alleviation by the act of the Executive, or shall be exempted from the operation of the vindictive laws by accidental peculiarities of their circumstances; or if an infusion of northern men shall be introduced among the people; those who are thus fortunately raised above the calamities of their fellow-citizens, will be "rari nantes in gurgite vasto," a few scattered loyalists in a nation of sufferers, seething with hatred and suppressed rebellion. Such will be the people who are to exercise the almost unlimited power of a sovereign State by means of universal suffrage. And it is expected that this power will be exercised, voluntarily or through fear of consequences, in harmony with and in subordination to the Government by which they have been ruined, degraded and oppressed. I will present a few suggestions, to show that such a scheme is impracticable, although a simple statement of the facts seems to me so forcible, that argument can add but little to it. I have endeavored in vain to discover in any public speech or document, or to procure in private conversation with those who believe in the possibility of the restoration of the Union by force and a policy of severity, any lucid explanation of the manner in which such a scheme

is to be *practically* carried into effect. To me it
appears that the only escape from the conclusion
that the country would be delivered up to hopeless
anarchy and perpetual civil strife, is to suppose that
a state of things would supervene similar to that
which attended the attempt of President Buchanan
to restore by force the authority of the United
States over the rebellious Territory of Utah.
Although the Mormon rebels were the objects of
universal detestation throughout the civilized world;
although our people were united as a man in the
determination that they should be put down;
although a force was sent against them which rendered open resistance hopeless; although they at
once nominally yielded, and our troops occupied
their country without opposition; and although
they wielded only the limited power of a territorial
government, yet the result showed how utterly
dependent is the operation of our whole political
system upon the wishes and affections of the people
of the different localities over which it extends.
The laws of the United States were practically nul-
lified; its actual jurisdiction was circumscribed by
the line of sentinels around the encampments; its
loyal citizens were plundered with impunity under
the forms of law; its judicial and civil officers
owed their lives only to the continual protection of
a guard; every species of crime was committed by
the Mormons with impunity; in short, a nest of

outlaws, contemptible in numbers, and thoroughly
depraved in morals, but united in purpose, and
wielding the numerical majority of the territory, set
at utter defiance the authority of the whole nation.
What then can we expect as the result of placing
the whole power of a State in the hands of a people
animated by such sentiments as I have described?
An utter abandonment for a season of the authority
of the United States within the State, and a surrender of all rights acquired under the penal statutes or
proclamations, would prevent collisions, and consequently avoid the continued irritation to which this
would give rise; and when the lapse of time had
assuaged the violent passions of the people, and
repaired the immense damage which the war has
occasioned to individuals and the public, the complete absorption of the State into the Union might
possibly be effected. But such a course is utterly
impracticable and inconsistent with the object of the
war; and whether practicable or impracticable, it
is the exact reverse of the policy to which the nation
now stands pledged, a policy which involves a perpetual collision between the Federal authorities and
the infuriated people. Apart from the negro controversy, there will be an abundant crop of quarrels
springing daily from the dragons' teeth which have
been so plentifully sown by the war. The collection of the customs and the administration of
justice by the Federal courts in ordinary cases,

could not fail, under the disqualifying statutes, to keep up a perpetual irritation. What then may be expected from an attempt to enforce the internal revenue law—a measure, the operation of which, extending as it does into nearly every portion of the every day business of every man, is exceedingly galling to our own people? Can any one doubt what will be the result of an attempt to collect from a conquered people, the price of their own subjugation by means of a law so vexatious in itself, and administered by men the very sight of whom, and the recollection of the oath they have taken are a perpetual reminder to the people of their own misfortunes and degradation? What will be the result of an attempt to enforce the confiscation law, by officers of the same character? What popular demonstrations will accompany the march and follow the train of a Federal judge, with a standing panel of jurors, and an army of marshals— every man, judge, juror and marshal, considered by the people a traitor or a foreigner—travelling around the southern country to enforce the vindictive penal statutes to which I have referred? What protection will the purchaser of a confiscated estate find for his life and his property in the State tribunals and from State officers, elected by the free votes of the sufferers and their fellow-countrymen and friends?

Here are but a very few of the questions which

will arise as a consequence of an attempt to restore
the independence and sovereignty of the southern
States after conquering their armies, and occupying their soil, without having secured the coöperation of a majority of the people; but I think that
whoever attempts to answer them will find himself
compelled to give up the problem as insoluble,
except by one of these two alternatives, viz., (1) the
people must be exterminated, or (2) a new element
must be introduced in sufficient numbers to reverse
the present majority. As I have already said
several times, the first of these two alternatives is
out of the question. There are many persons, however, to whom the second seems to afford a means
of escape from the difficulties with which the
question is surrounded; but a careful examination
of the subject will dissipate this illusion in the
minds of men yet open to conviction.

Whence is the "new element" to come? Some
will answer, from the negroes. Supposing it were
possible to transform the negroes into voters, the
difficulty would be but partially overcome, for only
in Mississippi and South Carolina do they exceed
the whites in numbers. In some of the seceded
States the disproportion is so vast that the newly
introduced element would not affect the result. In
Arkansas the whites outnumber the blacks three to
one; in North Carolina, Texas, and Virginia, about
two to one. But a difficulty meets us at the very

threshold, in the circumstance that every one of the State constitutions rigidly excludes negroes from voting or holding office; and hence the Federal Government, in order to entitle them to exercise the elective franchise, must commence by overthrowing the State constitutions and creating new ones, or, in other words, must *subjugate* the South. Apart from this consideration, it seems impossible that any sane man can seriously propose to endow the semi-civilized negroes of the South, whose whole lives have been passed in the most degraded ignorance and bondage, with the responsibility of exercising the elective franchise. A community composed of such a population would at once fall into hopeless anarchy, and the ordinary instinct of self-preservation would compel its neighbors to seize its country, abolish its government, and to establish over it a protectorate, in order to insure that ordinary security of life and property, without which even the most rudimentary government cannot exist. And would any State inhabited by the white freemen of the North, be willing to acknowledge such a State as its equal? Would our senators allow blacks to sit with them as equals in the Senate? Would our representatives tolerate the presence of black delegations in the House?

I do not think that any considerable number of reflecting men of our country would hesitate to reject the theory of superseding or nullifying the

political power of the whites of the South by en-
dowing the negroes with the elective franchise.
But many talk of an immigration of whites as a
means by which order may be established, and a
population created capable of sustaining a State
government. A few figures will, I think, dissipate
this theory. The following table shows the total
white population of the several seceding States, by
the census of 1860, omitting Tennessee, for reasons
which I have already given.

	White Population.
Virginia (less Western Virginia), . .	712,490
North Carolina, ...	631,100
South Carolina, ...	291,338
Georgia, ...	591,588
Florida, ...	77,748
Alabama, ...	526,431
Mississippi, ...	353,901
Louisiana, ...	357,629
Texas, ...	421,294
Arkansas, ...	324,191
Total in ten seceded States, . .	4,287,710

Whence is to come the deluge of immigration that
is to neutralize the votes of these four and a quarter millions of population? From Europe? The
total arrivals of immigrants from foreign countries
into the United States since 1854, when the effects
of the Irish famine ceased to influence the course of

immigration, did not exceed two hundred and fifty-two thousand in any one year, and the yearly average for the six years ending January 1, 1861 (when the census tables end), is about one hundred and seventy-six thousand. Of these a large portion merely pass through our country and ultimately settle in Canada. If, therefore, the population of the seceding States should remain stationary, and all the inmigrants from Europe should settle among them, it would still take over twenty-four years to enable the immigration to equal in numbers the native white population. But what inducements are to be offered to the foreign emigrant to persuade him to go to the southern States instead of to the West? The inevitable negro will continue to confront him at the South as he does now; and the negro's freedom, if it shall be secured to him, will not make a place for the European. For if the freed negro will be willing to labor, there will be a labor market already overstocked with men who can work during the whole year, in a climate which compels the white man to be idle during about one-third of the time. If the negro will not work, he will become a vagabond, a thief, and a nuisance, whose presence will afford a white man no additional attraction to the prospect of labor under a broiling sun, in the rice swamps, the sugar plantations, and the cotton fields, in a climate notoriously fatal to the stranger.

What privilege or bonus can the Government offer which will be adequate to induce even one million of foreign emigrants to settle in such a country, when the West lies before them with a demand for labor and a rate of wages increased by the war, with a climate similar to that in which they were born and brought up, and countless acres of the best land at almost nominal prices ?*

Most clearly nothing can be done to make any appreciable change in the course of immigration. Were the contrary possible, can it be supposed that the western States, which employ (or until recently employed) agents to reside abroad to compete with each other for the foreign emigration, would tolerate for any length of time an attempt on the part of the Government to turn the stream of immigrants away from them?

The same remarks apply to a northern immigration. If abolition of slavery and confiscations are to be the order of the day, a considerable stream of immigration southwards from the northern States may set in at the close of the war. It is not impossible that these immigrants may, in the three or four large cities of the South, soon constitute a class of the population, engaged in industrial occupations of all kinds, and sufficiently numerous to stand alone,

* It is hardly necessary to say that the whole European continent, except a portion of Portugal, Spain, Italy, and Greece, lies north of the parallel of New York.

socially and politically. But when that period shall
have arrived, no serious impression will yet have
been made by them upon the politics of the State.
The rural districts must also be overrun, and what
attraction is it proposed to offer to induce the settlement of the interior by northerners? Is it to be a
general confiscation of the estates of the conquered
rebels under the savage penal laws, and the sale of
those estates at low rates to "loyal" men, or a do-
nation of them to the volunteers? But the capacity of the Government to supply a population in
this way must be very limited; and I surmise that
any northern gentleman, who may propose to enjoy
his "otium cum dignitate" upon an estate so acquired, will find it essential to his comfort, to say
nothing of the security of his life and property, previously to surround himself with a population whose
interests and sympathies are similar to his own.
In other words, the masses in the rural districts
must also be composed of immigrants; and what are
to be the inducements for the laboring men of the
North to expatriate themselves? and how are we
to spare from among us the vast numbers of them
requisite to create a new political power in the
South?

In fact the more we study the problem of establishing by force one of our free State governments
over an unwilling people, the further its solution
recedes. It has no solution; it is an utter impos-

sibility; an absurdity; "ægri somnium." As Mr. Seward truly says, our federal republican system is of all forms of government the very one which is the most unfitted for the subjugation of "thoroughly disaffected and insurrectionary members of the State." It is true that all the inhabitants of a State owe an allegiance to the general Government as indissoluble as that which they owe to their own State authorities; it is true that the acts of secession were usurpations of power, and the insurrection a criminal rebellion against a lawful government. But although the rebellion may lawfully be suppressed by force, yet the fruits of victory will be worse than apples of Sodom in our hands, if we are to rely upon force and fear to retain dominion after the victory shall have been achieved. For baseless as the theory is that States have *the right* to secede, yet, as a *practical* proposition, it is utterly impossible permanently to retain eight or ten States within such a Union as was established by our fathers, against the will of a preponderating majority of their inhabitants. Although the Constitution, as we construe it, neglects to provide for a separation from the Union, and evidently intended to make that Union perpetual, it did provide, by the mere fact of establishing a popular form of government, that its own existence should depend upon the Union retaining the confidence and affection of the people in all sections of its territory.

All governments have the same general powers
and functions; but with governments, as with individuals, one system will permit without hazard the
exercise of particular functions to an extent which
would endanger or destroy the life of the other.
Despotic governments find their strength in the
very place where popular governments find their
weakness; for while the one rests on force, and its
prolongation by force is a mere question of the
extent of force at its command, in the other, every
successful exercise of force beyond the ordinary
administration of the police laws, is a stab at its
own vitals, which must always inflict a dangerous
wound, and the frequent repetition of which must
inevitably be fatal. Hence, when the majority, the
embodiment of whose wishes forms the governing
power of a free nation, only slightly preponderates
in numbers over the minority, although it has the
undoubted right to perpetuate its sway by force,
yet freedom is sure to perish if the necessity for the
exercise of force is imminent and continued. This
may be laid down as an axiom of political science
in nations where the party divisions are denomina-
tional merely. But when they are sectional other
considerations supervene. For if a contest arises
between the two sections, whether it be constitutional or revolutionary, rational or physical, whenever it has attained such intensity and duration,
that the people of the two sections have become

thoroughly and permanently alienated from each other, in thoughts, feelings, wishes and interests, the name of their common country becomes but a geographical designation. *They are to all practical intents and purposes two separate nations,* and if the bond of union is preserved by force of the arms of the stronger against the will of the weaker, by whatever designation they may formally style the relation between them, it is that of conquerors and conquered; a relation in which even the forms, and above all the spirit of a free popular government, can have but a transient existence.

The dissolution of the Union and its forcible restoration have from time to time been the subject of the speculations of American statesmen; but until within the last three years, I have never heard or read of any person of note advancing the proposition that it can be permanently maintained by force. Certainly the republican party did not advocate any such theory in the canvass of eighteen hundred and sixty. The argument that their success would lead to disunion and civil war, though vehemently urged by their opponents, was regarded even by most of the democratic party at the North, more as the statement of the ultimate tendency of republican tenets, than as the announcement of the immediate and direct result of their triumph. By the Republicans themselves it was received with such incredulity as to elicit no response but ridicule.

The progress, either of wisdom or its reverse, has been so great since that time, that the doctrine is now maintained with seriousness by some of the most eminent politicians of the day, that force and fear alone will be sufficient to reëstablish the Union in its original integrity. If I am wrong in the conclusion which I have endeavored to maintain, that this is a dangerous fallacy, I have the satisfaction of knowing that my error has been shared by the most distinguished jurists and statesmen of the present as well as of the past generations. I will select a few quotations from the expressed opinions of those whose names may possibly carry a weight which would be denied to my reasoning alone.

And first let us hear Andrew Jackson. Or rather before I quote his *words*, let me advert for a moment to his *deeds*. His great name is daily appealed to by those who believe or affect to believe in the possibility of restoring the Union by fear and coercion alone. How little our present policy accords with that of Jackson in the Nullification controversy will appear by a brief reference to any history of the times—say Mr. Benton's *Thirty Years in the United States Senate*. Jackson's theory, by which he redeemed his famous pledge, that the Union must and shall be preserved, was *that force and conciliation should go hand in hand*, and he therefore devoted as much energy to build-

ing up a party in South Carolina favorable to the
repeal of the Nullification ordinance as to overawing the promoters of the latter. I quote from Mr.
Benton: "His proclamation, his message, and all
his proceedings therefore bore a two fold aspect—
one of relief and justice in reducing the revenue to
the wants of the Government in the economical
administration of its affairs; the other of firm and
mild authority in enforcing the laws against offenders. . . . Many thought that he ought to relax
in his civil measures for allaying discontent, while
South Carolina held a military attitude of armed
defiance to the United States, and among them Mr.
Quincy Adams. But he adhered steadily to his
purpose of going on with what justice required for
the relief of the South, and promoted, by all the
means in his power, the success of the bill to reduce
the revenue." How little he relied upon force
to maintain the Union will appear from the following extract from his farewell address to the American people.

"If such a struggle (civil war) is once begun, and
the citizens of one section of the country arrayed in
arms against those of another in doubtful conflict,
let the battle result as it may, there will be an end
of the Union, and with it an end to the hopes of
freedom. The victory of the injured would not
secure to them the blessings of liberty; it would
avenge their wrongs, but they would themselves

share in the common ruin. But the Constitution cannot be maintained, nor the Union preserved in opposition to public feeling, by the mere exertion of the coercive powers confided to the general Government; the foundations must be laid in the affections of the people: in the security it gives to life, liberty, character and property in every quarter of the country; and in the fraternal attachment which the citizens of the several States bear to one another, as members of one political family mutually contributing to promote the happiness of each other."

Mr. Madison, in the convention which framed the Constitution, said: "Any government for the United States formed upon the supposed practicability of using force against the unconstitutional proceedings of the States, would prove as visionary and fallacious as the government of Congress" (the confederation). He nevertheless approved of the proceedings of General Jackson, because they were characterized by conciliation and not a reliance upon force alone; but he distinctly admitted the "impracticability of retaining in the Union a large and cemented section against its will." Mr. Benton, the friend and supporter of General Jackson throughout the whole of the Nullification controversy, says: "The authors of our present form of government . . . formed a government in which the law and the popular will, and not the sword, was to decide questions, and they looked upon the first resort to the sword for the decision of such questions as the death of the Union."

Mr. Edward Everett (now " quantum mutatus ab illo ") expressed himself to the same effect as General Jackson, in his letter of acceptance of his nomination for the vice-presidency in 1860.

" The suggestion that the Union can be maintained by numerical predominance and military prowess of one section, exerted to coerce the other into submission, is in my judgment as self-contradictory as it is dangerous. It comes loaded with the death smell from the fields wet with brothers' blood. If the vital principle of all republican governments is the consent of the governed, much more does a Union of co-equal sovereign States require as its basis the harmony of its members, and their voluntary coöperation in its organic functions."

Mr. Douglas went even further. He maintained that the inauguration of civil war would forever destroy the possibility of reunion. On several occasions during the second session of the thirty-sixth Congress, while addressing the Senate in support of the Crittenden compromise, he asserted this opinion in emphatic terms : " An amicable settlement is a perpetuation of the Union. The use of the sword is war, disunion and separation ; now and forever." . . . " I repeat, then, my solemn conviction, that war means disunion—final, irrevocable, eternal separation."

: *

Daniel Webster had previously expressed the same opinion.

"In March, 1850, when I found it my duty to address Congress on these important topics, it was my conscientious belief, and it still remains unshaken, that if the controversy with Texas could not be amicably adjusted, there must in all probability be civil war and bloodshed ; and in contemplation of such a prospect, although we took it for granted that no opposition could arise to the authority of the United States that would not be suppressed, it appeared of little consequence on which standard victory should perch. . . . . But what of that ? I was not anxious about military consequences; I looked to the civil and political state of things, and their results, and I inquired what would be the condition of the country if in this state of agitation, if in this vastly extended though not generally pervading feeling of the South, war should break out, and bloodshed should ensue in that quarter of the Union ? That was enough for me to inquire into and consider ; and if the chances had been one in a thousand that civil war would be the result, I should have felt that that one-thousandth chance should be guarded against by any reasonable sacrifice ; because, gentlemen, sanguine as I am of the future prosperity of the country, strongly as I believe now, after what has passed, and especially after the enactment of those measures to which I have referred, that it is likely to hold together, I yet believe that this Union once broken is incapable, according to all human experience, of being reconstructed in its original character, of being recemented by any chemistry, or art, or effort, or skill of man."

While I cannot doubt the correctness of the conclusion, in which all these great men agree, that constitutional Union cannot be preserved without the cordial coöperation of the people of every section of the country, I am unwilling to surrender the hope that common interests, mutual dependence, and the associations of the past will not suffice again to bind together the dissevered parts of the nation, if we shall adopt a policy of moderation and magnanimity which will permit the jealousies and fears which caused this great convulsion to be allayed, and the angry passions which it has aroused to subside. But the policy of coercion contemplates another alternative: that of subverting the existing constitutions of the States now in rebellion, and readmitting them into the Union with such modifications and restrictions of their constitutional rights as we shall deem most consistent with our own future prosperity. The consequences of such a course to them and to ourselves will form the subject of the following chapters.

CHAPTER IX.

Senator Sumner's Plan of Territorial Governments for the South—
The President's Plan of "Reconstruction"—A detailed Explanation of the latter—Delusive character of the apparent Intention to
submit the Emancipation Proclamation to the Supreme Court—
The Plan contemplates the Abolition of Slavery by a revolutionary overthrow of the State Constitutions—Nature of the Popular
Element of the "reconstructed" State Governments—Probability
of the acceptance of the Terms of Amnesty by the Southern
People now within our Lines—Readiness of the Baser Element
of a Conquered People to ingratiate itself with the Conqueror—
Illustrations of this Principle by the Conduct of Individuals in
New York, New Jersey, Pennsylvania and South Carolina during
the Revolutionary War—Efforts of the British Authorities to
reëstablish Civil Rule in South Carolina in the years 1780–1781—
Their apparent success in bringing the People back to their
Allegiance—Their Severities towards those who refused to ac-
knowledge themselves British Subjects.

I ASSUME that the people are nearly unanimously
of the opinion that the existing military governments of the southern States must be superseded by
civil governments of some kind, as soon as it is
practicable to do so, with safety to the authority
of the nation, and with due regard to the principles
which pervade our political framework. I need
not, therefore, consume any time in pointing out the
inconveniences and dangers, attending an attempt
permanently to maintain the present system.

There are two schemes of reëstablishing civil rule, which have met with favor among those who desire to escape, for a time at least, from the necessity of confiding the reins of Government in the States to the hands of officers elected by the people, and responsible to the people. One of these is the plan, the recommendation of which is the object of the article which has already been frequently commented upon in these pages, entitled, "Our Domestic Relations." It is stated in the words of that article to be "the establishment of provisional governments under the authority of Congress, or simply by making the admission or recognition of the States depend upon the action of Congress." The latter clause of the sentence is not very intelligible, if the whole is regarded as the statement of two alternatives; but as the article commences with an attack upon the system of military governments, and as its whole scope is designed to show that the southern States have been reduced to the territorial condition, and that the public interests will not for the present allow the participation of the people in the Government, the author's meaning is sufficiently clear. It is that Congress shall create in the conquered region, governments corresponding to those which have formerly been erected in the western part of the country, in the first stages of territorial existence; that is to say, that the legislative, executive, and judicial functions shall be

administered by officers nominated by the President, and appointed by him, with the advice and
consent of a Senate, composed wholly of members
from the States which have remained loyal throughout the war. Whether the boundaries of the new
territories are to correspond with those of the existing States, is not very apparent, nor, as I should
judge from the author's course of reasoning, is it
considered as very important. The time during
which the territories thus erected, would be governed in the manner pointed out, is not designated ;
except that it is said in terms rather vague and
indefinite in themselves, but sufficiently intelligible
to those who are familiar with the idiosyncrasies of
the class of politicians to which the author belongs,
that the jurisdiction of Congress is to be " employed
for the happiness, welfare and renown of the American people, changing slavery into freedom, and
present chaos into a cosmos of perpetual beauty
and power." And when the indefinite future shall
have brought around the period in which the
" cosmos " alluded to shall be in full working order,
it is proposed that Congress shall erect new States
out of the territories, and admit them into the
Union. Such is the future to which a senator of
the United States, the idol of his own State, and
one of the recognized leaders of a great and now
dominant party, invites the American people.
Startling as it may appear ; dangerous and destruc-

tive to peace, public order, public liberty and national prosperity as it is sure to prove, it will lead us to our ruin by a less direct road, and topple the nation over a precipice less awful than the other plan, the deformities of which are disguised under an appearance of respect to popular rights, and observance of the forms of popular government. I refer to the "plan of reconstruction" proposed by the President of the United States in his message to Congress of the eighth of December, eighteen hundred and sixty-three, which derives a peculiar importance from the official station of its author, and which I shall therefore consider at some length.

In discussing this proposed measure, it must be observed at the outset, that the scheme is as yet (January, 1864) but partially developed. The proposed "reconstruction" cannot be completed without the action of Congress. For the Constitution reserves to each branch of the national Legislature the exclusive right "to be the judge of the election returns and qualifications of its own members;" and consequently it will devolve upon Congress to provide, by legislation or by the separate action of the two Houses, in what manner and upon what terms the "reconstructed" States shall be represented in that body. This the President concedes; and at the same time he intimates his willingness to accept such modifications of his plan as shall not be inconsistent with its leading features.

We may therefore reasonably expect that the President's plan will receive further developments of its details, and probably some new features, before it will be adopted as the *one plan*, which commands the approbation of all those who are unwilling to have the war close with a simple restoration of the seceding States to the Union, so that "their constitutions and laws, customs, habits and institutions will remain the same." * But it is not probable that its foundation or its framework will undergo any material alteration; and these contain within themselves the germ of mischiefs and dangers, which cannot be averted or indeed appreciably diminished by any modification of its details. We will therefore consider it with reference to such of its features as are likely to remain unaltered.

The foundation of the plan is contained in an executive proclamation, a copy of which, bearing even date with the message, is appended to the latter, and in which the President declares and makes known to all persons who have participated in the rebellion, with the exceptions thereafter specified, that a full pardon is granted to them, with the restoration of all rights of property (except as to slaves and in cases where the rights of third persons have intervened), "upon the condition that every such person shall take and subscribe an oath,

* Mr. Seward to Mr. Dayton, April 22, 1861.— *Ante*, p. 80.

and thenceforward keep and maintain said oath inviolate," which oath is then set forth in the following words:

" I, ———, do solemnly swear, in presence of Almighty God, that I will henceforth faithfully support, protect and defend the Constitution of the United States and the union of States thereunder, and that I will in like manner abide by and faithfully support all acts of Congress, passed during the existing rebellion, with reference to slaves, so long and so far as not repealed, modified or made void by Congress or by decision of the Supreme Court; and that I will in like manner abide by and faithfully support all proclamations of the President made during the existing rebellion, having reference to slaves, so long and so far as not modified and declared void by the Supreme Court. So help me God !"

The President excludes from the benefit of the proclamation, all who are or have been civil or diplomatic officers or agents of the Confederate government, or military officers above the rank of colonel, or naval officers above the rank of lieutenant ; all who left judicial stations under the United States, or seats in the United States Congress, or resigned commissions in the United States army or navy to aid the rebellion ; and all who have been engaged in treating colored soldiers or persons captured while in the United States service, or white persons in charge of them, otherwise than as prisoners of war. It is proper to say in this place, that the message obscurely intimates that at some future time (not specified) some of these exceptions may possibly be removed; but as it is obviously impossible to give any practical effect to such a vague and indefinite intimation, it must necessarily be laid entirely out of view in considering the working of the scheme.

Upon this foundation the President proposes to erect the superstructure of State government. He declares in the proclamation that whenever in any of the seceding States, except Virginia, a number of persons, equal to not less than one-tenth of the voters at the last presidential election, " each having taken the oath aforesaid, and not having since violated it, and being a qualified voter by the election law of the State existing immediately before the so-called act of secession, and excluding all others, shall reëstablish a State government, which shall be republican, and in no wise contravening said oath, such shall be recognized as the true government of the State," and shall receive from the United States the benefit of the constitutional guaranty of a republican form of government, and against invasion or domestic violence.

The first question which will naturally suggest itself to the mind is, what is to be the constitution of a new State formed under this scheme? Does the President contemplate merely that loyal and anti-slavery persons are to be designated to fill the offices created under the existing constitution, and that they are to administer the functions of government under that constitution, leaving it to the Supreme Court to decide whether the emancipation proclamation has had the effect to alter it by abolishing the institution of slavery? Or, on the other hand, is his scheme an invitation extended to one-tenth of the inhabitants of a State, to organize a new political community with such a constitution as they may choose to adopt, provided that it shall be republican in form, and shall prohibit slavery? This doubt arises in consequence of the obscurity which lurks in the phrase, " shall reëstablish a State government, which shall be republican, and in no wise contravening said oath." It would seem at first sight, from the fact that the decision of the Supreme Court is apparently invoked, that the first of these two alternatives is the one contemplated; and yet if that is the case, why did the President provide that the new State government was to be " republican," thus intimating that its form was not to depend upon the existing constitution, but to be prescribed by him ; and why did he not say expressly that it was to be established under the former constitution? A further examination of the details of his scheme will show that with respect to the proposed submission of his emancipation proclamation to a judicial decision, the word of promise is merely kept to the ear; and that what he really requires, as a condition of recognizing the new government, is that the loyal one-tenth shall ASSUME TO FORM A NEW CONSTITUTION, which shall by its terms MAKE THE PROCLAMATION VALID, and thus preclude the possibility of procuring a judicial decision upon it. I quote from another part of the proclamation of December 8, 1863, italicizing two passages, which show conclusively that abolition of slavery by the authority of the new government, is a condition of recognition sine qua non :

" And I do further proclaim and make known that any provision which may be adopted by such State government in relation to the freed people of such State *which shall recognize and declare their permanent freedom*, provide for their education, and which may yet be consistent *as a temporary arrangement* with their present condition as a laboring, landless and homeless class, will not be objected to by the national executive."

And in the passage which immediately succeeds, the design thoroughly to revolutionize the State is openly avowed. So little concealment is attempted, that the "loyal" one-tenth are left to decide for themselves, the name, constitution and boundaries of the new State which they may elect to form; and the President "engages" that it shall not be deemed "*improper*" for them to retain in those respects,

the characteristics of the particular State in which
the new government shall be established, provided
that the other "conditions" are duly complied
with. I quote :

" And it is engaged as not improper that in con-
structing a loyal State government in any State,
the name of the State, the boundary, the subdivisions, the constitution, and the general code of
laws as before the rebellion, be maintained, subject
only to the modifications made necessary by the
conditions hereinbefore stated, and such others, if
any, not contravening said conditions, and which
may be deemed expedient by those framing the new
State government." *

* If further proof of the design to revolutionize the
constitution of the State is needed, it may be found in the
circumstances which attended the germination of this plan,
which did not, as many suppose, originate with the message
of last December. On the 12th of June, 1863, General
Shepley, military governor of Louisiana, ordered a registration of all free white adult male citizens, who should
take an oath of allegiance to the United States, of renun-
ciation of allegiance to the Confederate government, of the
necessary age, and that the registration was made " for
the purpose of organizing a State government in Louisiana loyal to the Government of the United States." A
short time previously, a committee of citizens of that State
had addressed to the President a request that he would
permit an election to be held under the existing constitution.
On the 18th day of June, 1863, the President denied the
request, alleging among other reasons, " that a respectable
portion of the Louisiana people desire to amend their State

The reader will therefore perceive that I was not lacking in charity towards the Executive, when in my comments upon the emancipation proclamation, I asserted that it contained internal evidence of a revolutionary design upon his part, and that its preamble was either a premeditated deception of the public or a proof of self-deception on the part of its author. The new State governments thus ushered into being by an insignificant minority, and maintained by the Federal arms, will be entirely revolutionary, as well with respect to the persons who will administer them, as to the source of their authority, and the provisions of their organic laws. If I have not entirely mistaken the rightful object of the war, and the powers and duties of the national Government in its prosecution and at its termination, the successful establishment of these new State governments will be a naked, lawless, forcible usurpation. It will unsettle the very foundations of our whole political system, and set us afloat upon a sea of experiment, against the dangers of which we have been warned by every eminent statesman and political writer since the foundation

constitution, and contemplate holding a convention for that object." For some reason, doubtless in pursuance of orders from Washington, the further progress of the scheme has been suspended ; but we may look for its revival at an early day, with the oath modified as required by the proclamation.

of our Government. It will accomplish the conquest and subjugation of the South, and disgrace our national name by a shameless repudiation of the public faith pledged by the Crittenden resolution and Mr. Seward's assurances to foreign nations.* And I shall endeavor in this and the two succeeding chapters to show that it will bring upon us calamities, which, great as they are, the civilized world of to-day, and the historians of the future will

* The following is an extract from the inaugural address of Governor Bramlette, of Kentucky, a gentleman whose loyalty is so undoubted, that the interference of the Federal army was resorted to for the purpose of accomplishing his election, though, as the canvass proved, without necessity :

"No reconstruction is necessary. The Government is complete—not broken—not destroyed ; but, by the blessing of God, shall endure forever. A revolted State has nothing, therefore, to do but to cease resistance to law and duty, and return to its fealty, organize under its constitution, as it was before, and would be now but for the revolt, and thus place itself in harmony with the Federal Government. Thus, all that was suspended by revolt will be restored to action. But will not the dominant powers require terms other than these ? Will they not require the revolted States, as condition precedent to a restoration of their relations, to adopt either immediate or gradual emancipation ? These are grave questions, and suggestive of a dangerous and wicked experiment. We trust to plighted word and constitutional faith as guaranty against such an issue. Nothing but disregard of honor and the principles of humanity can force such an issue, and we will not invite an evil by battling it into being."

acknowledge to be only a just retribution upon a nation, which shall have signalized its career by so much perfidy, wickedness and folly.

In examining the practical working of this scheme, let us in the first place inquire who will set in motion the machinery of the new State governments, and what will be the composition of their popular element in the early stages of their existence.

It is not specified what tribunal is to determine whether the persons who, having taken the oath, shall present themselves as electors, are in fact qualified under the former State laws. It will be readily perceived that questions of great importance will at once arise upon this branch of the scheme. In two of these States, as we have already seen,* a property qualification or the payment of a tax is requisite to confer upon a man, otherwise qualified, the privileges of electorship ; and in all of them, residence for a period more or less extended, is indispensable. It will doubtless be determined by act of Congress, or by another proclamation, or by a special order of the commander-in-chief, whether the first of these conditions shall stand ; for of course it would be idle to quibble about the power of the executive or legislative department of the nation to maintain or dispense with a law of a State, whose

---

* Chapter vi., page 105.

whole constitution is about to be overthrown. But
with respect to the fact of *residence* of the proposed
voter, it is evident that some tribunal must be
created to pass upon each particular case as it
arises; and it will be readily seen that many of such
cases will present questions, which would cause no
little embarrassment and perplexity to any tribunal
having no other object to attain, than a fair administration of the law. In the ordinary operation of
the election laws, in quiet times, cases of this
character rarely occur, and provision is made for a
summary determination of them when they do
arise; but in putting the President's scheme into
practical operation in the South, they will be so
numerous that the *personnel*, nay the very existence
of the new State governments, will probably depend
upon the manner of their solution. Every cotton
or sugar speculator, every camp-follower, every tide-
waiter of Providence who has followed in the train
of the conquering army, will prefer his claim to be
considered a "resident," and consequently a voter
and prospective office holder. It is quite possible
that a considerable number of the soldiers will also
offer their votes; but without reckoning them, the
number of men belonging to the other classes, who
have already congregated in some of the States,
parts of which are occupied by our forces, is nearly
if not quite equal to one-tenth of the vote cast by
those States in the year 1860. And inasmuch as

9

the new government is to go into operation whenever the requisite one-tenth shall have been secured in any State, it is evident that if such men shall be admitted to vote (and their "loyalty" is not only unquestioned but uncompromising), they will constitute a very large, in some cases a preponderating part, of the persons who will control the new organizations in the early stages of their career. Whether provision will be made by legislation, to establish some tribunal to determine this question, or whether its solution will be left to appointees of the military power, we are yet uncertain. But we shall doubtless be safe in assuming that whichever course may be adopted, a very great liberality will be exercised in admitting such "loyal" applicants to vote, either directly and at the outset of the experiment, or indirectly, by prescribing in the new constitutions such qualifications as will include them.*

* It is assumed that those who favor the scheme under discussion, will not consider this remark as unfair towards the President or his party. It is not made in a satirical spirit, but merely as the statement of a natural conclusion from the principles which they profess. For if the scheme is a good one, it is of course expedient to facilitate and expedite its operation by every lawful means ; and the greater the number of thoroughly loyal persons which a liberal construction of the law, or liberal provisions in the constitution, will admit to a participation in the elective franchise, the greater will be the basis upon which the new governments will rest. There can be no doubt that the power of

Supposing therefore that such men as I have described will constitute a considerable proportion of the popular element of the new State govern-

appointment of the officers charged with the duty of passing upon the qualifications of the voters, will be so exercised as to insure that this principle will be fully recognized in one of the modes suggested.

We have had practical proof in one instance that such will be the case, although I will not charge in advance that the precedent which was then set, will be followed out in all its details. I refer to the elections for representatives in Congress, which were held in Louisiana under the administration of General Butler, in December, 1862. It has never been denied that the liberality practised upon that occasion in the reception of votes, was, to use no harsher term, excessive. I have taken considerable pains to ascertain the extent of the abuses which were alleged, upon newspaper authority, to have existed in that canvass; and for that purpose I have corresponded with Union men of high character, residents of New Orleans at the time of the act of secession, and also during General Butler's administration. I annex extracts from two of the letters upon the subject which I have received. One of my correspondents writes :

" The Federal officers at the polls decided who should and who should not vote. I do not know of more than five or six of the old residents who voted at that election. No registry was required, and I have always been surprised, *under all the circumstances*, that the vote was so small."

The following is an extract from another letter, written by a gentleman who held a high official position at New Orleans in the year 1860, now, I believe, permanently a resident of New York :

" According to the laws of Louisiana, the names of the qualified voters in the city of New Orleans must be regis-

ments, let us inquire whether any great number of
the native population will probably join with them,
either in inaugurating the new system, or in volun-

tered." (By an order of General Shepley, dated November 22, 1862, this registry was dispensed with.) "Under
the administration of General Butler, no one was allowed
to vote without having previously taken the oath of allegiance. The great majority of the voters were in the
employment of the Federal authorities. Col. Thorp, the
street commissioner, had in his employment a large number
of Irishmen and Germans (not qualified voters) to clean
the streets and the levee, and dig canals, &c. They took
the oath to get work, and having taken it, they were
allowed the privilege of voting, provided they voted as they
were told to. Soldiers and foreigners voted because they
had been six months in the State, and because it was for
their interest to declare themselves Union men. Naturalization papers were not required—it was enough to have
been six months in the State, and to be a 'loyal' citizen.
Great frauds were perpetrated; tickets thrust into the box
by the quantity, in order to make it appear that the vote
was large. Such were the results of a popular election held
under the benign influence of bayonets."

I procured an early copy of Mr. Parton's new work,
"General Butler in New Orleans," expecting to find in so
bulky a history of so brief a period a detailed account of
the circumstances attending this election—certainly one of
the most important events of General Butler's administration, and affording conclusive evidence of that wisdom and
ability which the author claims for his hero, if it constituted a true test of the loyalty of the people of New
Orleans. But it is disposed of in a few brief sentences on
page 595 of the book; and the character of the vote is
described in words, which, if they were intended to bear
their most obvious signification, afford a rare instance of

tarily accepting it after it shall be in operation; and if so, what will be the character and social status of the repentant rebels.

I have already alluded to the feelings of the people in the State of Tennessee. The adherents of the Southern Confederacy being now pretty effectually driven out of that State, and a large part of its population having been not only Unionists but anti-slavery men, during the whole of the controversy, probably a much larger proportion of the actual and *bonâ fide* residents than the required one-tenth will be willing to take the oath, and to set the wheels of the new government in motion. In Arkansas there have been, since its occupation, some very unequivocal manifestations of Union feeling; but to what extent it prevails, and whether any considerable number of the people yet remaining in that State, have become not only Unionists but anti-slavery propagandists, we are yet without sufficient data to determine. In those parts of Louisiana which we hold, there is a class of men (most of them, I am informed, original advocates of secession), whose numbers it is as yet impossible to estimate, who are not only ready to take any oath which may be prescribed as a con-

ingenuous candor, Mr. Parton says: "The canvass was spirited, *and no restriction was placed upon the voting,* except to exclude those who had not taken the oath of allegiance!"

dition precedent to holding office, but are now so
intensely anti-slavery, that they propose to admit
the blacks to the exercise of the right of suffrage.
Inasmuch however as our troops only hold in Louisiana the west bank of the Mississippi river, with
that portion of the State which lies between the
State of Mississippi and the Gulf, and a strip of
coast west of the mouth of the river, it is impossible
to determine at present by practical proof, whether
any considerable number of the population are
willing to return to their allegiance upon the terms
proposed. For a similar reason, we have no sufficient means of ascertaining the sentiments of the
people of North Carolina, Texas, or the dismembered State of Virginia. In the other seceding
States, we do not occupy soil enough to call it correctly a foot-hold.

Within the districts over which our lines extend,
there are a number of persons who have been prevented by age, sickness, poverty, accident, or other
causes, from leaving the country when the Confederate army retired. Some of these persons are
doubtless Unionists from conviction, possibly also
anti-slavery men ; but I have already assigned my
reasons for believing that outside of the State of
Tennessee, the class even of sincere Unionists comprises but a comparatively small number of the
population. To these unfortunates the President
proposes to offer Mahomet's choice, the Koran or

the sword. And human nature is so weak, that it is not at all improbable that a considerable number of them will take the requisite oath, rather than expose themselves to their only other alternative of military plunder, civil confiscation, and criminal prosecutions. And we may also be sure that the number of those who will have the constancy to hold out against such powerful inducements to submit, will be greater or less, as fortune shall in the ensuing campaigns favor or frown upon the Confederate arms. For modern history offers no exception to the proposition that among every people struggling for independence, however high-minded the general tone of the national character, there will be found many who, whenever the tide of success has apparently turned against their cause, will hasten to give in their adherence to that of the conqueror, and purchase his forgiveness and their own security upon any terms, however humiliating. This proved to be true even among our ancestors of the revolutionary war, whom we are accustomed to regard as the purest people, engaged in the holiest cause of which history makes mention. And as I have already * stated in what manner the ministerial party in England continued from time to time to buoy up the hopes of their party with assurances of a speedy triumph over the colonists, I

* See note at the conclusion of chapter vii.

will conclude this chapter with some passages from
"Botta's History of the War of Independence,"
which will exhibit some of the foundations upon
which they built their expectations. I insert these
extracts, chiefly because I shall use them in the
next chapter to fortify the *à priori* argument that a
government resting upon a hollow oath, compul-
sorily administered to the southern people, will
endure just as long as it is sustained by military
force and no longer. But incidentally the passages
in question may guard us against the error of
anticipating too speedy a downfall of the Southern
Confederacy, from causes which were in full operation, it will be seen, among their and our common
ancestors, and which, nevertheless, did not prevent
the ultimate success of the Revolution.*

The first period to which the extracts relate, is the
fall of the year 1776, immediately after the battle
of Long Island, the battle of White Plains, and

* It is perhaps proper that I should say here that the
extracts contained in this and the next succeeding chapter
are introduced into the text, merely as aids in the prosecution of a philosophical inquiry, and not actually to compare
the Confederate cause with that of our ancestors. To the
mind of the southerners there appears to be not merely a
resemblance, but a perfect coincidence between the two ;
and hence their conduct will in all probability be governed
by the same feelings, principles and motives as those which
actuated the revolutionary patriots under similar circumstances. But my comparison goes no further, and Dr.
Botta's expressions of partiality for the American side of

the loss of Forts Washington and Lee. Dr. Botta
says :

"These successive checks, the loss of the two
forts, Washington and Lee, and especially the excessive vigor of the attack, which had constrained
the first to surrender, produced a deplorable change
in the fortune of the Americans. They beheld all
at once what the fatal battle of Brooklyn had not
been able to operate—the dissolution of their
army.

"The militia disbanded, and precipitately retired
to their habitations ; even the regular troops, as if
struck with despair, also filed off, and deserted in
parties.

"Everything, at this period of the war, threatened
America with an inevitable catastrophe.

"The army of Washington was so enfeebled, that
it scarcely amounted to three thousand men, who
had lost all courage and all energy, and were
exposed in an open country, without instruments to
intrench themselves, without tents to shelter them
from the inclemency of the season, and in the midst

the war are transcribed, only because the sentences which
contain them contain also facts and illustrations which my
argument requires me to use, and they could not be altered
or suppressed without garbling his language or rendering
his meaning obscure.

I should not have thought this explanation necessary .
were it not that much of the loyalty of to-day is, in every
sense of the word, suspicious.

of a population little zealous, or rather hostile towards the republic.

"The general of Congress had to face a victorious army, more than twenty thousand strong, composed entirely of disciplined and veteran troops. The excellent generals who commanded it, using the ardor inspired by victory, pursued their advantages with vivacity, and flattered themselves that a few days would suffice to crush the wrecks of the republican army, and put an end to the war. . . . . The greater part of their " (the Americans) " feeble army consisted in militia, almost all from New Jersey. These were either of suspicious fidelity, or desirous of returning to their habitations, to rescue their property and families from the perils that menaced them. The few regular soldiers who still remained with their colors, completed their term of service with the expiration of the year; it was therefore to be feared that this phantom of an army would vanish entirely in the space of a few days.

" In so profound a distress, the American general could not hope to receive prompt or sufficient reinforcements. . . . . Upon the heel of so many disasters, was the imminent danger of seditions on the part of the disaffected, who in various places loudly invoked the name of England. An insurrection appeared ready to explode in the county of Monmouth, in this very province of New Jersey, so that

Washington found himself constrained to detach a part of his army, already a mere skeleton, to over-awe the agitators. The presence of a victorious royal army had dissipated the terror with which the patriots at first had inspired the loyalists. They began to abandon themselves without reserve to all the fury which animated them against their adversaries. The English commissioners determined to avail themselves of this disposition of the inhabitants to revolt against the authority of Congress. Accordingly, the two brothers Howe drew up a proclamation, which they circulated profusely throughout the country. They commanded all those who had arms in hand to disperse and return to their habitations; and all those who exercised civil magistracies, to cease their functions and divest themselves of their usurped authority. But, at the same time, they offered a full pardon to all such as within the space of sixty days should present themselves before the civil or military officers of the crown, declaring their intention to take the benefit of the amnesty, and promising a sincere return to the obedience due to the laws and to the royal authority. This proclamation had the effect which the commissioners had promised themselves from it. A multitude of persons of every rank, availing themselves of the clemency of the victor, came daily to implore his forgiveness, and to protest their submission.

"It was remarked, however, that they belonged, for the greater part, to the class of the very poor, or of the very rich. The inhabitants of a middle condition manifested more constancy in their opinions. Several of the newly reconciled had occupied the first stations in the popular order of things; they had been members either of the provincial government, or of the council of general safety, or of the tribunals of justice. They excused themselves by saying that they had only acted, in what they had hitherto done, with a view to promote the public welfare, and to prevent greater disorders; they alleged, finally, that they had been drawn in by their parents and friends, whom they were unable to refuse. Those who had contemplated them in all their arrogance, and who saw them then so meek, so submissive, and so humble in their words, could scarcely persuade themselves that they were indeed the same individuals. But men of this stamp dread much less to be considered inconstant and perfidious, than rebels to the laws of the strongest; they much prefer to escape danger with infamy, than to encounter it with honor. Nor was it only in New Jersey, and in the midst of the victorious royal troops, that these abrupt changes of party were observed; the inhabitants of Pennsylvania flocked in like manner to humble themselves at the feet of the English commissioners, and to promise them fealty and obedience. Among others, there came the Galloways, the family of the Allens, and some others of the most wealthy and reputable. The example became pernicious, and the most prejudicial effects were to be apprehended from it. Every day ushered in some new calamity; the cause of America seemed hastening to irretrievable ruin."—*Otis's Translation*, vol. i., pp. 389–391.

Mortifying as this chapter of history cannot fail to prove to our northern pride, the conduct of many of our southern brethren, under similar circumstances, was even more abject. The next period to which I will ask the reader's attention, is no less than four years later. It is that which succeeded the fall of Charleston, in the year 1780. Our author says:

"As soon as General Clinton had taken possession of that capital, he hastened to take all those measures, civil as well as military, which were judged proper for the reëstablishment of order; he then made his dispositions for recovering the rest of the province, where everything promised to anticipate the will of the victor. Determined to follow up his success, before his own people should have time to cool, or the enemy to take breath, he planned three expeditions. . . . . All three were completely successful; the inhabitants flocked from all parts to meet the royal troops, declaring their desire to resume their ancient allegiance, and offer-

ing to defend the royal cause with arms in hand.
Many even of the inhabitants of Charleston, excited
by the proclamation of the British general, manifested a like zeal to combat under his banners. . . .
Such was the devotion, either real or feigned, of the
inhabitants towards the king; such was their terror,
or their desire to ingratiate themselves with the
victor, that not content with coming in from every
quarter to offer their services in support of the royal
government, they dragged in their train, as prisoners, those friends of liberty, whom they had lately
obeyed with such parade of zeal, and whom they
now denominated their oppressors."—*Id.*, vol. ii.,
p. 251.

The author then describes Tarleton's victory over
Colonel Buford at Waxhaw Creek; after which he
continues :

"This reverse destroyed the last hopes of the
Carolinians, and was soon followed by their submission. General Clinton wrote to London, that
South Carolina was become English again, and
that there were few men in the province who were
not prisoners to, or in arms with the British forces.
But he was perfectly aware that the conquest he
owed to his arms could not be preserved but by the
entire reëstablishment of the civil administration.
To this end, he deemed it essential to put minds at
rest by the assurance of amnesty, and to oblige the
inhabitants to contribute to the defence of the

country, and to the restoration of the royal authority. Accordingly, in concert with Admiral Arbuthnot, he published a full and absolute pardon in favor of those who should immediately return to their duty, promising that no offence and transgressions heretofore committed in consequence of political troubles, should be subject to any investigation whatever. . . . . General Clinton, seeing the province in tranquillity, and the ardor, which appeared universal, of the inhabitants to join the royal standard, distributed his army in the most important garrisons; when, leaving Lord Cornwallis in command of all the forces stationed in South Carolina and Georgia, he departed from Charleston for his government of New York."—*Id.*, pp. 252, 253.

Measures were then taken to reëstablish completely the English administration, which had the greater effect, because the impression spread among the people that Congress had abandoned them to their fate. In truth, however, the expedition of General Gates was rapidly organizing for their relief. "But," says our author, "the prisoners of Carolina knew nothing of what passed without, and from day to day they became more confirmed in the idea that their country would remain under British domination. Thus, between choice and compulsion, the multitude resumed the bonds of submission. But the English could have wished to have all under their yoke; they saw with pain that within as well as without the province, there remained some individuals devoted to the party of Congress. Their resentment dictated the most extraordinary measures against the property and families of those who had emigrated, and of those who had remained prisoners of war. The possessions of the first were sequestrated and ravaged; their families were jealously watched, and subjected, as rebels, to a thousand vexations. The second were often separated from their hearths, and confined in remote and unhealthy places. These rigors constrained some to retract, and bend the neck under the new slavery; others to offer themselves as good and loyal subjects of the king. Among them were found individuals who had manifested the most ardor for the cause of liberty, and who had even filled the first offices under the popular government. They generally colored their conversion with saying that they abhorred the alliance of France. Thus men will rather stain themselves with falsehood and perjury, than live in misfortune and poverty! . . . . . Hence arose a distinction between subjects and prisoners. The first were protected, honored and encouraged; the second were regarded with contempt, persecuted and harassed in their persons and property. Their estates in the country were loaded with taxes, and even ravaged. Within the city they were refused access to the tribunals, if they had occasion to bring suits against their debtors; while, on the other hand, they were abandoned to all the prosecutions of their creditors. Thus forced to pay, they were not permitted to receive. They were not suffered to go out of the city without a pass, which was often refused them without motive, and they were even threatened with imprisonment unless they took the oath of allegiance. Their effects were given up to the pillage of the soldiery; their negroes were taken from them; they had no means of redress, but in yielding to what was exacted of them; while the claims of subjects were admitted without question. . . . . In brief, threats, fraud and force were industriously exercised to urge the inhabitants to violate their plighted faith, and resume their ancient chains. The greater part had recourse to dissimulation, and, by becoming subjects, were made partakers of British protection; others, more firm, or more virtuous, refused to bend. But they soon saw an unbridled soldiery sharing out their spoils; some were thrown into pestilential dungeons; others, less unfortunate or more prudent, condemned themselves to a voluntary exile."—*Id.*, pp. 259, 260.

CHAPTER X.

The Facility of putting the President's Plan into Execution in the
early Stages of the Experiment—The Difficulties will thicken as
the Problem approaches Solution—Feelings with which the un-
corrupted Part of the Southern People will regard the Tender of
the Oath—Nature of the Undertaking which it requires from the
Pardoned Rebel—Character of the first Officials under the new
State Governments—Feelings of Animosity which will exist
between them and a large Portion of the Conquered People—
The Necessities of the National Government will require that
such Men shall be kept in Power—The Aid of the Military will be
invoked for that Purpose—Impossibility of effecting the Pacification of the Country under such Circumstances—Worthlessness of
Forced Oaths of Allegiance—The inevitable Tendency of Military
Rule over a Conquered People is to Severity—The Evil is thus
increased by the Means employed to remove it—These Propositions illustrated—Results of the British Efforts to reëstablish
the King's Authority in South Carolina in 1780–1781—How
Military Force agrees with a Popular Form of Government in
Maryland and Delaware—The Military Establishment which the
Policy of Subjugation will require us to maintain—Expense of
such an Army—Questions as to our Ability to defray the
Expense or to keep the Ranks filled—Other Questions relating to
the Subject.

HUMAN nature being the same now as at the
time of the Revolution, we may reasonably conclude,
not only from our experience of its operations, but
from the practical illustrations that have been fur-

nished, that the President's plan is capable of
being put into execution with a degree of success,
in its earliest stages, which will encourage its
adherents to expect its ultimate acceptance as a
permanent system of government by the bulk of the
southern people. The same result would however
attend an attempt to carry out any similar scheme,
which might meet with the approbation of the
commander-in-chief of the army. For as long as
war is actually raging, and the civil Government,
whatever may be its form, must be upheld by the
sword, it matters little what conditions of its exercise may be prescribed by him in whose hands the
sword is placed. He is to all practical intents a
despot; and the civil as well as the military rulers,
whom he may set up over the country which his
armies occupy, however distasteful they may be to
the people, will receive prompt and implicit obedience. If it suits his fancy that a portion of the
people should manifest their adherence to his
government by some outward act of submission,
he possesses the ability to gratify his wish, provided he shall take care so to limit the requisite
number, that it will not exceed that proportion of
the population who are accessible to the influences
of fear or corruption. And if he shall also hold or
assume the power to manufacture new citizens out
of an immense horde of his own fellow-countrymen,
who have been attracted to the conquered country

by the almost illimitable opportunities of gain which
it offers to them, it is easy to see that he may
readily establish a system which will present the
outward appearance of commanding a considerable
degree of popular support.

But although it is highly probable that the President's plan may be inaugurated in a few of the
conquered States, under apparently flattering auspices, it is evident that the difficulties of establishing it as a general system throughout the South,
and of maintaining it in the regions where it shall
be established, will increase as the problem approaches its final solution. For if the present rate
of progress of our arms should be maintained, the
time must ultimately come when it will no longer
be possible for us, as we are now doing, to drive the
physical and intellectual flower of the people before
us. When the cause of the Confederacy shall be
completely overthrown, those who have now fled
from the approach of our armies, must return to
their homes and mingle again with the rest of the
population. This must take place in all the States—
the semi loyal as well as the ultra-secessionist—in
Tennessee as well as in South Carolina. Let us
therefore inquire in what manner the tender of the
oath and submission to the new constitution, will
be really regarded by that part of the southern
people, from whom alone we can construct a stable
popular Government. I mean the men who pos-

sess to an average degree the noble as well as the sordid traits of our common nature.

And first, I will consider a circumstance which will be operative only while the war is still raging, which is therefore principally important, at present, for the purpose of determining the number and character of the people now within our lines, who will voluntarily take the oath with an intention to observe it; and also of those who are yet within the Confederate lines, as soldiers or as civilians, and who will be tempted by the proferred amnesty to seek our military stations, with a view of availing themselves of its benefits. I refer to the fact that a large number of the insurgents are expressly excepted from the provisions of the proclamation.

On perusing the list of the proscribed, it will at once be seen that no person who has voluntarily participated in the rebellion, can procure his pardon without committing an act of such unequivocal baseness, that every praiseworthy instinct of the human soul will recoil from it. For he is required to abandon to the vengeance of a hated and hating enemy—not merely the political "chiefs of the rebellion," against whom the advocates of the presidential scheme suppose the mass of the people to have become incensed—but a large number of men whose only crime was an erroneous political creed, or an inability to resist the strongest emotions which influence mankind—men, many of whom battled

for the Union during the political conflict which
preceded the act of secession, and whose motives in
taking up arms were as pure and as praiseworthy
as those which have actuated the most virtuous of
our own citizens. All the leading civilians of the
South, irrespective of their comparative complicity
in the outbreak of the rebellion, are to be left to
the clemency of a government, of whose embittered
feelings against their adversaries, the character of
the warfare which has been waged, and the civil
rule of many of our military proconsuls, afford to
the southern people the most conclusive evidence.
Whatever *we* may think of those men, they are the
most honored and trusted of the citizens of the
South, and are regarded by their fellow-countrymen
with the respect and affection which patriotism,
however mistaken, preëminent ability, undoubted
integrity, and great sacrifices in a common cause,
always command even from indifferent lookers-on.
And as if this was not enough, the same doom is to
await the gallant generals who have challenged
even our own admiration—the men whose names
are identified as household words, in the mind of
every southerner, with the most glorious reminis-
cences of southern valor and southern heroism.
The case is, in that respect, precisely the same as
if we were asked to purchase an ignominious peace
by the surrender to the gibbet of McClellan, Grant,
Rosecrans, Meade—all the long catalogue of heroes

who have inscribed their names in imperishable letters upon the most brilliant pages of our history.

We have therefore every reason to expect that, as long as resistance shall be possible, all those southerners who possess in any considerable degree the instincts of honorable manhood, will spurn an offer of reconciliation upon such degrading terms. But a shameful abandonment of the purest and bravest of his fellow-citizens is only the first step of the journey through the valley of humiliation which the repentant rebel must tread. The succeeding stages will be equally offensive to his prejudices and his pride, even if the amnesty should be extended, so as to include all those whose anticipated fate might awaken his sympathy, and induce him to repel with scorn the proposition to purchase his safety by his infamy.

For the terms of the prescribed oath could scarcely have been made more galling, if they had been framed for the express purpose of outraging the feelings of social order and constitutional law, which have been so instilled into the southerner from his childhood, that they have become, as it were, a part of his very nature. He must not only assume a title which he has always regarded as one of the most reproachful epithets which could be applied to a human being, but in so doing he must pledge himself to accomplish the objects which it implies by a crime. He must swear to become not merely

an abolitionist, but a revolutionary abolitionist.
Nay more, he must swear in advance that he will
abide by any abolition scheme that may hereafter
be devised by the masters, to whom he must surrender the keeping of his conscience. Nor does the
obligation of the oath stop even here. He must
swear not only to " abide by " but "*faithfully support* " all past and all future measures which the
President or Congress may adopt to accomplish
abolition. That is to say, he must consent to become an abolition propagandist—he must agree to
aid in forcibly depriving the unpardoned rebels of
other States as well as his own, of the right of self-
government which he has himself surrendered.
And as if all this was not sufficiently degrading,
his own pardon is made conditional that he shall
" thenceforward keep and faithfully maintain said
oath inviolate ;" so that he must continually crouch
under the impending sword, which his failure to
keep the oath at any time will let fall upon him.

The proposed terms of reunion are therefore such
as none will voluntarily accept save the ignorant,
the mean-spirited, and the venal. The occupants
of official station among the rebels not only are not
invited but are repelled ; the generous will find
themselves precluded from a pardon by the circumstances of dishonor and degradation which will
accompany its acceptance ; the wealthy will not
voluntarily submit to a government which proposes

to requite their submission by forcibly stripping them of the most valuable part of their property. All these classes will hold out as long as their aid can support the tottering cause of the Confederacy. Meanwhile, a new class of political leaders will spring up among the "loyal" population of the South— composed partly of the soldiers of fortune whom I have already described, and partly of a class of venal wretches, lately the loudest in their championship of the rights and blessings of slavery, and the most bitter and uncompromising revilers of the "Yankees," to whom the power and profits to be derived from adherence to the new order of things, will prove irresistible attractions. These men, like their prototyes whom Botta describes, will of course fall in with the theories so prevalent among a certain class of politicians at the North, that they were misled or coerced into rebellion. Like all other apostates, they will seek to prove the sincerity of their conversion by the intemperance of their denunciation of the principles which they have abandoned, and by the persecution of those whose manly endurance of the frowns of fortune, will shame their own tergiversation and venality. We may confidently look to see the ancient Herods of abolitionism outheroded by this new generation which will spring up at the South. We have indeed already seen the first fruits of the "new reckoning."

This class, and the northern immigrants who will

hasten to declare themselves citizens of the "reconstructed" States, will, from the absence of all other prominent men, as well as from other obvious causes, furnish the political leaders of the new State organizations. And when the fortune of war shall compel the rest of the southern people to submit to the power of the nation, they will find themselves obliged to live under State governments founded in usurpation, and controlled by such men as these. To reconcile a high-spirited people to such a fate—to induce the reputable, intelligent, educated and gifted among them to participate in the administration of such a government, would require years of labor on the part of the wisest and most moderate statesmen. But there is not the slightest probability that those who have heretofore pursued a policy, which relied for its success upon fear and compulsion only, will adopt the measures which will be requisite to soothe the feelings of an exasperated and humiliated people. Even were they so disposed, it is impossible to point out the means whereby they can carry out their good intentions. To do so, they must commence by discarding, or allowing the people to discard, the men who will be found in power under the new State governments when the conquest of the country shall be completed. These men, however, will be the true and original "loyalists"— they will have claims upon the party in power which cannot be ignored—and unless they belie the nature and history of their kind throughout the world, they will have aroused such feelings among the people, that the protection of the Federal authorities will be essential not merely to their continuance in power, but to their personal safety. If however an enlarged patriotism and sense of justice should so far prevail with the Federal authorities, as to make them willing fairly to commit to the people the reins of government, a more appalling embarrassment will at once present itself. I allude to the impossibility of preserving public order unless the State and the national governments shall act in harmony with each other, and to the necessity which consequently exists that the popular element which controls the elections in a State, shall be sincerely attached to the Union. In the eighth chapter of this work, I have illustrated the working—or rather the failure—of any attempt to carry on such a State government as our Constitution provides for, unless the people shall heartily co-operate in the endeavor. The very case which I have supposed, will be presented in every southern State in which the President's policy of "reconstruction" shall be put into operation, whenever the people shall be left free to control the result of the elections.

The result will add another to the many proofs which the history of the world furnishes, that—

"A sceptre, snatched with an unruly hand,
  Must be as boisterously maintained as gain'd."

The necessities of the national Government will require repressive means to be employed, in order to prevent " loyal " incumbents of office from being superseded by those who may be, and probably justly, suspected of an intention to use their official positions to foment another rebellion, or at all events to embarrass the Federal Administration in the performance of its functions within the State. The officers of the State government will thus necessarily become the mere creatures of the military power—they will be, in substance, civilians administering a military government—and the commonalty will continue to be a subjugated people, enjoying only the form of liberty without its substance.

This state of things must continue for an indefinite period; for every day of its duration will only make more apparent the impossibility of abandoning it. Those who fancy that the southern people will be induced, through fear of consequences or from regard to their personal interests, to become at first the peaceable, and in time the willing subjects of a government owing its origin to usurpation, and sustained in its earlier stages by military power, found their hopes upon their wishes, rather than the lessons of experience. There is no part of a statesman's art which demands such consummate tact and ability as to close a breach between governors and governed—it is in the nature of such a breach to widen from day to day, even when it occurs between a people and their legitimate ruler—but when the latter is a usurper and a conqueror, the task becomes hopeless till time shall have supplied him with a new patent of sovereignty.

History affords no instance to my knowledge, where any people have immediately become willing and loyal subjects to a government imposed upon them by conquest, and sustaining itself by military force. It will perhaps be said, in answer to this suggestion, that a conquered people were never before required to submit to so mild a government as that under which the southerners will live. But the intensity of the feelings of animosity which will exist between the rulers and a large number of the governed, and the probable character of the former, forbid us to entertain the expectation that the new governments will pursue a career of mildness towards the political and social enemies of those by whom they are administered. The essence of military rule is despotism, and it knows but one way to escape from the difficulties and embarrassments of administration; that is to remove all obstacles by force, and to compel obedience by terror. And after a career of repression has once been entered upon, it cannot be abandoned—the policy of the Government becomes fixed, and a change impossible. This is the history of all military governments. Very few conquerors have adopted a policy of severity towards the conquered as a matter of choice, but only as a matter of necessity, and because it has been found impossible to govern a conquered people without severity. However much we may theorize about a Southern Utopia, in which a ruined and vanquished people, prostrate at the feet of a hated enemy, with the bayonets of his infantry at their throats, and the hoofs of his cavalry upon their bosoms, are to be coaxed into love of the conqueror, or frightened into willing submission to and participation in the usurping government which he has established over them, the result will prove that human nature in this country is the same as in every other part of the world, and that the same causes will produce the same effects in this, as in every other case of conquest and subjugation.

The extracts from Botta's history, with which the preceding chapter concluded, described some of the results of the attempt to reëstablish by force British rule in the Carolinas. They demonstrate the correctness of my assumption, that a government established in such a manner over a high-spirited people, will pursue a career of repressive severity as a necessary law of its being. The impossibility of checking such a career. when it has been once entered upon, and the feebleness of the tie between governors and people, created by a compulsory oath of allegiance, will become apparent by pursuing the same subject a little further. The English authorities soon discovered that the apparent loyalty of the people was but a mask assumed for temporary purposes. Disturbances of all kinds speedily arose—Sumpter, Marion, and their associate commanders raised the standard of revolt, and numbers of the inhabitants hastened to join them. "They had no pay, no uniforms, nor even any certain means of subsistence; they lived upon what chance or their own courage provided them. They experienced even want of arms and munitions of war; but they made themselves rude weapons from the implements of husbandry; instead of balls of lead, they cast them of pewter, with the dishes which the patriots gave them for that purpose. . . . . . They were seen several times to encounter the enemy with only three charges of ammunition to a man. While the combat was engaged, some of those who were destitute of arms or ammunition, kept themselves aside, waiting till the death or wounds of their companions should permit them to take their place." Soon Gates arrived with his army; and he immediately issued a proclamation, inviting the people to rise, and promising forgiveness to all those who had taken the oath to the king, except such individuals as had exercised acts of barbarity or depredation against the persons or property of their fellow-citizens. The result showed how futile it was

to expect to bind a people to the support of an
unpopular government by oaths extorted from their
fears. "Not only the people ran to arms in multi-
tudes to support the cause of Congress, but even the
companies levied in the province for the service of
the king either revolted or deserted." Lord Raw-
don had sent to Georgetown a convoy of sick
soldiers under escort of a regiment of Carolinians.
"About the middle of the route, these militia
mutinied, and having seized their officers, conducted
them with the sick English to the camp of General
Gates. Colonel Lisle, one of those who had taken
oath to the king, gained over a battalion of militia
that had been levied in the name of Cornwallis, and
led it entire to Colonel Sumpter."—*Botta*, vol. ii.,
pp. 286–288.

The battle of Camden followed. It terminated
in a disastrous defeat of the Americans, but the
weather prevented Cornwallis from effectually pursuing his advantage. He availed himself of the
breathing spell which it secured him to undertake
new efforts for consolidating the royal authority.
. . . . "Unable to operate in the field, Cornwallis
turned his attention towards the internal administration, in order to consolidate the acquisition of
South Carolina. Resolved to have recourse to extreme remedies for terminating the crisis in which
that province found itself, he purposed to spread
terror among the republicans by the rigor of pun-

ishment, and deprive them of the means to do harm,
by depriving them of the means to subsist. Accordingly, he addressed orders to all the British commanders, that without any delay they should cause
to be hung all those individuals, who, after having
served in the militia levied by the king, had gone
over to the rebels; that they should punish with
imprisonment and confiscation those who, having
submitted at first, had taken part in the last rebellion, to the end that their effects might be applied
to indemnify those subjects whom they should have
oppressed or despoiled. . . . . All minds were pene-
trated with horror; all hearts were inflamed with
an implacable and never-dying hatred against such
ferocious victors. A cry of vengeance resounded
amidst this exasperated people. All detested a king
who had devoted them to the oppression of these
brutal executors of his will. His standard became
an object of execration. The British generals
learned by cruel experience, that executions and
despair are frail securities for the submission of a
people planted in distant regions, actuated by a
common opinion, and embarked with passion in a
generous enterprise. Nor were these the only rigors
which Cornwallis thought it expedient to exercise,
in order to confirm the possession of the provinces
conquered by his arms. To complete the reduction
of the patriots, he employed arrests and sequestra-
tions. . . . . . These different measures, combined

10*

with a vigorous watchfulness over the movements of the suspected, appeared to the English a sure guaranty for the return of tranquillity and obedience in the province of South Carolina."—*Id.*, pp. 295, 296.

But the remedies only aggravated the evils which they were designed to cure. The severities of the British generals produced no other result than to inflame the people with a still deeper detestation of the royal government and ·of its adherents. Their anger was specially directed against those of th.ir own fellow-citizens who remained faithful to the crown. "They observed the laws of war against the English, but they displayed an excessive rigor against the loyalists. They hung several without listening to their remonstrances." The battles of Cowpens, Guilford and Eutaw followed, and the English were compelled to retire within their intrenchments at Charleston and Savannah, which two cities, with a slender portion of territory in their immediate vicinity, alone continued to acknowledge the royal authority.*

* The case of Colonel Hayne affords another instance of how little obligation even men occupying the highest social position, and distinguished for the noblest traits of character, attach to an oath of allegiance extorted from them by threats of violence and plunder. After the surrender of Charleston, Hayne, who was in every respect one of the most honored and influential citizens of South Carolina, was prevented by the dangerous illness of his wife and

Should the Southern Confederacy be completely overwhelmed, the resolution of the inhabitants of the States which we shall have subjugated, may not alone be able to accomplish such decisive results. But the parallel will hold good in all other respects. Notwithstanding that we may compel an outward submission to our rule and to the usurped State governments which we may establish, it will be impossible to subdue the spirit of such a brave, proud, and passionate people, as those who have so effectually made a stand for nearly three years against our immensely superior power. Those who will take the oath, will do so only through fear of the immediate consequences of their refusal, with hatred in their hearts, and with a settled purpose

children from fleeing the country. He surrendered himself as a prisoner of war, and sought leave to return to his home on parole. But the British officers would allow him no alternative, except to acknowledge himself a British subject, or to undergo a rigorous captivity, with the certainty that the soldiery would sack and devastate his plantations. He consented to take the oath of allegiance, and received permission to return to his residence. Being ordered (contrary to the promise which the British commander had given when his submission was accepted) to take up arms for the king, instead of complying, he raised a force for Congress. He was taken prisoner by the British and executed at Charleston. The usual result followed. Universal sympathy for his fate pervaded the whole country, and " the aversion of the Americans for their barbarous foes acquired a new character of implacable animosity."—*Botta*, vol. ii., pp. 377–379.

of seizing the earliest opportunity to throw off a
detested yoke; and a large number, exasperated by
the losses and sufferings which the war has brought
upon them, by the humiliation of defeat, by the bitterness of conquest, by the political degradation to
which the exclusion acts condemn them, and by the
execution or exile of their leaders, will prefer to
endure every extremity, rather than submit to the
degrading terms, upon which alone they can purchase the privilege to drag out a dishonored existence. If these men shall be left unmolested, they
will constitute a dangerous class, whose presence
will be a source of perpetual and well-founded
apprehension to the Government. If, as is most
probable, an attempt shall be made to compel them
to take the oath by enforcing the penal and confiscation laws against them, they will imitate their
ancestors, and betake themselves to the swamps and
forests, whence they will wage an unrelenting war of
extermination upon the conqueror, and those of their
own fellow-countrymen who may have made themselves obnoxious by their zeal in his service.

But we need not resort to the records of the time
of the Revolution, or to the experience of other
countries, or to abstract speculations upon the operations of human nature, to learn what will be the
effect of an attempt to carry on a popular form of
government under the auspices of military power.
We have at the present time and in our own country

abundant instances of the working of such a system. We need not even inquire how such a government is now carried on in the conquered State of Louisiana. We have but to look to Maryland, a State in which no ordinance of secession was ever passed, which has never been humiliated by conquest, in which the existing loyal State government commands, I hope, a larger popular support that one of the President's governments could possibly command in Georgia, Alabama, Mississippi, or South Carolina. My readers are familiar with the compulsory prayers for the President, the displays of flags by military orders, the domiciliary visits, the seizures of songs, photographs and music, the constant succession of arrests, trials and punishments of citizens by court-martial, sometimes for words spoken or written, sometimes for gestures, sometimes for silence, and the thousand nameless other familiar incidents of military rule, all of them intolerably galling to a people born to freedom, which increase disaffection, harden the disaffected, and from the force of mere sympathy, weaken the loyalty of the well-affected.* This is not the place to criticise the

* "Ex uno disce omnes." The following newspaper extract is a recent instance of the working of the system. The language in which the writer relates the incident would alone suffice to prove his "loyalty"—in fact, the extract is part of the Baltimore correspondence of the New York *Evening Post :*

"A knot of cowardly traitors were arrested the other

necessity of such acts when they have occurred. I
refer to them to show that they are the unavoidable
concomitants of such governments as it is proposed
to establish throughout the South.

In Maryland and Delaware it has been supposed
that inferior numbers, the overwhelming prepon-
derance of the military power, and the geographical
situation of the States, have overawed the disaffected, and either banished them or reduced them
to sullen submission. But the events of November,
1863, demonstrate either that the spirit of disaffection is yet so rife even in those States, that the pub-

night in the act of drinking the following infamous toast :
' Damn the goose that grew the quill that made the pen
that wrote the Proclamation of Emancipation !' They
were about to start on their travels to Jeff. Davis's domini-
ons for this offence, when their wives and children appeared
on the scene. Provost-Marshal Fish, moved by their
entreaties, released the offenders on their taking the oath
of allegiance."

There is an English precedent for this kind of treason,
but it is as old as the reign of King Edward the fourth.
A gentleman, whose favorite buck the king had killed in
hunting, said that he wished that the animal was, "horns and
all, in the belly of him who counselled the king to kill it ;
and as the king killed it of his own accord, or was his own
counsellor, it was held to be a treasonable wish against the
king himself." Even in those days, however, there were
some who thought his " a hard case," and the chief-justice
(Markham) chose rather to resign his office, than assent to
the judgment.—*Chitty's Blackstone*, Book iv., p. 80, *and
note.*

lic safety will not permit freedom of elections, or
else that politicians, wielding military power, will
not tolerate freedom of elections when the popular
majority is against them. If we assume that the
military severity to which citizens have been subjected, and the measures by which the popular
vote was controlled by the military, were essential to the public safety in States situated like
Maryland and Delaware,* what measures may
we not expect in the more distant regions and
immense territories of the South, and with a whole
people disaffected? In those sections of the country, even the enormous military force of which I
will presently give an estimate, will be unable to
suppress the spirit or the outward manifestations of
disaffection. The military authorities will be per-
petually engaged in detecting or punishing real or
pretended plots and conspiracies. The presence of
the soldiers of the conqueror will lead to continual
collisions with the conquered people. The greater
the number of arrests, imprisonments and courts-
martial, the greater will be the necessity for them,
and the more frequent their recurrence. The hatred
of the conquered people will thus increase with
the means adopted for its suppression; its circle will continually widen; it will be transmitted

* See in a note to the twelfth chapter, a detailed
statement of some of the acts which attended the military
interference with the elections in those States.

from father to son; and no man can foresee the end
of the contest. It is the old story over again—the
same sad old story, which, told of other lands, has
so often aroused our sympathies for the conquered
and our indignation against the conqueror, in days
when none of us dreamed that he would live to see
the stars and stripes float over a Venetia, or a
Poland. And is it possible to suppose that while
in one-half of the nation, the people are seething
with a rebellion suppressed by the armed hand, and
continually struggling against a usurped government, and the military power by which it is upheld;
in the other half, an opposition, *and such an opposition as will be created by such events,* can be allowed
free scope in the press and upon the rostrum daily
to inveigh against and denounce this system of
government, as a violation of the Constitution and
an outrage upon human rights, and to array the
Administration which has adopted it before the bar
of public opinion? That the opposition will do so
if permitted, and that nothing but force or fear will
prevent them from so doing, no reader will for a
moment doubt; and yet it is entirely clear that the
Government cannot exist and keep the South in
subjection if such a political warfare is allowed at
the North; and it is equally clear that the latter
cannot be restrained without the presence of a large
military force scattered throughout the country.
Let us inquire how large a force will be requisite

to carry out the scheme which I am discussing, and what will be its annual cost.

And first, a few words respecting the burdens to which we shall be subjected, irrespective of the cost of the army. The Secretary of the Treasury, in his last annual report, estimates that the amount of our public debt, on the first day of July, 1864, will be $1,686,956,641 44, and that if the war should continue with an undiminished expenditure, till the first day of July, 1865, the debt will then reach the amount of $2,231,935,190 57. The average rate of interest, on the first of October, 1863, was 3.95 per cent—this low rate being produced by the large amount of the debt which bears no interest, the lowest rate at which the funded debt is now negotiated being six per cent. per annum, payable in coin. The average rate of interest has, in fact, been increasing since the first of July, 1863, and as the Secretary states, "it is obvious that it must continue to increase with the increase of the proportion of the interest bearing to the non-interest bearing debt ;" and the utmost limit of the latter having now been reached, the average increase must in the future be very rapid. I know of no causes which will operate to diminish the expenses of the war, in any material respect, until it shall be closed, an event which, if force alone shall be resorted to, can hardly be expected earlier than the campaign of 1865. On the contrary, as it is pro-

posed to augment the pay of the army, the next year
will probably see the expenses of the Government
consideraby increased over those of the last year.
But I will suppose that the end of the war will find
us with a debt of only $2,000,000,000 upon our
hands, and that the average rate of interest will not
go higher than five per cent. Upon this calculation,
we must raise annually the sum of $100,000,000
to pay the interest upon our debt alone. But it
must be remembered that this is payable in coin,
and unless the very improbable contingency should
occur, that our paper money will then equal coin in
value, there must be added to this sum the premium
upon gold to such an amount as shall equal the
difference between the receipts from customs (last
year $69,059,642 40) and the interest upon the
debt. To this sum, enormous as it is, which must
be raised annually by direct or indirect taxation of
the wealth and industry of the country, must be
added the amount of the current expenses of the
Government. Let us inquire in what manner these
will be affected by the policy which we are considering.

The returns of the census of 1860, show that
there were in that year the following number
of free white male inhabitants between the ages of
eighteen and forty-five years, in each of the seceding States:

Alabama	.	.	.	.	99,967
Arkansas	.	.	.	.	65,231
Florida .	.	.	.	.	15,739
Georgia .	.	.	.	.	111,005
Louisiana	.	.	.	.	83,456
Mississippi	.	.	.	.	70,295
North Carolina	.	.	.	.	115,369
South Carolina	.	.	.	.	55,046
Tennessee	.	.	.	.	159,353
Texas	.	.	.	.	92,145
Virginia	.	.	.	.	196,587
Total in eleven States .	.	.			1,064,193

In this table are included many in Tennessee and in the dismembered State of Virginia, who will be a source of strength instead of weakness, in endeavoring to carry out the policy of subjugation. The number which would remain, after making a deduction for those, must undergo a still further diminution for physical disabilities; although in estimating the portion of the population which is capable of causing uneasiness to an unpopular government, the percentage to be allowed for that cause is much less than if we were estimating how many men were capable of regular field duty.

Making all due allowances for each of these causes, it will be seen that the population of the States, over whom it is proposed to establish and maintain by force, the new State governments, contained in the year 1860 an enormous number, probably not less than from six to seven hundred thousand of arms-bearing men, who are or have been secessionists and rebels. It is of course impossible to compute accurately how large a force will be required to keep those men in subjection. Many of them have been, and more will be killed or disabled in the course of the war; and on the other hand, in time of peace, a population rapidly fills up gaps of that kind, and the show as well as the reality of military power is essential to keep down a spirit of rebellion. Many of them will submit to the new system outwardly—a few cordially— and on the other hand, the number of such men will be greater or less, according as the military force is of itself adequate or inadequate to sustain the new governments. Considering these circumstances; the vast extent of the southern territory; the character of the country over which the sway of the nation is to be maintained by the armed hand; and the necessity of overawing the opposition party by a strong military force stationed at different points in the North, I think, after mature reflection, that no prudent man would take the responsibility of carrying on the government, unless when the new policy is ushered into existence, it is sustained by a military establishment of at least three hundred thousand men. These figures may perhaps at first impress the reader as an exaggeration; but when it is remembered that every large city North and South will require a garrison; that in the South every custom-house must be guarded; and that military stations must be scattered throughout the whole country to suppress guerrillas, to keep the highways open by land and by water, to protect obnoxiously "loyal" citizens, to enable the State authorities to carry on the machinery of government, and to act generally as a Federal and State police, I think that the number of men which I have named, will be found inadequate to all the duties required of them, rather than a useless burden upon the treasury.

It is impossible for an unofficial person, and probably equally impossible for an official, to get at the exact cost per man of maintaining the army at the present time; but we have a few data upon which to base a tolerably accurate calculation. Several years ago it was estimated that the army annually cost the Government about one thousand dollars for each enlisted man. But as the establishment was small, the number of officers and the expenses of the ordinance and engineering departments was then greatly disproportioned to the number of the rank and file; and the restoration of the proper proportions in those respects will probably offset the increase of pay, &c., for the purpose of determining the present expense which the ratio bears to the number of men. In December, eighteen hundred and sixty, the Secretary of War asked for an appropriation of about three hundred and sixty millions of dollars to sustain for a year a force of five hundred thousand men, which is at the rate of seven hundred and twenty dollars for each man.[*] I believe that the latter rate is too low, and that I have under-estimated the number that the subjugation policy will require; but taking my estimate of numbers, and the lowest estimate of expense per man, as a basis of a calculation, the cost of the army will reach the appalling sum of two hundred and sixteen millions of dollars per annum. When to this we add the expenses of the civil establishment, the interest upon the debt, and the expenses of the navy, which must be kept up to a considerable proportion of its present size, the mind becomes overwhelmed

---

[*] According to the budget of 1862–3, it costs the British nation £15,139,379 to maintain an army of 145,450 men, or in round numbers $520 per man. But nearly every item of the expense of the British army is much smaller than the corresponding item in our service. An English infantry soldier gets 13 pence per diem, from which there is an abatement for rations of about $8\frac{1}{2}$ pence, leaving him for his daily pay $4\frac{1}{2}$ pence, or $2 70 per month. The monthly pay of an American infantry soldier is $13 besides his rations, which are estimated at 30 cents per diem against 17 for the Englishman. A corresponding difference against us exists in every branch of the service, and also, but to a less degree, in the expense of clothing, arms, ammunition, and supplies of all kinds. Upon the whole, I doubt if the army costs the Government less than $1,000 for each enlisted man.

in attempting to devise any plan by which our commerce and industry can exist under such frightful loads. And in what a condition will the nation be to carry on a foreign war, already burdened with such an enormous annual expenditure, and with a rebellious population in its midst, whose repression taxes its utmost energies in time of peace? The theorizer who believes that we can safely consult only our own interests or the gratification of our own passions in dealing with the southern people after their subjection, overlooks that law of retribution by which foreign nations avenge the injuries which sovereigns inflict upon their own subjects. The more completely a conquered people is crushed, the more eagerly do they turn their eyes in hope, and stretch out their arms in supplication to some rival or hereditary enemy of their oppressor. Are we prepared to create in our midst a people which will look for the display of the "meteor flag" upon their coasts and in their country, with the same feelings with which Irishmen for more than one hundred years longed to see the white flag of the Bourbons and the tri-color of Napoleon?

And again, whence is to come the vast army which is to keep our brethren in chains? Does anybody believe that it can be kept up by voluntary enlistments? Is the population of the North to be subjected to a perpetual conscription to maintain it? Can we permanently spare such a force

of laborers from our country at any time—especially
at the close of a war, which has made such huge
gaps in the laboring population, and when the pro-
ductive capacity of the nation will be strained to its
utmost tension to raise the means to pay the interest
on our enormous debt?

To many persons the problem of a supply of men
for the army will appear to admit of an easy solution; they will tell us to fill up the ranks with
negroes. But such a remedy would but aggravate
the disease. The employment of negro soldiers to
keep the white men of the South in subjection,
would add immeasurably to the difficulty of doing
that, which under any circumstances presents difficulties apparently insurmountable. Should such
a policy be adopted, the number of those in the
"reconstructed" States who would take, or having
taken, would keep the President's oath, would be
too small to affect appreciably a calculation based
upon the active hostility of the whole population.

It would intensify beyond calculation throughout
the whole South the fierceness of the smothered
passions, and it would add a large population in
Missouri, Tennessee and Kentucky to the number
of those who must be kept down by forcible repression. Nor would the white men of the North submit to be overawed by a negro army. No plan
could be devised better calculated to strengthen the
opposition and reduce the administration party to a

shadow, than that of carrying out the repressive policy by means of an army of blacks. The statesman who shall attempt it will need a force sufficiently large to establish at once a naked despotism over the whole nation.

But I forbear to pursue the subject further. There are two other grave questions involved in the policy of subjugation, the discussion of which I will waive. They are—of what use to us will be the impoverished and ruined country acquired and retained by such prodigious sacrifices? And its kindred question—will the freed negro work? Under any possible solution of those two problems, as a mere matter of profit and loss, balancing the expense of forcibly retaining the South in the Union, against the expansion of commerce, the increase of revenues, the military strength, or any other elements of national greatness which we fancy will result to us from so doing—the speculation will be the most disastrous that any nation ever undertook.

But considerations much graver than those of revenue and expenditure are also involved in the issue, to which I will now ask the reader's attention.

.

CHAPTER XI.

Consideration of the Policy of Subjugation, under Mr. Sumner's Plan or the President's Plan, with reference to its effects upon Popular Institutions at the North—The Constitutional Restrictions upon the General Government were framed for the purpose of preventing the Downfall of Public Liberty—The tendency of the Government to disregard them—The Barriers erected to check that tendency—The Independence of the States was one of those Barriers—The effect of the proposed "Reconstruction" will be to destroy it—The Independence of the Legislature and Judiciary constitutes another Barrier—It was secured by the Dependence of the President upon them and of the Legislature upon the People—It was further secured by the President's Personal Responsibility—The Provisions to protect the Liberties of the individual Citizen added to give it greater Strength—Consideration of the Doctrine that the Provisions protecting Personal Liberty are not applicable to a time of Civil Commotion—Its effect in destroying the Responsibility of the President and of the Legislature to the People—Its effect in destroying the Independence of the Legislature and Judiciary, and rendering the President independent of both—The President's Plan is even more dangerous than Mr. Sumner's—The policy of Subjugation under either Plan frees the Executive from Control or Responsibility, and leaves the Liberties of the People at his mercy —Effect of the vast Increase of the Annual Expenses of the Government which it involves, in disposing the Wealthy Classes to the Abolition of Popular Government—The presence of a large Standing Army will destroy the Popular Appreciation of the existing Form of, Government.

On the sixteenth of December, 1861, Senator Hale, of New Hampshire, in the course of a debate

in the United States Senate upon the arbitrary
arrests made in the loyal States by direction of the
Administration, spoke as follows :

" You may gain your victories on the sea, you
may sweep the enemy from the broad ocean, and
from all its arms, and from all its rivers, until you
may hoist, as the Dutch admiral once hoisted at the
head of his flag-staff, a broom, indicative that you
have swept the ocean of your foes ; and you may
crush every rebel that is arrayed against you and
utterly break their power; and when you have done
all that, when you have established a military
power such as the earth never saw, such as England
never aspired to be, and constitutional liberty shall
be buried amid the ashes of that conflagration in
which you have overcome and destroyed your foes,
then, sir, you will have got but a barren victory,
and with all your glory you will but have achieved
your everlasting shame."

I shall discuss in this and the next succeeding
chapter, the effect upon the free institutions of our
country, of the establishment throughout the South
of any system of government which must be maintained by military force against the will of the
people, whether it shall consist of territorial governments under Mr. Sumner's plan, or of revolutionary
State governments as contemplated by the President's scheme of " reconstruction." I shall endeavor
to show that such a termination of the war must

inevitably be followed by the abolition of the right of the people to choose their rulers, or its corruption to such an extent as to reduce it to a mere formality. The system of arbitrary arrests, from which Senator Hale apprehended the consequences so graphically described by him, will constitute the principal element of a political complication that will render the maintenance of constitutional liberty impossible, and at the same time furnish one of the chief instruments of its overthrow. For that reason, I have here put his warning upon record. The words are those of an eminent and enthusiastic supporter not only of the war, but of the objects with which it has been prosecuted, and the means which have been employed to accomplish them—of an extreme anti-slavery man—of a zealous, not to say an intolerant partisan—of a man whose political principles and party standing preclude the supposition that they were spoken for effect or for factious purposes. Coming from such lips, and uttered in such a debate, they possess a significance and importance which cannot be over-estimated. Let them fall upon the ears of the American people "like a fire-bell in the night;" arousing the nation from a fatal slumber—the torpor of indifference and incredulity—during which the flames which are now raging around the edifice of the Union, threaten also to destroy the kindred fabric of public liberty.

I have referred in a preceding part of this work

to the balance of power which the Constitution establishes, and which I contended could not rightfully be disturbed in any part of the country without infringing upon the rights of every other part.* I said that the exercise by the general Government in any State of powers and authority which the Constitution has withheld from it, would be an injury not only to that State and its people, but also to every other State, and to every citizen of every other State—that it would be a usurpation by which every individual in the nation would be wronged. As the principles upon which this proposition depends have an important bearing upon the subject which we are now considering, I will state them somewhat in detail.

The Constitution was intended to be framed so as to insure its own perpetuity, and its wise framers taxed their utmost ability to foresee and provide against the dangers to which it might be exposed. One of those dangers—the one in fact from which the greatest apprehension was entertained—was the tendency of the central Government to draw to itself the powers and functions of internal administration. These were (with a few exceptions which have been specified) reserved jealously to the States; and the utmost care was taken to exclude the general Government from their exercise. This

* See Chapter iii., pp. 71 to 73.

jealousy of the central power proceeded from a well founded apprehension, that a government to which should be confided the internal administration of such a vast extent of territory as the Union comprised, must soon degenerate into a despotism. It was thought that it would be entirely too colossal to survive; that the diversity of interests between the different portions of such an immense empire would lead to the tyranny of one section over the other, or of the larger over the smaller States; that the passions which would be aroused thereby would create too eager a contest for the possession of its immense power and patronage; and that popular liberty must soon perish, if such a brilliant prize was subjected at short intervals to the result of a heated canvass among the masses of the people. The evils of an elective chief-magistracy in a single State has been apparent to the whole world by the disorders and corruptions to which the kingdom of Poland* had been for centuries exposed, although the power of election was confided in that country to a diet controlled by the nobles and men of wealth, and the State itself was insignificant in territory and population, compared with the mighty domain that our fathers expected would grow up under the Constitution which they were framing. Hence the statesmen of

* Poland styled itself a republic, and it was, in fact, an aristocratic republic, with an elective chief magistrate.

that day were almost unanimously of the opinion
that the powers of the general Government should
be restricted to the smallest possible compass, consistent with the discharge of the functions for which
it was created. In this manner it was supposed
that the danger of the conversion of the republic
into a monarchy would be averted. It was held,
first, that such a restriction, by confining the Government chiefly to the management of the external
affairs of the nation, would greatly limit the amount
of its power and patronage, and prevent its opera-
ting directly upon the interests and feelings of the
masses of the people ; thus the prize to be contended
for would be less brilliant, and the competition for
its possession would provoke less popular passion ;
and secondly, it was supposed that the force of the
periodical struggle for power in the nation would
be greatly weakened by creating a similar struggle
for power in the States, the legislation and administration of which more directly affected the people.*

But the limitations having been established, the
next question was, how should the national Govern-

---

* "Into the administration of these (the States) a
greater number of individuals will expect to rise. From
the gift of these, a greater number of offices and emolu-
ments will flow. By the superintending care of these, all
the more domestic and personal interests of the people will
be regulated and provided for."—*The Federalist*, No. 46.

ment, powerful as it must be even with the restrictions to which it was to be subjected, be prevented from overstepping them and usurping the powers which belonged to the States?

Many opposed the adoption of the Constitution, because they could see no means of escape from this danger, without so circumscribing the powers of the central authority as to render it but little more efficient than the Congress of the Confederation. But the friends of the Constitution answered their opponents, by a reference to certain features of the system, which had, they said, erected two ample barriers against usurpation. The first of these was THE INDEPENDENCE AND SOVEREIGNTY OF THE STATES, and I find the argument as to its sufficiency, admirably condensed in the twenty-eighth number of *The Federalist*, from which I make the following extract:

" In a single State, if the persons intrusted with the supreme power become usurpers, the different parcels, subdivisions, or districts of which it consists, having no distinct government in each, can take no regular measures for defence. The citizens must rush tumultuously to arms, without concert, without system, without resource, except in their courage and despair. The usurpers, clothed with the forms of legal authority, can too often crush the opposition in embryo. . . . . But in a confederacy, the people without exaggeration may be said to be entirely the masters of their own fate. Power being almost always the rival of power, the general Government will at all times stand ready to check the usurpations of the State governments, and those will have the same disposition towards the general Government. The people, by throwing themselves into either scale, will infallibly make it preponderate. If their rights are invaded by either, they can make' use of the other as an instrument of redress. How wise will it be in them by cherishing the Union to preserve to themselves an advantage which can never be too highly prized!

"It may safely be received as an axiom in our political system, that the State governments will, in all possible contingencies, afford complete security against invasions of the public liberty by the national authority. . . . . They can readily communicate with each other in the different States, and unite their common forces, for the protection of their common liberty. . . . . If the Federal army should be able to quell the resistance of one State, the distant States would have it in their power to make head with fresh forces. . . . . When will the time arrive that the Federal Government can raise and maintain an army, capable of erecting a despotism over the great body of the people of an immense empire, who are in a situation, through the medium of their State governments, to take measures for their own defence with all the celerity, regularity and system of independent nations? The apprehension may be considered as a disease for which there can be found no cure in the resources of argument and reasoning." *

Thus it will be seen that our forefathers anticipated danger to public liberty from the centralizing tendency of the national Government, and relied upon the States in their separate and collective capacities, to avert that danger by restraining the general Government within its allotted limits, by every means at their command, including force, if necessary. But how does the policy of subjugation propose to affect this safeguard of our liberties? Whether Mr. Sumner's or the President's plan shall be adopted, it is evident that we shall, to use a

* The paper from which this extract is taken, was written by Mr. Hamilton. Precisely the same ideas are expressed in the forty-sixth number, written by Mr. Madison, an extract from which is contained in the note to page 247. An unbroken series of commentators upon the Constitution attest the necessity, if we would preserve our liberties, of jealously maintaining in their full integrity the State governments, which Mr. Jefferson aptly calls "the surest bulwarks against anti-republican tendencies;" and Rufus Choate, even more tersely, "*the police of the Union.*" Until the war broke out, there was no difference of opinion among the people upon this subject. The "Chicago platform" of 1860 vies with the "Baltimore platform" in affirming this doctrine ; it declares that "the maintenance inviolate of the rights of the States" is "essential to that balance of power, upon which the perfection AND ENDURANCE of our political fabric depends."

popular phrase, burn our candle at both ends. The
one contemplates that the conquered territory shall
be, for an indefinite future, governed by executive
and judicial officers appointed by the President,
and confirmed by the Senate, and that its legislation shall be controlled either by the same officers
or directly by Congress; the other proposes that it
shall be governed by officers chosen by a minority
of the people. In either case the system rests upon
a high-handed and forcible usurpation; and in
either case, martial or military law must constitute
the most important ingredient of government;
indeed it will be, in most of the States, the only
element which gives the local government any stability, and insures the officers who administer the
latter personal protection, as well as the ability to
discharge their duties. So that in the one case the
general Government directly, and in the other case
the President indirectly, will control the *internal
administration* of the vast territory and population
of the South; and the patronage directly or indirectly at the command of the Executive will be
swelled to an amount exceeding, it is believed, that
of any crowned head in the world. Thus the prize
to be contended for at the national elections, will
be so immeasurably increased in value, as to offer
an irresistible temptation to such incumbents of
public office as we are likely to have in these

degenerate times, to retain their grasp of the reins
of power, by any measures, however violent and
illegal, which are consistent with their personal
safety. And at the same time the ability of the
States to check usurpation will be correspondingly
destroyed, first by the immense aggregation of
material power which either scheme will place
within the control of the central Government;
secondly, by the diminution of the importance of
the State governments which the process of centrali-
zation is sure to produce; and thirdly, by a diminution of the number of the States, whose combined
action was relied upon to make head against usurpation. Thus the policy of subjugation operates
directly to break down ONE OF THE TWO GREAT
BULWARKS WHICH PROTECT THE LIBERTIES OF THE
PEOPLE. And within seventy-five years after Hamilton characterized an apprehension, that the time
would ever arrive when the Federal Government
could raise and maintain an army, capable of menacing the independence of a people protected by
their State governments, as "a disease for which
there can be found no cure in the resources of argument and reasoning," eminent statesmen are recommending the American people to pursue a
policy, which will reduce the States everywhere to
but little more than boards of local police; will
convert eleven of them into mere satellites of the

general Government; and will place at the disposal of the latter an army exceeding a quarter of a million of men!

The second great bulwark of popular liberty established by the Constitution, was THE INDEPENDENCE OF THE LEGISLATIVE AND JUDICIAL DEPARTMENTS,* which it was said rendered them amply able to protect themselves and the people against the encroachments of the executive department, from which the danger of usurpation was mainly apprehended; while the immediate dependence of one branch of the Legislature upon the people, and the fact that the other branch represented the States in their sovereign capacity, was a sufficient guaranty against the Legislature becoming so corrupted or influenced by the head of the executive department, as to tolerate any attempt which he might make upon the liberties of the nation. And it was supposed that any such attempt, without their toleration, was sufficiently guarded against by the liability of the President to impeachment. That feature of the proposed system which exposes the President to punishment, was kept prominently before the people in the discussions which preceded the adoption of the Constitution, for the purpose of

* See *The Federalist*, Nos. 47 to 51, written by Mr Madison. His conclusion is, that the greatest danger to be apprehended from usurpation, is that the Legislature will usurp the prerogatives of the Executive

allaying their apprehensions respecting the possibility of his subverting their liberties. Thus *The Federalist* says (No. 39), "The President of the United States is impeachable at any time during the tenure of his office;" and again (No. 69), "The President of the United States would be liable to be impeached, tried, and upon conviction of treason, bribery, or other high crimes and misdemeanors, removed from office. . . . . In this delicate and important circumstance of *personal responsibility*, the President of confederated America would stand on no better ground than a governor of New York, and upon worse ground than the governors of Virginia and Delaware." And again, "The President of the United States would be an officer elected by the people for four years; the king of Great Britain is a perpetual and hereditary prince. The one would be amenable to personal punishment and disgrace; the person of the other is sacred and inviolable." And again, in No. 70, treating of the Executive, "The ingredients *which constitute safety in the republican sense*, are a due dependence upon the people and a due responsibility."

Thus it was supposed, that by the independence of the Legislature and the President's responsibility to it, the *liberties of the nation* were effectually secured against the usurpations of the Executive. At the same time, great dissatisfaction was manifested at the omission of the convention to incorporate a bill of rights into the Constitution, so as to secure the *liberties of the individual* against the exercise either of unlawful powers, or of lawful powers in an oppressive manner. The eighty-fourth number of *The Federalist* is principally devoted to showing that the Constitution is not open to any solid objections by reason of that omission ; but the alarm which the absence of a bill of rights aroused was so great, that although, after a long hesitation on the part of some of the States, the Constitution was ratified by the requisite number, several of the conventions expressed officially an earnest wish to have amendments immediately incorporated into it, which should supply that omission. And accordingly, several "declaratory and restrictive" amendments to the Constitution were at once adopted, in order, as expressed in their preamble, " *to prevent misconstruction or abuse of its powers*," among which were the following :

" Congress shall make no law . . . . abridging the freedom of speech or of the press, or the right of the people peaceably to assemble, and to petition the Government for a redress of grievances. The right of the people to be secure in their persons, houses, papers and effects, against unreasonable searches and seizures, shall not be violated ; and no warrant shall issue but upon probable cause, supported by oath or affirmation, and particularly describing the place to be searched or the person to be seized. No person shall be held to answer for a capital or otherwise infamous crime, unless upon a presentment or indictment of a grand jury, except in cases arising in the land or naval forces or in the militia, when in actual service, in time of war or public danger; nor shall any person . . . . be deprived of life, liberty, or property, without due process of law. In all criminal prosecutions the accused shall enjoy the right to a speedy and public trial, by an impartial jury of the State and district where the crime shall have been committed; which district shall have been previously ascertained by law; and to be informed of the nature and cause of the accusation; to be confronted with the witnesses against him; to have compulsory process for obtaining witnesses in his favor; and to have the assistance of counsel for his defence."

These provisions for the " due responsibility " of the Executive, the independence of the legislature, and the protection of the individual from arbitrary punishments or seizures, in person or in property, were therefore regarded by our forefathers as *essential to the preservation of public liberty*, even in a time when corruption and unregulated ambition were almost wholly unknown, and party spirit comparatively so, in the administration of our public affairs.

Now let us examine in what manner the efficiency and stability of this, the second of the constitutional bulwarks against usurpation, will be affected by the subjugation policy, under either of the two plans to which I have referred. And for that purpose I must consider the nature, extent, and practical operation of the power which the President assumes to exercise over the persons and property of individuals during invasion and rebellion.* I do not intend to discuss the question whether he is correct in his conclusion that the Constitution confers such power upon him. I will assume, for the purpose of considering the question, that it does; and this involves necessarily the further assumption that he will use and exercise this power until the complete pacification of the country, and consequently during all the time when the aid of the military is necessary to compel obedience to the Government. For whatever opinion may be entertained respecting the existence of this particular power, I apprehend that it will not be denied that any power, which is in fact confided to the President's

---

* The reader will readily perceive that in my future comments upon the abuses to which this power will give rise, and the dangers to be apprehended from its exercise, in case the policy of subjugation shall be adopted, no personal allusion is intended to the present incumbent of the executive chair. My argument is confined to what may be expected during the term of office of his successor ; and it is entirely immaterial to my conclusions whether the next President shall be Mr. Lincoln himself, or any other gentleman professing the principles of constitutional law and of political science, under which he is now administering the government

hands, to be exercised during invasion or rebellion, will continue in full force until the one is completely repelled or the other effectually subdued, so that they are no longer *imminent.*

There have been, since the commencement of the war, many military, or as they are called, arbitrary arrests of citizens, for words spoken, written, or printed, in addressing their fellow-citizens in condemnation of the war, or the general policy or particular acts of the administration. But before the spring of 1863 it was generally supposed that these acts were conceded by their authors to be illegal violations of the clauses of the Constitution which I have cited, and that they were justified solely upon the ground of extreme public necessity. It was said that the constitutional prohibitions and guaranties were overridden by the supreme law of self-preservation, applicable to nations as well as individuals, and embodied in the maxim "Salus populi suprema lex." Such was the character of the debate in which Senator Hale made the speech with an extract from which this chapter commences,* and in the letter of the President to the

---

* In the course of the same debate, Senator Dixon, of Connecticut, arguing in favor of the propriety of the arrests, said, "I shall not vote for an inquiry into the legality of these arrests. They find their justification in the dire necessity of the times." Senator Fessenden, of Maine, on the same side, said, "I will say here that I do not believe there is the slightest warrant of law for any

Albany committee, which will be presently referred to, the latter admits that it is only "by degrees" that he has been "forced to regard" these measures "as being within the exceptions of the Constitution," as well as "indispensable to the public safety." Accordingly a statute of indemnity was supposed to be necessary in order to avoid the legal consequences of such acts, and such a statute was passed at the third session of the thirty-seventh Congress. It appears however by two semi-official letters of the President explaining the proceedings in Mr. Vallandigham's case, one addressed to a committee of citizens of Albany, and dated June 12, 1863, and the other to a committee of the Ohio Democratic State Convention, and dated June 26, 1863, that the power to arrest and imprison citizens in any part of the country, for using language which he shall judge to be calculated to diminish the efficiency of the army, is lodged with him by the Constitution itself during an invasion or insurrection. It is therefore not subject to regulation, modification, or repeal, by the legislature, but it is to be exercised without any accountability on the part of the President, except to his own con-

such proceeding, and I do not suppose you will find a lawyer in the country who does think there is any warrant of law for any such proceeding, and yet I do not shrink from it. . . . . I justify the act although it was against law ; I justify it from the necessity of the case."

science, and his ultimate liability to impeachment.
And the President does not leave us in doubt respecting the character of the language which he con-
strues as being calculated to impair the efficiency of
the army, or the circumstances of its use which expose the speaker to arrest and imprisonment. For
he says expressly that the man who excites hostility
to the continuance of the war, and appeals to the
people to elevate to power men who will make
peace, is employing language which damages the
army, and therefore gives the military jurisdiction
over him : and he implies, almost expressly avows,
that any language tending to bring the military
policy of the administration into disrepute, is to be
regarded as falling within the same category. The
use of objectionable words, he says, amounts to
" warring upon the military," whether they are
addressed directly to soldiers or to individuals in-
tending to enlist, or whether the same result is
effected " by getting a father, or brother, or friend
into a public meeting and there working upon his
feelings till he is persuaded to write to the soldier-
boy " in such a manner as to tempt him to desert.

I need not spend any time in showing that the
same argument by which it is proved that such
power exists over individuals, will also establish
the fact of its existence over a much more powerful
organ of the expression of public or individual
opinion, the newspaper press; and in fact ob-

noxious newspapers have been repeatedly silenced. And without discussing the question whether the President's arbitrary power has been already abused in any instance of its exercise, either over individuals or newspapers, I may say that its *use*, in truth the very object for which it is evoked from the constitutional shades in which it has so long lain hidden, is to repress criticism of the acts of the President and his subordinates, *to whatever extent the President himself may deem proper*, without regulation, control, or review, by any other department of the Government. As I have already stated, the President will, if the subjugation programme is carried out, enjoy this prerogative during the indefinite future which is to elapse before the execution, imprisonment, and confiscation of the property of the principal citizens, and usurped military dominion over the whole community, will have won back the affections of the southern people to the national Government, and rendered them proper subjects for the enjoyment of free institutions. And although his own sense of propriety, or a fear of arousing public feeling to such an extent as to affect the next Presidential election, has of late greatly limited its exercise, it rests entirely within the President's own discretion to what extent and for what causes it shall be employed in future.

Let us now consider what effect the exercise of

such a power will have upon the President's
responsibility, in the discharge of the vast functions
of administration which either plan will devolve
upon him. And in the first place, it may be remarked that the very object of its exercise is to
fetter the expression of *public opinion*, which even
when confined to public discussion, is one of the
most powerful checks upon misgovernment. The
importance even of public discussion to the liberties of the people is recognized in its careful preservation by the amendments to the Constitution
which I have quoted—an importance which is not
diminished by the circumstance, if such be the fact,
that those provisions were only intended to be
operative in time of peace. But our Constitution
provides for the expression of popular opinion by
periodical *acts*, which are to have a direct and controlling influence upon the action of the Government—the election of public officers to various
stations, high and low, in the Federal and the State
Governments. And liberty of speech and liberty
of the press have been for centuries recognized as
indispensable to the preservation of popular liberty
in all free governments, and to a fair expression of
the popular will at the polls. Their suppression is
invariably the first step accompanying the establishment of a despotism. To suppress them and yet
allow popular elections to be held, amounts to
turning against the people their own weapons of

self-defence. Dr. Lieber, from whom I have already quoted, emphatically states that an election conducted under such circumstances is absolutely valueless as an exponent of the popular will. I copy from his work " On Civil Liberty and Self-Government:"—" An election can have *no value whatever* if the following conditions are not fulfilled : the question must have been fairly before the people, for a period sufficiently long to discuss the matter thoroughly, and under circumstances to allow discussion . . . . The liberty of the press, therefore, is a condition sine qua non. . . . . The indecency as well as the absurdity and immorality of the government recommending what is to be voted, ought never to be permitted. . . . . If *any one* of these conditions is omitted, the whole election or voting is vitiated."

Thus the direct result of the exercise of the arbitrary power over the citizens and the public press, which the President will assume to wield for an indefinite future time, if the South shall be successfully subjugated, will be to render the elections of executive officers and members of the State legislatures in the North, as well as representatives and senators in the Congress of the United States, valueless as exponents of the popular will, and to produce an antagonism of interest, principle, and feeling between the Government and the people. How greatly that tendency will be aggravated by the passions to which such a system will give rise in both of the antagonistic parties, and the results to which it will lead in rendering it impossible for the President to surrender his power to the people, will be the subject of particular consideration in the next chapter. At present, my object is rather to show the means by which free institutions may be destroyed, than the motives which will lead to their destruction.

But while I am upon this subject, I must not overlook the fact that military interference with the exercise of the elective franchise, will not be confined to the indirect suppression of the popular will by stifling free discussion; but it will also be employed actively and affirmatively, by compelling the election of persons who will coöperate with the administration. That feature of the system under discussion will also be the subject of particular illustration hereafter; at present, I will only allude to it as an experiment which has already been successfully tried, and of which we can therefore confidently affirm that it will be tried again, whenever and wherever it shall be necessary for the administration to resort to such a proceeding, in order to secure the support of the local officials or of the national Legislature.

But the corruption and emasculation of the Legislature will not stop here, if the President's plan shall be adopted, and I now come to the features of the latter, which render it even more dangerous than that of Mr. Sumner, ruinous and disorganizing as the latter is sure to prove. For under Mr. Sumner's plan, all the members of each branch of Congress, even if many of them shall be elected by minorities, will represent actual constituencies; and it will be impracticable, or at all events very difficult to secure a controlling majority in either House, of men utterly destitute of personal dignity, independence, and a sense of ultimate responsibility for their conduct, even if suppression of popular discussion and military interference with the elections shall attain its utmost possible limit. A President aiming at the overthrow of his country's liberties, or unconsciously driven on to that consummation by events beyond his control, will therefore be compelled to stop short, whenever he shall have reached that point beyond which neither intimidation, corruption, fanaticism or inflamed party-spirit, will carry the bulk of his supporters. And although the process of disintegration of the Constitution is equally certain under either scheme, it will be more gradual under Mr. Sumner's plan than under that of the President; and if the former shall be adopted, there may be a possibility that the fears or the scruples of his followers will arrest the Executive at some point short of the grand catastrophe, and produce a disruption of his party; when the people, by an armed or a bloodless

12

revolution, will regain power, and by the reversal of a suicidal policy, save their liberties from annihilation, ere it be too late.

But the President's plan, in connection with the power of arbitrary arrests, will give the Constitution a speedy and effective *coup-de-grace*. For when eleven subjugated States, controlled by military power, shall enjoy the rights and privileges of eleven of the free and sovereign States which the Constitution recognizes, the Executive will be practically free from all personal responsibility, and he will need but a small auxiliary body of mercenaries in either House—much smaller than military regulation of elections and the unlimited means of corruption in his hands will enable him readily to command—to place the entire affirmative action of either House of the national Legislature within his control. In the first place, he will have, in the House of Representatives, fifty-eight of his creatures—men whose oath of office requires them to be strangers to the people whom they profess to represent, or to have gone counter to the whole course of public sentiment and every tie of neighborhood, friendship or affection, at a time when the lives, liberty and property of their supposed constituents were at stake—men, most of whom will owe their nomination, their election, their personal safety, and their ability to keep a house over their heads, to the military power which he will control, and

to the system of which it will constitute the sole
prop and support. This is the number of representatives to which the seceding States are entitled
under the last apportionment, in a full House consisting of two hundred and forty-one members, of
whom one hundred and twenty-one constitute a
quorum. His power to arrest any citizen without
warrant or explanation, or review by any tribunal, will secure at any critical period the absence
of those representatives whose influence or whose
votes might endanger the success of any scheme
which he might have at heart; and fifty-eight votes
lack only three of being the majority of a quorum.
Terrible as it is to contemplate the possession of
such a power by the executive department of the
Government over the popular branch of the Legislature, the worst has not been told. For the eleven
" reconstructed" States will send twenty-two senators to a Senate consisting of seventy members—
only fourteen less than a majority of the whole, and
three more than the majority of a quorum. And
in the court of impeachments, these twenty-two
creatures of the President will have an absolute
veto. They will constitute more than one-third of
a *full* and *hostile* Senate; and the Constitution explicitly requires the concurrence of two-thirds of the
senators present to warrant a conviction.

I have alluded to the President's ability to affect
the affirmative action of either House by the use of

his absolute and uncontrollable power of military arrest. In truth this prerogative adds to the unlimited means of corruption at his command, not only unlimited means of intimidation, but unlimited power to annihilate every form of constitutional check or opposition, whether it proceeds from the State authorities, or the judiciary, or the legislature of the nation. For there is no tribunal to review his acts, and no class of citizens, official or unofficial, who are not entirely at his mercy. *The United States judges, the representatives who impeach, the senators who try*, hold their liberties, and consequently their power to discharge their official duties, entirely at his good pleasure. Even the presidential electors who will choose his successor, are completely at his mercy. Whatever suspicions may be excited, that he is wielding his uncontrolled power over individuals, so as to establish an imperial throne for himself, there is no remedy but submission or revolution. He can proceed step by step to grasp the reins of absolute power, WITHOUT OVERSTEPPING IN ONE INSTANCE HIS CONSTITUTIONAL AUTHORITY. It will be impossible at any stage of his career, until he shall have reached the crowning catastrophe, to place the finger upon any one of his acts and say, *this is unlawful, and it therefore justifies resistance.*

By the adoption of the policy of subjugation, the American people will therefore deliver themselves

over, bound hand and foot, into the power of the
individual who shall fill the office of President.
They will voluntarily part with every safeguard of
their liberties; they will place the whole destiny
of the republic in his hands, without check or
restraint; they will grant him for four years patronage almost boundless, and unlimited, imperial, despotic power over every individual and every political
institution in the country. As security for the discharge of this immense trust with wisdom, fidelity
and integrity, and with a view solely to promote
the common welfare, and for its surrender to the
people at the end of the allotted period, they have
. . . . what?

History says—nothing. Psychology says—nothing. Political science says—nothing. But those
who assume to be wiser than history, psychology,
or political science, say that we shall have abundant security in the attachment of the people to
their form of government and in the conscience of
the Executive.

These prophets are the same, the falsification of
whose many confident prophecies during the past
four years, is indicated by the very condition of the
country which gives rise to the doubt. But inasmuch as they still appear to have credit with the
people, notwithstanding their past failures, it becomes necessary to examine whether their present
opinion rests upon grounds any more solid than

those, the falsity of which has been so conclusively demonstrated by events.

In truth, the apparent conviction of a large part of the American people, that they can safely pursue a career which has never before been pursued by any other free nation upon record, without resulting in its ruin, and that the laws of political science, and the experience of history are to be falsified in order to preserve our liberties, is a marvel to thoughtful observers throughout the world. It is only paralleled by a similar infatuation which prevailed in 1860, respecting the preservation of the Union, and which could not be removed by arguments or warnings, or anything but the actual crash of the falling edifice. To combat the present delusion, when a man has deliberately allowed it to take possession of his mind, is an impossibility; for its existence presupposes the discredit of the only sources from which arguments against it can be drawn. But many who have adopted it have done so without reflection, and in consequence of a hasty assent to the opinions of others; and to a mind open to conviction, the proposition that liberty cannot endure, even among such a people as ours, if a large military force shall be maintained for the purpose of keeping one section of the nation in subjection to the other, while the Executive is rendered practically independent of the people, is as susceptible of a demonstration as complete as any of the laws of natural science.

The next chapter will be devoted to a considera tion of the causes which will render the attachment of the people to the republican form of government, and the conscience of the Executive, utterly inefficient to prevent that destruction of constitutional liberty, to which irresistible events will impel any President who shall undertake to carry out the policy of subjugation. But before concluding this chapter, I desire to call the reader's attention to two circumstances, which will greatly smooth the way for such a consummation, by weakening that very preference for a popular form of government which is now so universal among the people.

The first of these is even now in partial, I may say in formidable operation. I allude to the creation of a class among the people, holding the obligations of the Government to such an extent as to render the payment even of the interest, a very onerous burden upon the masses. At present, while the war fever rages so high, and a sudden and enormous expansion of the currency has created a fictitious appearance of prosperity among the people, there is but little difficulty in raising the necessary means to meet the interest upon the public debt with punctuality, and thus to create a feeling of security among its holders. And it may be that if the current expenses of our Government shall be so reduced, before the debt shall receive a very formidable addition to its present volume, as to constitute, together with the interest, an annual burden upon the industry of the people which shall not be too insupportable, we shall continue to be able to pay the latter. Still many reflecting men are even now doubtfully putting to themselves the question whether, after the excitement of the war shall have subsided, and the country shall be suffering from that distress which will inevitably succeed the present apparent prosperity, it will be possible to induce a people governed by means of universal suffrage, voluntarily to impose upon themselves such fearful burdens.

These men see that whatever form of taxation may be devised, its principal weight will fall upon that class of the community, which receives nothing in return, and which is at once the most numerous, and the least affected by appeals to a sense of national honor, and by enlarged considerations of future welfare to proceed from immediate sacrifices. They know that it is now accepted as an unanswerable objection to the demands of the people of Great Britain for a further extension of the right of suffrage, that the interest of the holders of the Government stock, and consequently the honor and prosperity of the nation, require that the elective franchise should continue to be controlled by the men of property. They know also that the

history of the northern, as well as the southern section of the country, shows that in such a form of
government as ours, there is a limit to popular
endurance of taxation in times of scarcity. Hence
a grave doubt is even now arising in their minds
whether the time may not come, when the repudiation of our present national debt will become a
political principle, which will command the support
of a majority of the people, whatever efforts may
be made to lighten its annual burdens by a rigid
reduction of current expenses of the Government to
the smallest possible compass.

But whatever weight such apprehensions may at
present be entitled to, there can be no doubt that
they will address themselves with irresistible force
to the holders of Government securities, if we shall
enter upon a career which will involve the increase
of the current expenses of the Government by the
enormous sums, which the adoption of the policy
of subjugation will require. As I have already
stated, the expenses of the military establishment
will alone be more than double the interest upon a
national debt of two thousand millions of dollars.
To these must be added the expense of a correspondingly powerful navy and of a swarm of office-
holders. And it may be affirmed without hesitation,
that whenever it shall become apparent that Government cannot go on, without raising every year
over four hundred millions of dollars, by direct or

indirect taxation upon the industry of the country, all the persons whose fortunes are involved in the collection of such a tax, will become either secret or open opponents of a system of government which places all political power in the non-debthold-ing masses. Those persons constitute the wealthy classes; and the direct operation of the policy of subjugation will thus be to render them the allies of the Government, in any scheme which will have the tendency to prevent power from returning to the hands of the masses of the people.*

While a direct antagonism of interest is thus being created between the Government and the governed, and the rich and the poor, another cause will be in powerful operation to prepare the minds of the people to witness passively the overthrow of popular institutions. I allude to the presence among them of an immense standing army, a cir-cumstance which will have the direct effect to blunt the popular sense to the importance of free institutions, especially when it is accompanied with the constant interference of the army in the regular operation of the laws, to which the disturbed con-dition of the country and the political necessities of the Administration will give rise. I find the opera-tion of this cause described by Alexander Hamilton, in the eighth number of *The Federalist*, in language

* See Note at the end of this chapter.

so much more forcible than any which I can command, that I will insert it in place of any observations of my own :

" There is a wide difference also between military establishments in a country, which by its situation is seldom exposed to invasions, and one which is often subject to them, and always apprehensive of them. The rulers of the former can have no good pretext, even if they are so inclined, to keep on foot armies so numerous as must of necessity be maintained in the latter. These armies being, in the first instance rarely, if at all, called into activity for interior defence, the people are in no danger of being broken to military subordination. The laws are not accustomed to relaxation in favor of military exigencies ; the civil state remains in full vigor ; neither corrupted nor confounded with the principles and propensities of the other state. . . . . But in a country where the perpetual menacings of danger oblige the Government to be always prepared for it, her armies must be numerous enough for instant defence. The continual necessity for his services enhances the importance of the soldier, and proportionably degrades the condition of the citizen. The military state becomes elevated above the civil. The inhabitants of territories of the theatre of war are unavoidably subjected to frequent infringements of their rights, which serve to weaken the sense of those rights ; and by degrees the people are brought to consider the soldiers not only as their protectors, but as their superiors. The transition from this disposition to that of considering them as masters, is neither very remote nor difficult ; but **it is** very difficult to prevail upon a people under such impressions, to make a bold or effectual resistance to usurpations supported by the military power."

It will be noticed that the distinguished writer did not contemplate the possibility that a large army would be kept up in this country *to repress our own citizens.* I need not say that its employment for that purpose would vastly increase the evils and dangers which he describes. Considering the centralizing effect of the proposed policy of subjugation, the destruction of the constitutional antagonism between the States and the general Government which it involves, and the manner in which the laws are already " accustomed to relaxation in favor of military exigencies," the words which I have quoted may almost be called a prophetic warning addressed to the men of to-day.

Having thus adverted to two of the means by which the way will be rendered smooth and easy to the tread of a usurper, I will now consider the operation of much more powerful causes, which will irresistibly impel even a well-meaning President and his supporters to accomplish the overthrow of the Constitution, if the retention of the southern States in the Union against the will of their people shall be adopted as the permanent policy of our Government.

NOTE.—I append a few suggestions which may assist the reader in determining, whether the holders of Government securities will continue to feel perfect confidence in the disposition of the people, voluntarily to impose upon themselves the taxation which the policy of subjugation will require. Table 35, annexed to the preliminary report on the eighth census, (1860), contains the valuation of all the real and personal property in the United States. The superintendent informs us that the figures may be relied upon as accurate, the marshals having been instructed to add the proper amount to the assessed valuation, " so that the returns should represent as well the true or intrinsic value, as the inadequate sum generally attached to property for taxation purposes." The table foots up at $16,159,-616,048. The value of the slaves in the southern States is of course included in this computation, and if they are all to be freed, so much productive and taxable property will be stricken out of existence. I have not the necessary data to enable me to determine how much must be deducted from the sum total for this item, as the table gives only the gross value of property in each State, being $5,-202,166,107 for the seceding States, and $10,957,449,961 for the others. A very large portion of the property in the seceding States (besides the slaves) has been, and more will be, destroyed in the course of the war. The productive capacity of both sections has been, and will continue to be, greatly diminished by the fearful losses of life, limbs, and health among the producers ; and the negroes, even under the most favorable circumstances, will not produce any more as freemen than they produced as slaves. The extent to which the ability of the country to pay taxes has been lessened by the operation of these causes, can only be conjectured ; we may be sure however that it is very considerable.

The amount of the annual expenditure of the Government, under the subjugation policy, can only be estimated approximately ; but it is believed that we shall be safe in assuming it to be, at the very lowest calculation, $216,-000,000 for the Army, (300,000 men); $100,000,000 (five per cent. upon $2,000,000,000), for the interest on the debt ; $50,000,000 for the navy, (estimate for 1864–5, $142,-618,785), and $50,000,000 for the civil service, pensions, Indians, and miscellaneous items, (estimate for same year, $47,604,498). These figures foot up at $416,000,000, being about two and a half per centum per annum on the whole taxable property of the country, *as it existed before the war broke out, including slaves.* To this is to be added the local taxation, swollen in the loyal States to an enormous bulk by the bounties and other expenses of the war— the two together probably exceeding at the North, *five per centum per annum upon the actual value of all the property in the country ;* or if the same ratio of valuation prevails elsewhere, as in the rural districts of New York, about fifteen per centum per annum upon the assessed valuation.

The Secretary of the Treasury estimates the probable receipts, under existing laws, for the next fiscal year (exclusive of loans) as follows :

From customs, - - -	$ 70,000,000.
From internal revenue, - -	125,000,000.
From lands, - - - -	1,000,000.
From miscellaneous sources, -	5,000,000.
	$201,000,000.

So that our present rate of federal taxation, onerous as it is, must be more than doubled. Possibly a legislature, elected by universal suffrage, will continue to pass the necessary laws to compel the people to pay such sums of money, in a period of distress and scarcity, as well as of plenty ; but I am very confident that the time will come, when holders of Government securities will fancy (upon grounds either solid or insufficient), that their interest requires that the masses of the people shall no longer enjoy the power, to decide this question for themselves.

In considering these figures, and following out the train of reflections to which they give rise, two grave questions, and the consequences to which affirmative answers will lead, also force themselves upon the mind. Will not national bankruptcy overtake us before we have completed the subjugation of the South ? or, if we can sustain our national credit so long, can even a military government continue for any length of time to collect such fearful taxes from the people ? I suggest these questions for the reader's reflection ; they have not escaped my attention ; but this work was written with a specific object, and its plan precludes me from discussing them. I have assumed for the sake of the argument, that our arms would ultimately triumph ; and I have attempted to point out the consequences to which successful subjugation would lead. But in doing so I have arrested the discussion at the point where popular liberty falls.

CHAPTER XII.

The Danger to Popular Institutions from Party Spirit was overlooked by the Authors of *The Federalist*—The Honesty and
Patriotism of the present Executive and his Party conceded—
But their Political Training menaces Public Liberty with Destruction—The Dangerous Tendency of the Doctrine that Rulers must
be Unconditionally Supported, pending a Great National Crisis—
Causes of the excessive Party Spirit which has hitherto raged—
Alarming Results which it has already produced—Further Excesses which it threatens during the state of Civil Commotion
which will follow the Military Repression of the South—They will
render the Preservation of Popular Liberty impossible—The
situation of the President and his Necessities—Inefficiency of the
restraining Power of Conscience over a Ruler so situated—The
manner in which the Constitution will probably be overthrown
and the Pretexts by which its Overthrow will be justified—Viru-
lency of Party Spirit during Washington's Administration—His
Warning to his Fellow-countrymen against its Effects—His Warning against Usurpation—Results of the Teachings of all the
Writers upon the Constitution—Incidents of the Maryland Election of November, 1863.

HAVING thus shown in what manner the policy
of subjugation, in combination with the political
principles and administrative practices involved
in its adoption, will *enable* the Executive to accomplish the ruin of public liberty; and having also
explained how two causes will operate, the one to
create a powerful class disposed to sustain him in

an attempt to accomplish that result, the other to prepare the popular mind to acquiesce in its success; I will now proceed to consider what influences will reconcile the President's conscience to the commission of such an act, and overcome, in the minds of his supporters, their attachment to the principles which underlie our existing system of government. And the causes which will produce such a result may be all comprehended in one brief sentence—*they are the effects of excessive party spirit.*

The authors of *The Federalist*, far-seeing and sagacious as they proved themselves to be in other respects, had evidently no adequate conception of the extent and violence which party spirit is capable of attaining, in a country in which the whole policy of the Government, and the enjoyment of all the sweets of power in an immense empire, depend upon the direct result of popular suffrage. In truth, the political and social condition of our ancestors was such that party spirit, although it gave rise to numerous cabals, follies, and crimes, during the Revolution, could not have full scope to display itself in all its deformity, until the adoption of the Constitution relieved it from the trammels which had previously restrained its action, and afforded it an ample field for the display of its vices. For this reason, the argument of *The Federalist*, relative to the perpetuity of our system of government, admirable as it is in all other respects, contains a fatal flaw. It assumes that the principal danger to public liberty would proceed from the corruption, or the unprincipled ambition of rulers, acting in antagonism to the mass of the people; and having succeeded in demonstrating that those crimes would be ineffectual to deprive a people, living under such a government as it was proposed to establish, of liberties which they should unite to defend, the distinguished authors supposed that they had exhausted the argument. As we have already seen, from the copious extracts which I have made from their work, while they were considering the danger of the overthrow of the State governments and of popular liberty, through the encroachments and usurpations of the general Government, they overlooked the possibility of the existence of a political party in the States themselves, acting in harmony with those who were administering the general Government, to the ultimate destruction of the power and sovereignty of the States, and of the liberties of the people. But time has revealed the existence of this flaw in the panoply of the Constitution, and through it popular institutions are even now receiving the death-stroke. Unless we shall at once arrest the hand which is dealing the fatal blows, we may expect with entire confidence to witness at an early day their utter overthrow and destruction.

I am far from charging upon the present Executive, or his leading supporters, and still less upon the masses of their followers, any deliberate design to effect such a consummation. I frankly admit that they are as patriotic as men can be, whose first and principal thought is at all times in what manner to promote the ascendency of their party. I have no reason to doubt that they believe that the subjugation policy is consistent with the preservation of the forms and the substance of popular government, as firmly and sincerely as they believed in 1860, that their success was consistent with the permanence of the Union, the preservation of the Constitution intact, and a continuation of the peace and prosperity which the country then enjoyed. I will go further; I will say with entire candor, that they believe that if the President of their choice shall, at any future time lay violent hands upon the Constitution, they will themselves at once resist his unlawful attempt, pass into the ranks of the opposition, and if necessary, raise the standard of revolt.* But historical experience of

---

* As these pages are passing through the press, my attention has been attracted by a portion of the debate in the Senate on the 28th of January, 1864, upon the resolution of Senator Wilson to expel Senator Davis, of Kentucky, for introducing resolutions, intended, it was alleged, to excite the people of the North to revolt :—

"Mr. Howard (Adm., Mich.) expressed his dissent from the views of Mr. Fessenden yesterday. He never could

the conduct of men similarly situated—nay, their
own history during the last three years—proves
conclusively that they will gradually adapt their
own consciences to the real or fancied necessities
of the political complications that will from time
to time arise, till a complete revolution has gone
on in their own minds, and they are ready to
accept as wise, beneficent, and patriotic, principles and practices the bare suggestion of which
would now shock their convictions of right and
duty.

conceive it his duty as a senator, to call upon the people,
under any conceivable circumstances to rise in insurrection. When any senator rises in his seat here and invokes
the people to resort to insurrectionary measures, he is acting contrary to his oath.

Mr. Fessenden (Adm., Me.) asked what was to be done
if the Executive was trying to break up the Government.
Must we not save the Constitution and the Government?

Mr. Howard could not conceive of such a case. The
President himself would become a traitor, and deserve a
traitor's doom. He would not shield the Executive. He
held it right to express his opinion upon every act, though
they were acts sufficient to impeach. But when the question arises as to the guilt of the Executive, we must use
our proper judicial functions.

Mr. Fessenden said, 'Suppose the President had a large
army at his back. What would the senator do then?'

Mr. Howard said he would become a rebel. He would
fight him as sharply as the senator from Maine."

I doubt not the sincerity of both these gentlemen, but
as Shakspeare says, "use can almost change the stamp
of nature."

In truth, the political training of the administration party, since the outbreak of the war, is as admirably calculated to adapt them for acquiescing, if not actively participating in the downfall of public liberty, as the political training of the southern people was to adapt them to the purposes of the secessionists. For even those among them (and I know that there are many) who have condemned the facility with which the provisions of the Constitution have been set aside, and have regretted the existence of the rancorous spirit that the more unscrupulous, fanatical or thoughtless of their fellow-partisans have exhibited towards their political opponents, have also deprecated the public criticism of any act of those in power, however decided their own opinions may have been respecting its injustice, inexpediency, and unconstitutionality. They have contended that all such discussions should be discountenanced pending the war; that the exercise, no matter with what intentions, of the right of individuals to criticise and condemn the conduct of rulers, must necessarily have a factious effect; that at a great national crisis like the present, those who are charged with the duty of carrying on the war should receive the unhesitating and unconditional support of all loyal citizens, whatever folly or even wickedness they might commit; and that retribution for such offences should be exacted, if at all, only after peace shall have been restored to the country. I have never been satisfied with the wisdom of this reasoning, however great may have been my respect for the motives of those who have adopted it. But whatever weight may have been due to it in the past, I have now to consider its practical operation in the future. As I remarked before, respecting the President's assumption of arbitrary military power over the citizen, it is evident that whatever is lawful, right, and expedient while war is raging, is lawful, right, and expedient until a complete pacification has been effected. And therefore those men who have deemed it necessary in the past, tacitly to submit to whatever the Executive has thought proper to do, and to continue to sustain him with their voices and their votes, will deem it necessary to do the same in the future, at least until he shall openly avow a design permanently to subvert popular liberty, or shall pursue a course of conduct which leaves no room to doubt that such is his intention. But I do not suppose that any Executive will commit the inconceivable folly of avowing such a design, or of acting so as to leave no doubt of its existence, until it is too late to dispossess him without a civil war in which he will have all the advantage. It will be totally unnecessary for him to do so; for he can act for several years so as to consolidate his power, with a view to its perpetuation, without resorting to any measures which have not already been resorted to during the war, and the lawfulness of which will be established by his election, so far as it can be established without judicial sanction. And I have not supposed that the Executive will at the outset deliberately plan the subversion of the Constitution, and shape his course so as to carry out such a design. My theory has rather been that he would commence his career towards absolutism from praiseworthy motives, and in ignorance of its necessary termination ; and that in his eagerness to carry out a policy which he regards as essential to the interest of the nation, and to prevent the ascendency of opponents, from whose action he apprehends embarrassment to himself, or national disgrace or injury, he will be led on step by step, to measures, from which at first he would have recoiled, till he has gone so far that the way of retreat is closed behind him. That meanwhile his conscience will adapt itself to the shifting exigencies of the case, and to the advice of counsellors, some of them corrupt, and others doubtless misled in the same way as their chief ; and that the same process will go on to a greater or less extent, with the great bulk of his followers. To borrow the language of one of the keenest observers of human nature, himself a distinguished statesman (Sir E. Bulwer Lytton), "Among the marvels of psychology, certainly not the least astonishing is that facility with which the conscience, being really sincere in its desire of right, accommodates itself to the impulse which urges it to go wrong." And Lord Macaulay conveys the same idea in words still more appropriate to the present subject: " In revolutions men live fast; the experience of years is crowded into hours; old habits of thought and action are violently broken; novelties which at first sight inspire dread and disgust, become in a few days, familiar, endurable, attractive." My reader needs only to refer to his own experience during the last two or three years to acknowledge the correctness of these words. Let me ask him whether, starting from our present standpoint, the practical abolition of the system of popular government, would require a revolution of the thoughts and actions of men, more striking than that which has actually occurred since the outbreak of the civil war?

But in considering the process which will probably go on in the minds of the supporters of the next administration, if it shall be one committed to the policy which I have discussed, I must look beyond that class from which the greatest amount of opposition to the destruction of the Constitution may be anticipated. I mean the men whose motives are above suspicion, whose intelligence is at least above the average, and whose political convictions are moderate and untinged with fanaticism. They constitute, I am glad to believe, a considerable proportion of the present administration party; but in that, as well as in the other party, they are largely outnumbered by the herd of mere partisans. These consist in all political organizations, partly of men who are actuated by a purely selfish desire of personal profit or advancement through party triumph; partly of fanatics, who are blind to every consideration except the gratification of their fanaticism; and partly of that much larger class, composed of men sufficiently honest and well-meaning, but who have not the intelligence or education to form opinions of their own, and therefore adopt those of others. And whatever hesitation may show itself from time to time in individuals, the experience of the past two years shows that the great bulk of the mere partisans will be ready to sustain the President of their choice, in any measure which tends to prevent the opposition from coming into power, even if the Constitution itself should receive a mortal wound from the thrust aimed at their political antagonists.

I will endeavor to point out the causes that have led to party-spirit reaching its present alarming development, and the manner in which it has manifested itself; and I think that the result of our examination will show that the very political education of the citizens of this country, that apparently protected our institutions against those dan-

13

gers which have overthrown those of other free nations, has been warped by recent events so as to menace their destruction. For while many other republics have lost their liberties through excessive popular idolatry of an ambitious individual, our training has been such that the popularity of an individual among us could never equal the popularity of a principle. That fact formed a conclusive answer to those who feared the overthrow of the Constitution from the energetic and indomitable will of President Jackson, combined with the personal idolatry with which he inspired his partisans. Apart from his incapacity to entertain any idea of personal aggrandisement, at the expense of the liberties of his country, the frame of the popular mind and the tenets of his party were such, that General Jackson's first unequivocal attack upon the principles of constitutional liberty would have cost him the whole of that popularity, which alone rendered him dangerous. But exactly the reverse of that state of things now exists with the administration party. They are not actuated by devotion to any individual; so far from that, their present leader, until recent events gave him a sudden popularity, probably inspired less personal attachment than any of his elected predecessors, except perhaps the last incumbent of the presidential office. But the course of public events has been such, as to jeopardize the continued maintenance of an institution, for which every American has been taught in childhood to cherish an almost fanatical affection—the unity of the nation. It is alleged by all of the opposition that this jeopardy is due in a great degree to the tenets and conduct of the administration and its party; in other words that the Republicans are themselves measurably the authors of the calamities under which the nation is suffering. Some of the opposition also contend that the preservation of national unity has now become incompatible with the further existence of still more important constitutional principles. The consequence is, as would be natural under such circumstances, that the attachment of the Republicans to the Union, and their determination to maintain its ascendency, have increased with the dangers to which it is exposed, and which they are accused of having caused. In itself this disposition, so far from being censurable, is praiseworthy; but in politics, as in religion, and even in science, devotion to a sound and beneficent principle may lead to such excesses, as to make it the instrument of mischiefs even greater than those which would result from its converse, however unsound and pernicious the latter might be. That such will be the case in this instance is the danger to be dreaded. For the rebellion has intensified into fury and hatred the passions and prejudices against the southern people, to the existence of which the Republicans owed their own success, and many, I

think most of them, have allowed such feelings to
become so completely incorporated in their own
minds with their affection for the Union, that they
are unable to distinguish the operations of the latter
from those of the former. In this way they have
persuaded themselves that those emotions are
emanations of patriotism, which are in reality only
emanations of angry passions; and they confound
their thirst for revenge upon their enemies with
zeal for the cause of their country. This leads them
to regard an attack upon the expediency or lawfulness of any measure which may have the immediate effect of injuring the enemy, as an attack upon
the cause of the nation, and to regard the opponent
of the former as the enemy of the latter; and thus
they transfer to their own fellow-citizens, who have
the same object in view with themselves, but differ
with them respecting the means of attaining it, a
considerable portion of the hatred which they bear
to the enemy. The consequence has been that
men of northern birth and northern education;
whose patriotism and integrity do not admit of a
question; who have not a dollar of interest in the
South; whose future social, political, and pecuniary
prosperity or adversity, depends upon the prosperity
or adversity of the North; who have liberally spent,
and are still liberally spending, their own blood and
treasure to assist in the prosecution of the war; who
have not a friend or even an acquaintance south of

the Potomac outside of the national armies, have
found themselves daily charged in the public press
and upon the rostrum, with the crime of treason,
and the charge accompanied with every insulting
epithet which malignant passion can devise. And
this style of political warfare has not been a mere
partisan trick, confined to the low and irresponsible
instruments of faction : for thousands, yes, hundreds
of thousands of kind, sensible, and reasonable men,
have persuaded themselves that the opposition party
is in league with the South, to accomplish, by means
of the blackest of crimes, the dissolution of the
Union, irrespective of the consequences of such an
act to that section of the country, in which all their
own hopes and interests, present and future, are cen-
tered. And men high in office, even among the
highest, have been weak enough or base enough to
countenance such an opinion ; to encourage the
spirit which inspires it; and to enter into an ignoble
rivalry with the most vulgar instruments of faction
in a search for foul epithets, with which to accompany the foul accusation, that citizens, eminent for
virtue, patriotism, and public services, are guilty of
crimes too base for any but the most degraded out-
casts of society. Even the President is not guilt-
less of having encouraged this spirit; for although
he has hitherto exhibited a respect for his own character and the dignity of his office, which has prevented him from disgracing himself and the nation,

by a scurrility in which many of his nearest and most
confidential civil and military advisers have indulg-
ed, he has suffered the latter openly to administer
their respective departments in accordance with the
theory that the difference between the opposition
and the insurgents is only technical,* a theory
which he has himself publicly countenanced on
several occasions, though in language more decorous
than that employed by his subordinates.

These invectives have produced their natural result in arousing a bitter and revengeful feeling on
the part of the opposition; and the two great political parties are no longer composed of citizens differing from each other in their views of public policy,
but conceding to each other equal patriotism and
equal sincerity.   Party spirit has assumed on both
sides a character of personal rancor, which leads

---

* One instance, among thousands, will suffice to show
that this observation is not exaggerated : I copy it below :

"WAR DEPARTMENT,
SPECIAL ORDERS, No. 19.   ADJUTANT-GENERAL'S OFFICE,
        (Extract.)   Washington, March 13, 1863.

" By direction of the President, the following officers are
hereby dismissed from the service of the United States :
Lieutenant A. J. Edgerly, 4th New Hampshire Volunteers,
for circulating 'copperhead tickets' and doing all in his
power to promote the success of the rebel cause in his State.
  *   *   *   *   *   *

" By order of the Secretary of War.
        " L. THOMAS, Adjutant-General.
" To the Governor of New Hampshire."

men to distrust and hate their political opponents, as their own personal enemies and the enemies of their common country. To such an extent has this spirit developed itself, that it is but yesterday that heated partisans, high in office, high in the favor of the President, were clamoring for the blood of their political antagonists, amid the frantic applause of most of their adherents and the passive regret of a few. And it is at this time, when the public mind is in the precise state of all others most dangerous to the permanency of the Constitution, even if the original integrity of all its barriers against the excesses of party and of power was preserved, that it is proposed to govern one half of the nation by military force; and to place for an indefinite period in the hands of a partisan leader, entertaining such notions of public policy and such opinions of his political opponents, the command of an army of more than a quarter of a million of men, and that vast, overshadowing, irresponsible power, the extent of which I have described.

I have already hinted at the nature of the political warfare which the opposition would be sure to wage, upon an administration pursuing the policy of holding the southern States in subjection by the armed hand. There can be no doubt that fiercely as party spirit now rages, such a state of things would be certain to inflame it still further; and that the opposition, if unrepressed, would assail the administration and its policy with a bitterness of invective and vehemence of denunciation, even exceeding those which have, in the opinion of the President, rendered it necessary for him to employ his extraordinary military authority for their partial repression. But invectives and denunciations, however violent, do not at the present time affect any hostile population; they are addressed exclusively to our own people; and their most injurious tendency can only be to affect negatively the power of the Government, by producing alienation of feeling towards it, on the part of those who acknowledge its lawful title to their allegiance, and have never yet entertained the idea of open rebellion against it. But as soon as the system of subjugation is in full operation, there will be the same reason for preventing the public discussion of its policy and effects throughout the South, which there has been for years for preventing the public discussion in the same region of the policy and effects of the system of slavery; and as it will be impossible to close the avenues of communication between the two sections, the denunciatory speeches and newspapers will be scattered among a conquered people in that condition of discontent and quasi-rebellion which I have already described. Even moderate criticisms upon the administration, under such circumstances, would be susceptible of construction as instigations and encouragements to revolt, and even unprejudiced men would doubt whether it was possible to preserve order or administer the functions of government in the conquered States, while full liberty of discussion was allowed the presses and speakers of the North. That heated partisans holding the reins of absolute power, and unchecked, as they have been since the existence of that power was discovered, by the near approach of another Presidential election, would not hesitate under such circumstances to inaugurate a system of severe repression, there cannot be a doubt; and they will be, as they have been, enthusiastically supported in so doing by the most violent of their own party, while the doctrine of passive obedience will prevent the more moderate from remonstrating.

It is impossible to exaggerate the dangerous tendency of such a state of things, even if it was conceded that the only excesses to which it would lead, would be the injudicious and oppressive exercise of the lawful powers of the Government; but it must be also remembered that those who will thus feel the heavy hand of power, in the North as well as the South, will regard their injuries as proceeding from a lawless and criminal usurpation. For although I have waived all discussion of the arguments by which the President sustains his assumption of transcendent power over the citizen, in time of invasion or insurrection, yet the existence of such a power is not only doubted by large numbers of his supporters, but is vehemently denied by the

13*

opposition. The latter look upon every act of its exercise as a usurpation; a forcible prostration of the law before military power; a high-handed and outrageous invasion of individual right, for which redress will be exacted whenever the civil law resumes its sway in the land.* And I may also remark that although this question properly belongs to the courts of justice, it is, in all its aspects, purely political; that is to say, the principles upon which its decision will be predicated are political, not legal. The accession to power of the party which denies the existence of any such authority, therefore involves their ability to procure a legal adjudication against its existence; and the consequent exposure of every officer of the Government, who shall have been concerned in exercising it, to civil and criminal proceedings, ruinous to his fortune, and menacing even his personal liberty. Already a grave question is presented whether the

---

* I will remark here that the suspension of the writ of habeas corpus, under the act of Congress of March 3, 1863, does not affect the question of the *legality* of the exercise of the power claimed by the President. It merely takes away the most expeditious and summary remedy for testing the question. Whether such a power really exists or not, is, in the absence of the remedy by habeas corpus, to be determined in civil or criminal prosecutions at the instance of those who have suffered by its exercise. These may be instituted at any time before the expiration of the period prescribed by the statute of limitation applicable to the case.

personal safety and pecuniary interests of the present incumbents of public office, will allow the restoration to the ordinary courts of justice, of the ability to adjudicate upon the legality of the arrests and banishments which have already taken place, and the constitutionality of the law depriving the State courts of jurisdiction to entertain such questions, and fixing a limitation to actions founded upon them ; and it is to these as well as other considerations, that we owe the proposition to introduce into the Supreme Court new judges, whose political tenets will afford an unerring clue to their judicial action, in sufficient numbers to create a majority of the court. But such a measure, should it be adopted, will allay only temporarily the alarm of those who apprehend danger from an unbiassed decision ; for they will remember that the same process can be repeated with a directly contrary result, when the mutations of popular opinion shall transfer the political power to their opponents. Whenever the system of repression shall have proceeded to the extremities, which I apprehend from its unchecked continuance during another presidential term, the only method by which the incumbents of public office can feel themselves entirely safe, will be the retention of power in their own hands, by whatever means that object may be accomplished.

It is hardly possible however that the exposure to damages in civil actions, or to fines and imprisonment in criminal proceedings, will be the only consequence which those in authority will apprehend from the success of their opponents. The measures to which they will resort, in order to preserve their power or to carry out their policy, will result, as such measures have in all times resulted, in aggravating the evils which they were intended to remedy. They will increase the fury and audacity of those who will be subjected to them; measures of greater severity will soon follow; and the catastrophe from which we have already had such a narrow escape will ultimately fall upon us. We shall see the blood of American citizens spilled, for indulging in that freedom of speech and political action, which we have been taught from childhood to consider as our national birthright. The question will then pass, if it shall not have previously passed, far beyond the dominion of politics or of jurisprudence. The contest will then be no longer for office or for the ascendency of political principles; passion will be aroused on one side and the other to an extent of which our past history affords no example; and a desperate struggle will commence, in which one party will seek for revenge, and the other the preservation of their own lives from their infuriated enemies.

But even if its effects should stop short of this point, the system of subjugation of the South and repression at the North, will divide the people into

impassioned advocates of popular rights on the one
hand, and impassioned advocates of the prerogatives of power on the other. It will array these
two parties into irreconcilable antagonism and hostility to each other. It will lead to such a series of
injuries inflicted by the one upon the other, and
generate such an intensity of passion, that defeat in
the contest for political ascendency will involve the
ruin of the President and his leading supporters.
Can it be supposed that such an autocrat as I have
described; possessing the *power* to perpetuate his
authority ; surrounded by counsellors and accom-
plices whose stake in the result equals his own ;
supported by a powerful party whose passions are
aroused to the highest pitch, and by an army of
overwhelming numbers; believing that he and his
associates are the only friends of the country, will
allow such a contest to take place at the polls of a
free and fair popular election? Will he not remember
that law of political science, as unerring in its application as the law of gravitation, which renders it certain that under any form of government, the opposition will *in time* become the majority of the
people? Will he overlook its equally inevitable co-
rollary, that the use of violent means by a government to suppress the expression of popular feeling,
hastens the arrival of that period? Alas for the
country whose liberties are held by such a tenure
as the conscience of a man thus situated! Lord

Macaulay well says, that " men who have once engaged in a wicked and perilous enterprise are no
longer their own masters, and are often impelled
by a fatality, which is part of their just punishment,
to crimes such as they would have shuddered to
contemplate." The law of self-preservation; the
necessities of his anxious associates; the principles
for which he has risked so much, will impel him
irresistibly onwards in a road which presents no
turning-point. I will not attempt to point out the
mode in which the destruction of the Constitution
will be effected. It suffices for me to exhibit to
my readers the victim delivered over to the execu-
tioners, bound hand and foot for the slaughter,
without speculating as to the instruments which
will be used to accomplish the work; the places
where the mortal wounds will be inflicted; or the
extent of the convulsive struggles which will follow. But the past affords us data which enable us
to conjecture how the overthrow of our liberties
will commence, and at the same time remove any
doubt from our minds, respecting the adaptability
to the purposes of a usurper, of an army officered
by his instruments. No doubt the title of President, and the nominal coöperation of a legislature,
perhaps also the formality of popular elections, will
for a time be preserved; but we have seen within
a few months in what manner unscrupulous partisans, wielding unchecked military power, can ren-

der a popular election a mere machine for the
registry of a military edict. We have seen military
orders issued for the express purpose of warning
from the polls those electors who were unwilling to
vote in accordance with the wishes of their military masters; we have seen soldiers stationed at
the polls to prescribe the ticket to be voted, to interrogate, threaten, and arrest those who offered
any other; we have seen obnoxious candidates and
judges of election who hesitated to obey the unlawful orders of military tyrants, insulted, maltreated,
and imprisoned; we have seen such acts enthusiastically applauded by frantic partisans, as the bold
and energetic measures of rulers who would not
allow the cause of the Union to suffer from tender
adherence to formalities; we have seen men elected
by such means sitting unmolested in a House of
Representatives, blinded by its partisanship to the
insult to its own dignity, which their presence involves, and to the ruinous consequences of the precedent which has thus been established.* We can
therefore conjecture in what manner the early
stages of the usurpation will be accomplished—in
fact they have already been accomplished. With
a Constitution daily crumbling away, as the plea of
necessity saps its foundations; with every citizen's

* For a detailed account of some of the incidents which
attended the congressional elections of 1863, in Maryland,
see note at the end of this chapter.

life and liberty at the mercy of the Executive; with the laws insulted, despised and disregarded at the will of petty military commanders; with our legislature composed in part of nominees of military officers imposed upon the electors by violence, it is only because we have yet the means to redress our own grievances that we can properly be styled a free people. The struggle which we are about to enter upon is not so much to preserve our liberties as it is to regain them. The question is not whether we shall establish a despotism upon the ruins of popular liberty, but whether we shall permit a partial despotism to become total, a temporary despotism to become permanent. Every day that the present system endures increases the difficulties of abandoning it; and soon its abandonment will become impossible. The result to which it will lead is inevitable, and when the time comes that the final catastrophe can no longer be deferred, there will be no lack of pretexts, plausible enough to satisfy the usurper's conscience and the consciences of his partisans. Possibly the standard of revolt will be unsuccessfully raised in the early stages of the usurpation, and thus facilitate its subsequent steps. Possibly it will be said, as it has already been said to justify similar acts, that the absence of the " loyal soldiers " from the polls prevents the result of the elections from being a true exponent of the popular wishes; that " disloyal " men have no moral right to vote under a government which they oppose; or that the all-absorbing necessity of preserving the Union overrides all other considerations; possibly it will be discovered that the provisions for periodical elections and limited terms of office are, like the equally explicit provisions protecting the life and liberty of the citizen, inapplicable to a state of public danger. The history of the world is full of proofs of the facility with which the ruler of a free people can find an excuse for the overthrow of its liberty, when power and inclination combine to induce him to make the attempt, and of the large train of followers which he can at once command, if his attempt shall be successful.

I purposely refrain from pursuing the subject further. It is too soon to form anything beyond a conjecture as to the events which would succeed such a usurpation. We can only say, that so far no Napoleon, no Cromwell, has arisen among us; and the history of our sister republic of Mexico affords us some indications of the fate of a country in which petty usurpers overthrow a government, and raise a storm which they cannot rule.

Before I conclude this chapter, I wish to present to the reader an extract from the writings of a man whose foresight and sagacity equalled his purity, and whose purity has never yet been equalled by any public man of his nation. It needs only to add

that he was an American, and the reader will at
once recognize to whom I refer.

I have said that our forefathers had comparatively
little experience of the effects of party spirit, while the
Federal Government was administered by the Congress of the Confederation, and while the nation was
insignificant in population, and yet suffering from
the effects of the hardships of the Revolution.
But the adoption of the Constitution, and the altered
condition of our internal affairs which succeeded,
gave that spirit an ample field of action. Even the
purity of character and the distinguished services
of Washington did not avail to shield him from its
effects. His controversy with Genet, the treaty of
1795 with Great Britain, and the "whiskey insurrection" in Pennsylvania, were successively occasions of attacks upon his character as well as his
policy, which wrung his great and patriotic heart.
To such lengths did the virulence of party passion
lead the people, whose independence was due in
so great a degree to his wisdom and his virtues,
that he was menaced with the fate of Louis XVI. ;*
that his impeachment was publicly called for; that
"it was averred that he was totally destitute of
merit, either as a soldier or a statesman," and that
he was charged with having plundered the public
treasury for his private emolument.† Even the

---

* Irving's Washington, vol. v., p. 166.
† Marshall's Washington, vol. ii., p. 370.

equanimity which was such a conspicuous trait of
his character gave way under such provocation.
He repeatedly expressed his regret at having accepted the Presidency. He declared, in the bitterness of his spirit, that " he had rather be in his grave
than in his present situation;" and he asserted that
such " is the turbulence of human passions in party
disputes, where victory more than truth, is the palm
contended for, that the post of honor is a private
station." And when his approaching retirement
into private life had assuaged the fierceness of the
envenomed attacks to which he had been subjected,
and disposed all his fellow-countrymen to acknowledge the wisdom and perfect rectitude of his conduct during his presidency, he left upon record, in
his farewell address, this solemn warning against the
spirit of party, from his experience of which he fore-
saw a danger to the liberties of his country, greater
than any that could proceed from the ambition or
corruption of its rulers.

" I have already intimated to you the danger of
parties in the State, with particular reference to the
founding of them upon geographical discrimina-
tions. Let me now take a more comprehensive
view, and warn you in the most solemn manner
against the baneful effects of the spirit of party
generally.

" This spirit, unfortunately, is inseparable from
our nature, having its root in the strongest pas-

sions of the human mind. It exists, under different
shapes, in all governments, more or less stifled, controlled, or repressed ; but in those of the popular
form it is seen in its greatest rankness, and is truly
their worst enemy.

" The ultimate domination of one faction over
another, sharpened by the spirit of revenge, natural
to party dissensions, which in different ages and
countries has perpetrated the most horrid enormi-
ties, is in itself a frightful despotism. But this
leads at length to a more formal and permanent
despotism. The disorders and miseries which result gradually incline the minds of men to seek
security and repose in the absolute power of an
individual ; *and, sooner or later, the chief of some
prevailing faction, more able or more fortunate than
his competitors, turns this disposition to the purposes of his own elevation, on the ruins of public
liberty.*"

Startling as is the adaptation of these words
to the present condition of the country, they do
not constitute the only warning contained in the
farewell address, against the follies and errors
of the policy which I have discussed at such
length. For Washington does not confine himself
with pointing out the passion that will predis-
pose the nation to the overthrow of its liberties ;
he indicates as the very method by which the
catastrophe will be effected, *the destruction, by*

usurpation, of the checks established by the Consti-
tution. I copy :

"The necessity of reciprocal checks in the exercise of political power, by dividing and distributing
it into different depositaries, and constituting each
the guardian of the public weal against invasions
by the others, has been evinced by experiments,
ancient and modern, some of them in our country,
and under our own eyes. To preserve them must
be as necessary as to institute them. If, in the opinion of the people, the distribution or modification
of the constitutional powers be in any particular
wrong, let it be corrected by an amendment in the
way which the Constitution designates. BUT LET
THERE BE NO CHANGE BY USURPATION ; for though
this in one instance may be the instrument of good,
IT IS THE CUSTOMARY WEAPON BY WHICH FREE GOVERN-
MENTS ARE DESTROYED."

It has been my aim in this chapter to enforce
these emphatic prophecies; to show that Washington did not read amiss the signs of the times; to
satisfy my reader that his earnest and affectionate
appeal was something more than a mere flourish
of rhetoric. I have elsewhere cited the language
of Hamilton and of Madison ; and I could have
filled this volume with quotations to the same
effect from a long roll of statesmen, philosophers,
jurists, publicists, and historians, who have discussed the theory of our political system, and the

various provisions of the Constitution. They all
concur in their conclusions. They teach us that
a large debt, and a large national expenditure,
create a class of citizens inimical to popular institutions; and we have now a debt counted by
thousands of millions, and we propose to adopt
a future policy which will require an annual expenditure of four hundred millions. They teach
us that an uncontrolled and irresponsible executive
will ultimately convert himself into a despot; and
we propose to make our President an unchecked
autocrat. They teach us that a large standing army
is the instrument by which executive power strikes
down free institutions; and we propose to keep up
a standing army of more than a quarter of a million of soldiers. They teach us that the independent sovereignty of the States is the great
guaranty of the perpetuity of our Constitution; and
we propose to convert the States into mere bureaux
of the central power. They teach us that the
spirit of party creates a usurper, and furnishes
him with his instruments; and we propose to
arouse party spirit till the two political parties
shall be ready to imbrue their hands in each other's
blood.

Why so much incredulity as to a result so clearly predicted? Why this confidence that there is no
danger? Why this blind refusal to believe those
who have so often warned us of the precipice at

the end of the road down which we are so madly rushing?

For one, I cannot share the pleasing anticipations of those who believe that the Constitution can survive the proposed experiment; I cannot allow my apprehensions to be soothed by the assurances of optimists—the eager votaries of philanthrophical theories of government, panting with the excitement of a civil war which is yet raging, whose advent they derided with confident predictions that have scarcely died upon my ears. I prefer to rest my faith upon the teachings of the great and good men who framed the Constitution; of their successors who administered the government under it, in times favorable for the exercise of calm reason and the attainment of sound judgment; of the publicists and political economists throughout the world, who have carefully studied the science of government; and of the historians who have recorded the rise, progress, and fall of the republics which preceded ours. I can therefore anticipate nothing but the total overthrow of the Constitution, and the extinction of the bright hopes, which in this and other countries, have clustered around the American experiment of self-government, from any attempt to marry military rule to free institutions; under whatever name the monstrous alliance may be disguised, or with whatever specious pretext of philanthropy, or commercial or political ascendency, it may be commended to our favor.

Note.—The following account of some of the incidents which attended the Congressional elections held in Maryland in November, 1863, is copied from the newspaper press. It is, of course, not impossible that some of the details may be exaggerated, but the general accuracy of the narration is vouched for in the recent annual message of Governor Bradford of that State, and confirmed by documentary proof submitted by him to the Legislature.

Correspondence of the " New York Tribune."

A Provost-Marshal and Lieutenant-Colonel in Kent County, issued an absurd order in regard to the election, in which they undertook to designate who were loyal citizens, by saying that only those could be so considered who voted for the Government candidates, and then arrested and sent to Baltimore the entire Copperhead candidates on the county ticket. These unhappy gentlemen arrived in Baltimore the night before the election.

Correspondence of the Washington " National Intelligencer."

Mr. Arthur Crisfield advanced between the file of soldiers to the judges' desk and offered his vote ; Capt. Moore, who was standing by the desk immediately fronting the judges, challenged his vote and inquired his name. The reply was, " Arthur Crisfield."

Capt. Moore, pulling a paper from his pocket examined it, and proceeded to interrogate Mr. A. Crisfield, in substance as follows :

Capt. Moore.—" Have you ever been in the rebel service ? "

Mr. A. Crisfield.—" No."

Capt. Moore.—" Are you loyal ? "

Mr. A. Crisfield.—"I am."

Captain Moore.—"Have you ever sympathized with those in rebellion against the Government?"

Mr. A. Crisfield.—"I have never given aid, assistance or encouragement to the South."

Capt. Moore.—"Do you acknowledge this to be a rebellion against the Government?"

Mr. A. Crisfield.—"I acknowledge this."

Capt. Moore.—"Are you in favor of prosecuting the war to put down the rebellion by every means, and of voting men and money for this purpose, and that all your property may be devoted to the prosecution of the war?"

Mr. A. Crisfield.—"Define the means."

Capt. Moore.—"By blockade, cutting off supplies from the South, and by every means known in civilized warfare?"

Mr. A. Crisfield.—"I think the Government has the right to prosecute the war by all the means recognized by international law and civilized warfare, within the limits of the Constitution and the laws of the country."

Capt. Moore.—"Are you in favor of prosecuting the war by EVERY MEANS?"

Mr. Crisfield was repeating the same reply as that to the former question, when Capt. Moore turned to the judges and said, "administer the oath to him."

Mr. Pinto, one of the judges of the election, then rose and said : "We disapprove of this mode of conducting the election. We should never get through. We are sworn to conduct the election according to the laws of Maryland; and if we are not permitted to do so, we submit to arrest."

Capt. Moore.—"You refuse then to carry out the order of Gen. Schenck?"

Mr. Pinto.—"We decide to obey the proclamation of the Governor and the order of the President."

Capt. Moore then arrested the judges, and said, "the arrest is for refusing to obey the order of Gen. Schenck."

15

The judges then said the election was closed, and Capt. Moore required them to report themselves to him under arrest at Twilley's hotel, which they promised to do. Capt. Moore informed them they were to be taken to the city of Baltimore.

This statement is certified to be true by the judges of the election (who add that they were carried under a military guard to Salisbury, and then placed in the guard-house), and also by a large number of prominent citizens.

The sergeant in command at Potato Neck district, in the same county mentioned above, stated to the judges of election that he had received orders to enforce the Order No. 53 ; to challenge every voter ; to examine all tickets offered ; to administer the oath contained in the Order No. 53, and to decline to allow any tickets but the yellow or Creswell tickets to be polled. That after the proclamation was received at camp, he was ordered to enforce Order No. 53, as it had been modified by the President ; to administer the oath ; to challenge every man who offered to vote, and to prevent all from voting who presented any but the yellow or Creswell ticket ; that he would examine every ticket, and that if there should be a disturbance, soldiers enough could easily be got to wipe all out who attempted it. A very small vote was polled, the mass of the people being deterred from coming out by fear of the soldiers, who were reported to have received orders to arrest all who voted for Mr. Crisfield.

In Barren Creek, the sergeant in command pulled out of his pocket a yellow or Creswell ticket, and said, "This is the only ticket that shall be voted to-day." The window was guarded, and all were ejected who would not vote the yellow ticket.

At Chestertown, the Lieut.-Col. commanding, stated in a printed order :

" It becomes every true loyal citizen to avail himself of

the present opportunity offered, to place himself honorably upon the record, by giving a full and ardent support to the whole Government ticket, upon the platform adopted by the Union League Convention. None other is recognized by the Federal authorities as loyal or worthy of the support of any one who desires the peace and restoration of this Union."

Mr. Hamilton, in the sixtieth number of *The Federalist*, speaking of the apprehension that the power confided to the Union to regulate its own elections might be abused, among other things, "in such a manner as to promote the election of some favorite class of men in exclusion of others," says, " of all chimerical suppositions, this seems the most chimerical. On the one hand no rational calculation of probabilities would lead us to imagine that the disposition, which a conduct so violent and extraordinary would imply, could ever find its way into the national councils ; and on the other hand, it may be concluded with certainty, that if so improper a spirit should ever gain admittance into them, it would display itself in a form altogether different and far more decisive. The improbability of the attempt may be satisfactorily inferred from the single reflection, that it could never be made without causing an immediate revolt of the great body of the people, headed and directed by the State governments."

But Mr. Hamilton, as I have already stated, had no adequate experience of the lengths to which rulers will go, and of the usurpations which the governed will not only tolerate but applaud, under the influence of party-spirit.

CHAPTER XIII.

Suggestions as to the Possibility of restoring the Union without destroying Public Liberty—The most important Object to be accomplished is to impress upon the Public Mind a correct understanding of the Conditions of the Problem—Also to modify the Spirit with which the War has been carried on—There will be no difficulty in framing a plan when those Objects have been attained—Reasons for believing in the existence of a Disposition at the South to return to the Union upon honorable Terms—The Utility of a further prosecution of the War discussed—Purposes for which it should be prosecuted—The Effect of the Emancipation Proclamation should be left to Judicial Decision—The political Power of Slavery is at an end—Urgent Necessity of Remodelling the Constitution—Reasons why the holding of a National Convention at an early day is indispensable, irrespective of its Influence in promoting the Restoration of the Union—But such a Convention can be and should be made a Powerful Instrument to hasten the end of the War—Reforms which it should accomplish—Effect of those Reforms upon the Pacification and Prosperity of the Country, and the Future Permanence of the Union,

Is it then impossible to preserve at the same time the Union and popular government; or must the American people resign themselves to the hard necessity, of consenting to the destruction of one or the other of those cherished institutions? I feel reluctant to leave the reader who has patiently followed me so far, as long as it is possible that any suggestions which I can make, will aid him in any degree in the solution of this grand and absorbing question ; and yet it seems to me that I have already gone over the ground so fully, that I can add but little to the observations contained in the preceding pages, with any useful or satisfactory result.

I have fully laid down the principles applicable to our civil war, which distinguish right from wrong—the enforcement of constitutional jurisdiction from usurpation of the prerogatives of a conqueror. I have endeavored to portray the consequences which will ensue from an attempt to overstep the clear and distinct boundary line, which separates the one from the other. I have indicated in what manner, if we would preserve our national greatness and prosperity—nay, our existence as a free people—the exercise of indisputable powers must be controlled and regulated by the laws of humanity, the established principles of political science, and the theories upon which our government is based. And I have not confined myself to the elucidation of abstract principles ; but I have carefully applied them to the various measures which we have already adopted, and to the policy which is urged upon us in the future. I have done even more—for while condemning particular acts as unlawful or impolitic, and pointing out the mischiefs which they have already produced, or the fatal consequences to which they will lead in the future, I have also designated the lawful and regular mode

of meeting the same emergency, and the benefits
and advantages to ensue from its adoption.

So fully has this been done that it is scarcely
possible to suggest any plan (except disunion) by
which the war can be brought to a close, whether
it contemplates the preservation or the destruction
of the Constitution, whose general features will not
depend upon principles that have been condemned
or commended in these pages, with reference to
considerations of expediency as well as of right.
And if I should attempt to add another to the many
plans for the settlement of our difficulties, now
occupying the public attention, its general outline
would consist of a mère repetition of what has already been said; while it seems to me that it would
be worse than unprofitable to attempt to mark out
at the present time, the details by which the scheme
could be carried into effect. For there is not the
slightest possibility that this work, even if it should
fall under the observation of our present rulers,
would in any respect influence their action. They
are committed to "the President's plan;" and whatever may be its merits or demerits, they will occupy the remaining year of their power in efforts
to force it upon the southern people. And should
I attempt to devise, with reference to the present
situation of affairs, the details of a scheme that
will accomplish the results, by which alone we
can ' ope to preserve our freedom and the Union,

the rapid march of events might soon render some of them impracticable, and perhaps mischievous.

Indeed the only object of real importance at the present time, that should command the efforts of those who agree with me that the policy which we are at present pursuing, can end in nothing but involving the southern people and ourselves in a common ruin, is to impress that fact thoroughly upon the public mind. Whenever the American people shall fully appreciate the consequences of attempting to maintain the Union by force, and clearly understand the conditions of the problem involved in its maintenance by any other means, there will be no difficulty in settling the details of a scheme of pacification, which will ensure at all events the preservation of our liberties, and will also accomplish the restoration of the Union, if that event is yet capable of accomplishment by the art or the power of man. And we have reason to believe that the time has not passed when such a consummation can be attained, by a return to political and constitutional principles, that once commanded such universal acquiescence, and by the exercise towards the southern people of the great Christian virtues of forbearance, magnanimity and charity—traits which ennoble nations as well as individuals. I have referred in the seventh chapter to some of the reasons which authorize us to entertain such an opin-

ion.* It will be confirmed and strengthened by
observing the great change that has taken place,
within the last year or two, in the character of the
appeals by which southern newspapers and public
speakers animate their people to renewed efforts,
and the continued endurance of the hardships of the
war. At the commencement of the struggle, they
were never weary of depicting in glowing terms the
prosperity and greatness to which their section would
attain, by realizing the dream of Independence;
they ascribed its misfortunes and comparative
poverty in the past, solely to the baneful effects of
the Union; and they roused popular passion by re-
presenting the Northerners as lacking in every one
of the manly virtues, and unworthy to be the political associates of a chivalrous and high-minded people. But the burden both of vituperation and argument is now entirely altered. We hear nothing
more of northern cowardice; but little of northern
perfidy; still less of the glories and advantages
of Southern Independence, or of grievances sustained by the South in years gone by. Denunciations of our people are now levelled at the malignant and blood-thirsty spirit, with which the civil
and military policy of our Government proves the
ruling majority to be imbued; and arguments are

* See pages 139 to 141.

predicated upon the political ostracism, degradation, spoliation, and slaughter which await the insurgents, whether they shall voluntarily submit or be conquered. Those who still have faith in the success of their cause, appear to have diverted the stream of their vituperations from the administration party to its opponents, evidently through apprehension that a change of policy at the North will excite such dissensions at the South, as to compel the abandonment of the struggle. All this indicates very conclusively that a great change has come over the minds of the southern people since the commencement of the war, and that a large number of them, including several of their leading men, find their principal motive for continuing the struggle in the impossibility of abandoning it, without sacrificing their self-respect and the Constitutional rights of a whole people, and exposing the lives, liberties and property, of their most beloved and venerated citizens to the fury of a cruel and vindictive enemy.*

---

* The principal newspapers of the North copy from time to time the most interesting paragraphs which appear in the southern papers. Any person who has been in the habit of attentively reading those extracts will confirm my statements respecting their tone and spirit, heretofore and at the present time. I have only room here for a very few recent paragraphs, which I select as among the most significant indications of a disposition entertained by many at the South, to return to the Union whenever they can do so with safety and honor.

14*

To what extent this feeling extends is of course only matter of conjecture; but its existence authorizes us to believe that we may yet avoid the

From the *Mobile Register*, edited by Judge Forsyth :

" We thank God from the depths of our heart that the authorities at Washington snubbed Vice-President Stephens, in his late attempt to confer with them on international affairs, without form or ceremony.   .   .   .   .

President Davis gave him full powers to treat on honorable terms and started him off to the kingdom of Abraham. But Father Abraham told him there was an impassable gulf between them, and the Vice-President had to steam back to Richmond, a little top-fallen.   We hope this will put a stop forever to some croakers about here, who intimate that there are people enough friendly to the South in the North to restore the Union as it was. And we also hope the Government at Richmond will not humiliate itself any more, but from this time will look only to the one end of final and substantial independence.   .   .   .   .

" There is only one party in the North who want the Union restored, but they have no more power—legislative, executive or judicial—than the paper we write on.   .   .   .

Should a strong Union party spring up in Ohio, the third State in the North in political importance, it might find a faint response in some southern States and give us trouble. But as long as the Republicans hold power, they will think of conquest and dominion only, and we on the other hand will come up in solid column for freedom and independence, which we will be certain to achieve, with such assistance as we may *now* (after the refusal of the Washington Cabinet to confer) confidently expect, before the Democrats of the North get into power again, and come whispering in our ears—' *Union, reconstruction, Constitution, concession and guaranties.*'   Away with all such stuff !   We want separation.   Give us rather men like Thaddeus

disruption of the Union without trampling the
South and prostrating ourselves under the feet
of a military despotism. And although I shall

Stevens and Charles Sumner. They curse the old Union
and despise it ; and so do we."

From the *Richmond Enquirer :* " But for the poisonous
embrace of the Democratic party, these States would have
been free and clear of the unnatural Union twenty years
ago. The idea of *that* odious party coming to life again,
and holding out its arms to us, makes us shiver. Its foul
breath is malaria ; its touch is death. It was *not* the Sew-
ards and the Sumners, the Black Republicans and Abolitionists, who have hurt us. They were right all along.
Let our enemy appear as an exterminating Yankee host,
we pray, and not as a Democratic Convention ! Let him
take any shape but that ! Already we have visions of the
men of feeble knees, tender feet, and undulating spines,
losing their sense and manhood by the contact, as they did,
alas, so often before."

These are the expressions of those who *desire* separation ;
the extract which follows reflects the views of the class of
men referred to in the paragraphs quoted ; those who per-
severe because they have no other option. It is taken
from an address to the people of Georgia by the Hon. B.
H. Hill.

" Extreme men now govern the United States. They
mean our subjugation and ruin. We must fight as long as
those men are in power. When the people of the United
States shall drive these men from power, and repudiate
their extreme measures, and cease to invade and rob us,
there will be an honorable door open for discussion. But
never before. Until that door shall be opened by our enemies, let our people count no disaster as intolerable, and
regard every interest as protected only by a vigorous prosecution of the war. Let every man of the army be in

not attempt, for the reasons already given, to elaborate a scheme by which this result can be attained, I will briefly glance at some questions connected with the effort to accomplish it, the conditions of which cannot be materially affected by any
mutation in public affairs that the progress of the
war will occasion, unless unexpected disasters to
our armies, or the intervention of European powers,
should enable the Confederates to dictate the terms
of peace to us.

I regret that the possibility of settling our difficulties by negotiations with our adversaries, con-
templating their voluntary return to the Union, is
not one of these questions. Many of our ablest
statesmen and purest patriots believe that such a
settlement of the controversy could be attained at
the present time, in a manner and upon terms honorable to both parties, and which would ensure
the restoration of the feelings of fraternal attachment formerly existing between the different sections of the nation. But it is useless to inquire
whether these hopes are now well founded, since
there is no possibility, while the present Administration is in power, of testing the soundness of our
conclusions by a practical experiment. And it

camp, and let every man not of the army, produce something to sustain those in camp. To fight the extreme men
and keep our ears open to the reasonable and just men of
the United States, is the only road to peace and honor."

would be still more idle to speculate whether the events of the succeeding year will dissipate or confirm them.

But there is another question of paramount importance, and demanding a direct and immediate answer, the solution of which necessarily lies at the basis of an altered policy, in case negotiations shall fail in their object, or the state of the country shall be such that they could not be usefully or honorably attempted; and that is—*shall the war be further prosecuted?* And it must be acknowledged that an affirmative answer to this question can be justified, less by the inherent force of the arguments in its favor, than by a consideration of the consequences which will result from answering it in the negative. For I have endeavored to show that although the war is a lawful and constitutional mode of restoring the Union, yet that its object cannot be accomplished under our existing Constitution, unless it shall terminate with the voluntary and cheerful acceptance by the southern people, of the restoration of the Government to its former authority over them. To quote Mr. Seward again: "Only an imperial or despotic government could subjugate thoroughly disaffected and revolutionary members of the State. This federal republican system of ours is of all forms of government the very one which is most unfitted for such a labor." No candid man can doubt that the southern States are now thoroughly disaffected and revolutionary; and I have endeavored to expose the fallacy of the theory that they have been brought to that condition, or that they are maintained in it, in any other way than by the voluntary action of the great majority of their people. Hence it must be acknowledged that the attempt to inspire the southern people with attachment to the Union by the use of force presents a perplexing problem.

But on the other hand, we must inquire into the probable consequences of stopping the war. And doubtful and uncertain as the results of its further prosecution may appear, there can be but little doubt or uncertainty respecting the consequences of its cessation. To withdraw our armies from the southern territory, and announce to the enemy and the world that we had abandoned all attempt forcibly to reduce the insurgents to submission, would lead at once to the recognition of the Southern Confederacy by foreign nations, and to the complete and undisputed establishment of its sway over all the people within its boundaries. It would then become de jure and de facto one of the political sovereign communities of the civilized world; the separation would be complete; and the failure of the negotiations, or the fact that they were so manifestly useless that they were not undertaken, would lead to the conclusion that it was final.

It is true that such a result might be due to the

fact that power was in the hands of men, who in that respect did not truly represent the wishes of a majority of the southern people. For under their form of government, as well as under our own, the temper of the people and of their rulers may be for a time antagonistic to each other. But for us to assume the existence of such an antagonism, and to wait till the time should arrive when the men whom we should find in power, would be compelled to give place to other and truer representatives of the popular sentiment, would expose the cause of the Union to innumerable hazards during the intervening period. And on the other hand, if the people of the South, notwithstanding what we have done to merit their hatred, still cherish feelings which would render a voluntary re-union possible, there is no reason to suppose that such feelings would undergo any diminution, if we should destroy the power of their leaders by a further prosecution of the war, without adding to its horrors and the passions which it has awakened, by a perseverance in the policy of insult and aggravation that has heretofore accompanied it. Hence we shall gain nothing, and risk the loss of everything, by arresting the war, and leaving the Confederates at liberty to accomplish their own independence, or to reunite with us, as those who may then chance to hold the reins of power among them may think proper to determine.

Inconsistent as war may appear with the objects which we propose to accomplish, it seems impossible to avoid further prosecuting this bloody, hazardous and costly experiment of restoring the Union by force, till the progress of events has dissipated our present hopes that separation may be averted, or till we have achieved a victory in the field, which we must trust to statesmanship to convert into a bond of future affection and harmony. It is truly a sad necessity—but the follies of the past have left us no other alternative. We can only say with Macbeth—

> " I am in blood
> Stept in so far, that should I wade no more,
> Returning were as tedious as go o'er."

The gravity and importance of this question entitle it to a much more elaborate discussion; but the length to which these pages have already extended, admonishes me that I must subject these concluding remarks to a strict condensation. And I feel the less reluctance in dismissing the subject after such a cursory and imperfect examination, that its merits have apparently been already prejudged by the American people.

But I have written so far in vain, if I have failed to impress my reader with the conviction that a continuation of hostilities will be worse than useless, unless it shall be accompanied with an entire revo-

lution of feeling, and an abandonment of some of
the objects which we have hitherto sought to attain.
The first and greatest victory which it behooves us
to achieve, is a victory over ourselves. We must
go back not only to the objects expressed in the
Crittenden resolution, but to the sentiments with
which that resolution declares the rulers of the
nation to be inspired. We must banish all feelings
of mere passion or resentment, and recollect only
our duty to the whole country—to the South as well
as to the North. We must recognize and keep ever
prominently before us this great fundamental truth,
that the end of the war, if it shall be commensurate
with our hopes, will find the men now arrayed in
arms against us our equals and our brethren, under
a system of government depending upon the voluntary coöperation of the whole people—a system
that can endure only upon conditions, which have
been clearly and emphatically stated by one, whose
conduct at a similar political crisis I have repeatedly
commended as a model for imitation :

" *The Constitution cannot be maintained nor the
Union preserved, in opposition to public feeling,
by the mere exertion of the coercive powers confided
to the general Government ; the foundations must
be laid in the affections of the people ; in the security
it gives to life, liberty, character and property in
every quarter of the country ; and in the fraternal
attachment which the citizens of the several States*

bear to one another as members of one political family, mutually contributing to promote the happiness of each other."

We must therefore cease to look at the rebellion in its legal aspect, and consider it from a political point of view. We must abandon the idea of punishing our adversaries as traitors and disturbers of the public peace, and learn to regard them as a people imbued with political dogmas, prejudices, feelings, and passions, which force, severity, usurpation and humiliation will only strengthen, and which can only be removed by the exercise of justice, kindness, moderation and forbearance. The war must be regarded as a mere instrument to bring them within reach of those influences; and care must be taken that while hostile action is repressed, the tenacity of hostile opinion, and the intensity of hostile passion, be not left undiminished. And we must never forget that we shall ourselves be compelled in the end to heal every wound, which we shall have inflicted upon the pride as well as the sense of justice, of a high-spirited people, descendants of our common ancestors, and possessing the same faults and the same virtues as ourselves.

We must therefore utterly abandon the idea that we are fighting to accomplish the ends of public justice, to avenge the injured majesty of the laws, or to repair the defects of the Constitution. Still more emphatically must we renounce the expectation of attaining by means of the war, political advantages to our own section, beyond those which the Constitution secures to us ; the redress of grievances, real or imaginary, which we have sustained in times past ; the reformation of social institutions with which we have no rightful concern, or the promotion of philanthropic objects at the expense of others. We must reiterate our solemn pledge that it is waged SOLELY " to defend and maintain the supremacy of the Constitution and preserve the Union, with all the dignity, equality, and rights of the several States unimpaired." And we must firmly resolve that when those objects are accomplished, or when it has been conclusively demonstrated that they cannot be accomplished, the war ought to cease, and shall cease.

There are many at the North who would gladly welcome the adoption of an equitable, humane, and constitutional policy towards the southern people, and are willing, for the purpose of uniting upon such a policy with other conservative and moderate men, to waive all differences of opinion respecting every measure, except one. These men hold that the Emancipation Proclamation should be sustained ; some of them because they have faith in its expediency as well as its legality ; others, because, irrespective of its expediency, they believe it to be legal, and that the faith of the nation which it plighted to the blacks, would be dishonorably violated by its withdrawal. They assume that the South, and the majority of conservative men at the North, would be satisfied with nothing but its immediate and unconditional repeal, and the abrogation of all rights real or pretended, which may have been acquired under it. Hence they are unable to see any method whereby this stumbling-block can be removed.

It seems to me, however, that imagination has greatly overrated this difficulty, and that if the embarrassments which attend the settlement of the controversy with the South, or the union of moderate men at the North, can be narrowed down to this point, it can be easily overcome. For one, decided as my opinions are respecting the invalidity and inexpediency of military emancipation, I am willing not only to waive this question entirely, but even to support a candidate for the Presidency who entirely dissents from my views upon that subject, provided that he will pledge himself to abide by the regular operation of the laws. In truth the Emancipation Proclamation has already accomplished all its mission for good—would that I could say the same of its mission for evil! If the blacks have acquired their freedom under it, their right to freedom is as sacred and unalterable as our own; certainly neither the President as a military commander, nor the President and Congress as civil functionaries, can lawfully remand freemen into slavery. Its repeal or its reaffirmance will not therefore affect the condition of a single human being in the land. Its future career presents only three alternatives: it must pass the ordeal of a judicial decision; or it must be upheld by a lawless exercise of power; or it must be trampled upon by an equally flagrant usurpation. If our adversaries will pursue the second of these alternatives, let them stand alone in a career of lawlessness and violence. The first is the only one which we can adopt with consistency, safety and justice to all concerned.

The people of the South, if reason shall take the place of passion among them, cannot fail to recognize the force of these principles, and if the other conditions of reunion shall be favorable, the Emancipation Proclamation will not prove a serious obstacle. Whether it shall be repealed or allowed to stand, they must equally expect that its validity will be determined by judicial proceedings. They will demand a fair, competent, and impartial tribunal, and they should have one. They will demand that the President shall not forcibly interfere between them and the blacks till the relation between them shall be judicially determined, and this demand should also be acceded to. If, contrary to their expectations, the decision should be in favor of the blacks, it will be the duty of the Federal authorities to enforce the mandates of the Federal

Court. Such a decision would doubtless cause great disappointment and serious pecuniary loss to the slaveholding whites, but it would not interfere with the peaceful and regular action of the Government within their section of the country. The injury would be pecuniary merely; it would add another to the many calamities which the war has brought upon the southern people; but it would be unaccompanied with a sense of humiliation from which the greatest obstacles to future harmony are to be apprehended.*

The people of the North may rest assured that if all other questions can be equitably adjusted, the institution of slavery will never again lead to a disturbance of the public peace, whatever may be the

---

* "Fas est ab hoste doceri."—I find a sentence in a recent number of that "loyal" periodical, *The Atlantic Monthly*, which expresses so forcibly the comparative effects of insults and injuries upon the human mind that I copy it: "We doubt if any strong enmity was ever created in the minds of men or nations through the infliction of injuries, though injuring parties have an undoubted right to hate their victims; *and we are sure that an insult was never yet forgiven by any nation, or by any individual, whose resentment was of any account.*"

The writer states this undeniable proposition with a *naïf* unconsciousness of the force of the argument which he furnishes against the whole plan of subjugation. He is discussing, not the effect of injuring and insulting the southern people at the same time, but of the insults which we have received from England. Upon that subject his clearness of mental vision is beyond criticism.

result of the judicial test to which the Emancipation Proclamation will be subjected. As an engine of political controversy its doom will be sealed by the restoration of the Union. The misfortunes which excessive devotion to it have brought upon the southern people cannot fail to greatly discredit it in their estimation, if we shall cease to make its existence the symbol of their own civil liberty, and allow reason and reflection to combat it, without interference from the promptings of pride and passion. The destiny of the territories is fixed forever by the laws of God as well as the laws of man. Maryland and Missouri are now substantially free States, and Delaware, Kentucky, Tennessee, and Arkansas will soon follow their example, by the voluntary action of their own people, unless an unjustifiable attempt to destroy slavery by military force and usurped power, shall frustrate all efforts to accomplish its lawful and constitutional extinction. The States where it yet exists are already in a hopeless minority, in the Senate, the House of Representatives, and the Electoral College—a minority which must become more insignificant as time adds to the number of the free States, without increasing that of the others. In those States where the institution shall survive, it will exist purely as an industrial system, the preservation or extinction of which the people will regulate as their own interests may dictate; and we may be sure that the warnings of the past will not be lost upon either section of the nation.

If the people, by repudiating the policy of subjugation, shall manifest their determination that popular institutions shall survive this struggle, it will be necessary for our sake, as well for the sake of the southern people, that the Constitution should undergo an immediate revision. Before the war broke out, experience had already demonstrated its inefficiency to answer the requirements of such a populous, powerful, and wealthy people as we have become since its adoption. The events which led to the war admonish us that we have postponed for too long a period its adaptation to the altered circumstances of the nation. And the war itself has already destroyed its substance and reduced it to a mere shell. We have yet a judicial department, an executive department, and a legislative department, the latter consisting of two Houses, the members of one of which are elected by the people, with certain exceptions which have been noted; but what else remains of the Constitution? The ability of the judiciary to restrain the other departments within their allotted spheres is gone; and the President and the legislature acknowledge no limitation of their powers save their own ideas of public necessity. And, worse yet, the executive department is rapidly assuming the functions of the legislature, with the consent or at least the acquiescence of the latter.

It is true that the supporters of the administration allege that this state of things is merely temporary; but in the same breath they acknowledge its permanency, by felicitating themselves and the country upon the unexpected strength which the Government has been found to possess. It is also true that the opposition vehemently denounce the administration for its assumption of unconstitutional powers, but the precedents having been established, they will remain for the guidance of all future administrations, whatever may be their political principles. A wild beast newly caught is scarcely more impatient of its cage than power of the fetters which restrain it. And from the moment when a political emergency becomes recognized as a key which unlocks them, the line which bounds it and the features which distinguish it, commence to fade in the eyes of those, who are alone authorized to determine the application of the precedent. Soon they disappear entirely; and the limits of power no longer depend upon fixed boundaries, but fluctuate from time to time according to the ability or the disposition of him who wields it, or the strength of the party which sustains him. As the boundary lines of power advance, they push back those which define the rights of the people: as they recede the antagonistic force advances, and soon steps within

15

the legitimate territory of the other; and thus government becomes to-day a despotism, and to-morrow a mere advisory body. If such a state of things shall continue long, a bloody struggle will ensue, the result of which will be a permanent despotism, or a complete breaking up anew of that Union which we are now endeavoring to recon struct at such immense expenditure of blood and treasure.

It must be apparent to any reflecting man, even if he believes that necessity has justified the course of the administration during the past three years, that its acts cannot safely be allowed to pass into history, as precedents for the future action of whatever party shall be strong enough to follow them. As soon as comparative tranquillity allows the people to turn their thoughts, from the preservation of the Union to the preservation of popular liberty, a cry for a national convention will arise throughout the whole country. Would it not be wise to base negotiations with the insurgents upon this inevitable necessity, or in some other manner to take advantage of it, for the purpose of shortening the war? It seems to me that much might be gained by a standing offer to meet our rebellious fellow-citizens, whenever they shall lay down their arms, in a convention, composed of delegates freely and fairly chosen by the people of all the States, and called together for the purpose of amending the

Constitution, so as to redress all real or imaginary grievances, provide against the occurrence of quarrels in the future, and establish the Union upon a new and more satisfactory basis. Would not such an offer produce a powerful effect in hastening the period of submission, and possibly avoiding the embarrassments which even a successful exercise of force will entail upon us? It would certainly open to the southern people a door for their return to the Union without the humiliation of defeat and conquest, and in entire confidence that they would be received as brethren, equals, and fellow-citizens. If there is in truth a party among them disposed to abandon the struggle whenever they can secure honorable terms of submission, such an offer would tend to strengthen its hands and increase its numbers; and we may fairly indulge the hope that it would operate so powerfully in this direction, as to spare any further effusion of blood, by satisfying those who were still disposed to hold out, that the cause of southern independence could no longer command that united support among their own people, without which its success would be hopeless.

But even if the convention shall not meet till after the war shall be ended, it may still be made a powerful agency to allay the remnants of discontent, which the prostration of the rebellion, even under the most favorable circumstances, will leave behind. I will

not prematurely attempt an enumeration of all the
objects which it should accomplish. Certain evils,
however, obtrude themselves in such gigantic and
hideous forms upon the eye, that the bare suggestion of reform becomes at once associated with
their extinction. The most flagrant and abomin-
able of these is the practice of ignoring fitness, capacity, or integrity in the distribution of the enormous patronage of the Government; of making the
tenure of office depend exclusively upon the political opinions or party services of the candidates; and
of signalizing the advent of every new administration to power, by a radical change in all the public
offices throughout the country. It is impossible to
exaggerate the mischiefs to which this detestable
perversion of the executive power of appointment
and removal has already led, and to which its continuance will lead in the future. Its most obvious
effects are seen in the violence, mendacity, and un-
scrupulousness which characterize our political can-
vasses, the corruption which pervades every department of the Government, and the weakness and
incapacity of our public men. These are all trace-
able directly to a system which has driven the
purest and ablest men of the country out of public
life, and compelled us to trust the administration
of the Government in a great measure to those who
are morally and intellectually unfit for their post. In
this way I opine that the careful student of the

causes which led to the present war will find that this practice is really responsible for the creation of the jealousies, fears, misrepresentations, and heart-burnings, of which the institution of slavery was merely a vehicle and the pretext. And an infusion into our public affairs of the wisdom, moderation and integrity, in which of late years they have been so deficient, by approaching our presidential election more nearly to the character of a struggle for the simple ascendency of principles, would do more than any other measure to heal the wounds left open by the war, and to insure the nation against another disturbance of the public peace.

The attention of the convention should also be directed to precluding the possibility of future collisions between the general Government and the States. The former, strengthened by the addition of such powers as experience shows that its efficiency requires, should be limited by more clearly defined boundaries; and the language by which the grants or restrictions of power are regulated, should be so revised as to exclude or sanction the different interpretations to which it has already given rise. Greater and more lasting checks against the usurpations of the various depositories of power over the citizen, or over each other, should be introduced. The rights and powers of the States, the nature, character, and permanency of the Union, and the relations of the States to each other and to the central Government, should be as clearly defined as language will permit. And some great tribunal, with ample ability to enforce its mandates in time of war or in time of peace, and to protect its own independence against the encroachments, assaults or corruptions of any department of the Government, should be created, with a jurisdiction sufficiently enlarged to preclude the possibility of a resort to the sword, in order to settle such disputes as the imperfection of human language, and the narrow range of human foresight, render it impossible wholly to avoid. Other measures, tending to bind more closely together the now dissevered fragments of the Union, and to " establish justice, ensure domestic tranquillity, provide for the common defence, promote the general welfare, and secure the blessings of liberty to ourselves and our posterity," will suggest themselves to reflecting men, when the proper period shall arrive for their consideration. But the public mind is not yet ripe for a discussion of these measures, or of the means whereby the reforms suggested can be accomplished.

––––––

And here I will bring to a close these observations, which have already extended far beyond my original intentions, and to a length that nothing but the magnitude of the interests at stake could justify. Hopeful as I try to be, that my country will survive its terrible ordeal, I have not been able to banish from my mind the belief that it is rushing onward toward an abyss, at the bottom of which lie national destruction and individual ruin. Impressed with this conviction, I have endeavored plainly and earnestly, but I hope temperately and with charity towards those who differ from me, to point out the signs of the danger and the fatal consequences of the plunge. I have discharged my task with an ever-present sense of the reponsibility resting upon the man, who aims to influence public opinion at such a crisis of the nation's destiny. And I have been led at every step of my labors—and especially in this last chapter—to feel acutely how fearful and uncertain is the mysterious future which I have endeavored to explore, and how blindly we are all groping in the dark. In such a strait, while, as becomes men, we bend all our physical and intellectual energies to extricate ourselves, let us also trust that a kind Providence, in its infinite wisdom, will second our efforts, and ultimately lead us to the way, whereby we can emerge from this darkness into the light of peace, fraternity, civil liberty and prosperity.

> "O that a man might know
> The end of this day's business ere it come!
> But it sufficeth that the day will end,
> And then the end is known."

* 9 7 8 3 3 3 7 1 3 3 8 7 0 *